THE SPLENDOR OF THE MAYA

Twenty-Three

CAROLYN AND ERNEST FAY SERIES
IN ANALYTICAL PSYCHOLOGY
Michael Escamilla, General Editor

The Carolyn and Ernest Fay book series, based on the Fay Lecture Series in Analytical Psychology, was established to further the ideas of C. G. Jung among students, faculty, therapists, and other citizens and to enhance scholarly activities related to analytical psychology. The lecture and book series address topics of importance to the individual and to society. Both series were generously endowed by Carolyn Grant Fay, the founding president of the C. G. Jung Educational Center in Houston, Texas. The series are in part a memorial to her husband, Ernest Bel Fay. Carolyn Fay has planted a Jungian tree carrying both her name and that of her husband, which will bear fruitful ideas and stimulate creative works from this time forward. The Jung Center, Houston, and all those who come in contact with the growing Fay Jungian tree are extremely grateful to Carolyn Grant Fay for what she has done. The Frank N. McMillan Jr. Scholar at the Jung Center, Houston, functions as the general editor of the Fay Book Series.

THE

A Journey into the Shadows

SPLENDOR

at the Dawn of Creation

OF THE

NANCY SWIFT FURLOTTI

MAYA

Foreword by Michael Escamilla

TEXAS A&M UNIVERSITY PRESS: COLLEGE STATION

Library of Congress Control Number: 2025022450

Identifiers: LCCN: 2025022450 | ISBN 9781648433016 (cloth) |

ISBN 9781648433023 (ebook)

LC record available at https://lccn.loc.gov/2025022450

Unless otherwise indicated, all illustrations are by the author.

Cover: This Creamware Vase is in the private collection of Nancy Swift Furlotti, who supplied the photograph. It was also photographed by Justin Kerr on March 2, 2006, and is Kerr Number 8832 on his website, www.Mayavase.com. The vase is incised on both sides, depicting an Ajaw, or Lord, making an offering or sacrifice of an animal, perhaps of a coati, in a basket with its long tail curled in the air. The youthful lord wears an elaborate headdress incorporating a netted turban, jaguar head, and plumage. The glyphs include the name of the figures portrayed on both sides of the vase and the name of the carver.

Dedicated to James Hollis
Mentor and Friend

CONTENTS

SERIES EDITOR'S FOREWORD

The Swiss psychiatrist Carl Jung was an avid student of world cultures, as he strove to develop a psychology that incorporated both the conscious and unconscious aspects of the entire species *Homo sapiens*. Although recently criticized for his Eurocentric views of what constituted modern and primitive cultures, he consciously strove to gather his understanding of the human psyche both through the analyses of his clients (largely affluent individuals from Europe and the United States) and through visits to other countries where he sought to learn about other cultures (including India, Africa, and visits with Native Americans, African Americans, and European Americans living in the United States). His hypothesis of a collective unconscious and of a universal structure of the unconscious relied on similarities in archetypes and belief systems existing not only across different cultures but also over the millennia of time that the human species has existed.

Nancy Furlotti's book *The Splendor of the Maya* deepens and expands the knowledge base of analytical psychology through her in-depth look at the creation myths of Maya and Mesoamerican cultures, allowing us to explore the collective unconscious from a different angle and perspective than we have seen in the European, Slavic, Celtic, Asian, African, and Middle Eastern cultures. In my view it fills a relative gap in the Jungian world with respect to understanding the contributions of the Native American cultures of Mesoamerica to what can be understood about the collective psyche. In a time, currently, of threats at the global level to the human and all other species, we need more than ever to draw upon the deep knowledge of all our world cultures as we seek to understand the challenges of our day and hopefully find a way to be in better balance with nature—both nature that surrounds us (which we are part of) and (psychologically) the nature within us.

The Maya culture and the myths described in Furlotti's book offer an interesting contrast to the narratives and foundations of the scientific/rationalistic view predominant in the Western world since the Age of Enlightenment. In particular, the Maya myths and spiritual system are based on an idea of cyclic time, and they also portray a world where the human being is one among many animals and gods operating in a complex ecosystem. By contrast, the Western scientific method (the principal myth of our times) has relied on a narrative of linear development, progress, and (to our detriment now) the idea of mastering or harnessing "nature" to serve the needs and desires of our human ego.*

In Jung's time, the disasters of the two world wars and the development and use of nuclear weapons made clear to many that civilization was not necessarily progressing in a healthy way and that the seduction of the "Western" or "Enlightenment" philosophies was leading to a one-sided and dangerous way of life. Jung found, in his in-depth analyses of both his own psyche and the psyches of his patients, alternative viewpoints, systems, and archetypes, including the concepts of circular time, death and rebirth, and the alchemical processes of nature (which, although pointing to a process of transformation, also allowed for that process to be circular in nature). When Jung visited Taos, New Mexico (Jung and Jaffe 1965), and had his now famous conversations with Ochwiay Biano, it is perhaps no coincidence that one of the central symbolic systems they talked about was the movement of the sun across the sky—a daily revolution as experienced by us humans on earth, repeated ad infinitum, but core to all of existence for those on the earth. Indeed, an understanding of our universe as circular in nature (with respect to the changing of seasons; "movements" of the sun, planets, and moon; and cycles of creation and destruction) helps us see ourselves as part of a deep system of nature. It is no surprise that early mythic and spiritual beliefs around the planet developed based on the circularity of time and nature (as experienced

---

*I use the word "Western" to refer to the scientific and political processes and rapid technologies that began in Europe and developed over the last several centuries around the world, but truly all world cultures, from the earliest of times, have had rational, scientific developments side by side with other belief systems and philosophies.

by humans and other life-forms on the planet)—what is perhaps surprising is how, once the Age of Enlightenment and scientific technologies developed, the human race has shifted to a worldview that is linear, developmental, and reliant on the knife of logic to solve all problems and with which to understand the universe. The Maya mythologies and spiritual views help us see, from the perspective of ancient Mesoamerica, the "deep" unconscious structure of the human species. The human psyche is part of the ecology of the planet. Indeed, we can hypothesize that the human unconscious (a phenomenon shared by all humans living and past) developed on this particular planet, with a deep knowledge of our universe and our place in it, which, if tapped into, can help us overcome the dangers of our one-sided scientific/materialistic viewpoint (or, as Neil Young called it, the "aimless blade of science"; Young 1979). The Maya mythologies, developed—as far as we know—independently of other world cultures, resonate well with Hindu concepts of Brahma, Vishnu, and Shiva and the stories of the *Mahabarata*, as well as with the spiritual insights of the Tao in China and many of the myths of cultures around the world.

Carl Jung himself touched on some of the mythologies of the Mesoamerican cultures in his writings, but he did not write about these myths in detail. Since his time, research and knowledge about the Maya culture have greatly increased through the hard work and dedication of many persons, as described in *The Splendors of the Maya*, and not least through the active continuation of the tradition by the Maya themselves. Furlotti takes us through the historical, cultural, and anthropological knowledge of the Maya culture, but she also augments it with her own life experience and approaches this material from the standpoint of analytical psychology. It is clear that the Maya spiritual ideas are alive in the Maya people today (who, like all modern humans, can draw on ancient traditions as well as the current scientific/materialist view of the world) and that, through work such as this book, these ideas are also speaking to many other people from other cultures. The Maya have gone through their own historic cycle of developing into a large and sophisticated society, then seeing it fall to ruins, then reviving in a new form—something we may well be facing on a global scale now. No doubt our scientists and politicians may be needed to help us through the challenges we now face. But I would venture to say that the Maya culture can give us spiritual and psychological tools to utilize as well, and these may be needed more than ever.

All of this said, the Maya myths are not just "circular" in form, although their concept of the universe going through cycles of death and rebirth is central. As one will see in this book, with repeated cycles, there can be development and knowledge, and it is perhaps the fate of both the human species and the individual human to go through stages of failure and then regroup to find a different way of being. The flow of how the Maya stories develop reminds me of the work of therapy with individuals, which I see much more as a "spiral" process, where themes come and go in a sometimes circular fashion but, with some luck, also offer an increasing wisdom with every turn in the spiral. The Maya myths also seem replete with information (and examples) regarding how humans should behave, our place in relationship to each other, other animals, the spiritual world, and all of nature. They are filled with drama, tragic and comic, and tell us as much about our human nature and our place in the universe as the best of Shakespeare's works.

The Maya were students not just of this earth but of the universe, and no doubt their mathematical study of astronomy clued them in to the cyclic patterns of all nature. As seeing, hearing, feeling beings, with our minds and brains reflecting the nature that surrounds us, *Homo sapiens* have evolved as part of the cosmos, and our knowledge of the universe is both conscious and unconscious. The Maya astronomers were kindred spirits to later Europeans like Nicolaus Copernicus, using instruments, their senses, and careful recordings to discern the motions of the planets and stars. Copernicus upset the then current paradigm of the West by his insight that the earth and other planets revolved around the sun. But the fact that our existence on the planet, and the part of the cosmos we are embedded in, was tied to cycles, circles, and rotation, was knowledge deeply embedded in the psyche of the Maya and, one can surmise, all human beings, for many ages (Copernicus appreciated the cosmic design of rotations—he just intuited, built on the details of his observations, that our subjective frame of mind was preventing us from understanding that our own planet was moving in daily and annual rotations of our own). Perhaps a solution to how to live in a psychologically sound manner on our planet is to develop that dialogue between our collective consciousness and the collective unconscious, and to become more adept at a non-dualistic approach to objective and subjective experience. The Maya myths can help us better discern the unconscious wisdom of the psyche, as their history, mathematics, astronomy, civilization, and edifices have brought us much conscious knowledge.

Furlotti shares in these writings some of her own personal experiences, with the dream image of a black jaguar stalking her, an image not from her outward reality (growing up in Southern California) but an image comfortably a part of the *Popol Vuh*'s images and stories. Her telling of this reminded me of encounters that the early-American analyst Joseph Henderson (1903–2007) had when he was being analyzed by Carl Jung (Hill 1978). Jung believed that people from America could draw effectively on the collective symbols and myths of the native peoples, and Henderson himself incorporated symbols from Hopi and Maya mythology into his own analytic work. Henderson, like Furlotti, delved deeply into the Maya culture in his own journey to become an analyst. For those of us growing up in the Americas, living on the same land where Native American cultures developed their sacred myths, there seems to be a natural tendency for us to resonate at a deep level with the art, poetry, and religions of those who have lived here long before us. Jung thought that the psychology of Americans of European ancestry was especially complex, as it needed to also draw from and build a relationship to Native American and African traditions that are important factors in our cultural milieu. *The Splendor of the Maya* is an important step forward in integrating Native American concepts and spiritual ideas with Jung's European-based psychological and spiritual perspectives, psychological work that those of us living in the Americas would all benefit from doing.

On a personal level, as a Mexican American (my father, Hector, emigrated from Mexico to the United States) it has been especially meaningful for me to see the lectures and read the work of Furlotti on the Maya culture. My first analyst, Carlos Martinez, was born in Mexico, practiced in San Francisco, and taught at Jungian institutes in Northern and Southern California. As I worked through the material of my own dreams in my analytic work with Carlos (in the early 1990s) and we reflected on the symbols together, we both felt there was a rich resource for understanding the psyche in the cultures of Mexico and Mesoamerica. At the time, though, there was little written about these cultures in the Jungian world. It is interesting to note that, since that time, a Jungian institute has been founded in Mexico, and in 2022, the International Association of Analytical Psychology had its first meeting in Latin America. I believe the publication of this book by Nancy Furlotti is very timely. *The Splendor of the Maya* will be an important resource both for those interested in Jungian psychology and the particular contributions of the Maya myths and spiritual insights to analytical psychology. I hope that, in doing so, it will encourage more persons of Latin American background to also become aware of analytical psychology and perhaps be stimulated to become analysts themselves. I also would like to thank the Jungian analyst Alex Peer for making available his Truchas Peak retreat space in New Mexico, where I completed the editing for this book, not far from the location of Jung's visit to Taos in 1925.

September 2022, Truchas, New Mexico   *Michael Escamilla*
General Editor,
Carolyn and Ernest Fay Series in
Analytical Psychology

ACKNOWLEDGMENTS

This book reflects my lifelong pursuit to understand and shed light on a civilization and culture that was prominent in the area south of where I grew up. Its influence is still apparent in the soil I walk on and the mist that surrounds me, its ghosts and influence still very much present. My early dreams pointed the way to an understanding of a culture so different from my own, yet still so alive. A shadow jaguar in an early dream introduced me to the real jaguars and to the jaguar god that still roamed the area and the psyches that pay attention to their silent but powerful movement. Thank you Xbalanqué for making your introduction. This was the first of many such dreams expressing symbolism that was alien to my worldview, that led me south, into a world richer than I could ever have imagined. I am especially grateful to Richard Hansen, the archaeologist in charge of the Mirador-Calakmul Basin in the Petén in Guatemala. He has been a source of unending inspiration over many years after my first visit to the site in the early 2000s. The work he continues to do there is critical not only regarding the many Preclassic Maya cities but also for the remaining rain forest seriously under threat and the indigenous Maya still living in the area.

This book is the result of many years of research. My appreciation and gratitude go to my dissertation committee that gave me the encouragement I needed to complete my research: Eugene Taylor, chair, who unfortunately died suddenly during an early stage of my work; James Hollis, who stepped in with grace and support to see it through and never stopped encouraging me to give lectures and get this material published; and Priscilla Murr and Dennis Slattery for their interest and insights. A big heartfelt thanks goes to Frank Mc-Millan for his interest in my work and his friendship and for recommending me for the Fay Lecture, allowing me to have the opportunity to give voice to all the spirits that roam unrecognized.

Finally, I would like to thank all the wonderful people at the Jung Center of Houston who organized the details of the Fay Lecture held both in person and online, making sure we were safe during the COVID pandemic. A very special thanks goes to Michael Escamilla for his interest in my topic, his insightful questions, careful editing of the manuscript, his poignant foreword, and *his* calm and thoughtful presence. I am endlessly grateful to Texas A&M University for its willingness to publish this book, and to Thom Lemmons, editor in chief; especially Abagail Chartier, assistant project editor; and Cynthia Lindlof, copyeditor, for their help shepherding this book to publication. I hope it goes beyond borders, beyond the world of psychology, to offer further richness to the understanding of Maya culture.

THE SPLENDOR OF THE MAYA

INTRODUCTION

The focus of this book is to give you an overview of the Maya culture
as it existed from about three thousand years ago and to explore the
meaning, function, and continuing significance of the *Popol Vuh*, the
K'iche' Maya creation myth, from a Jungian psychological perspective. By examining the themes, metaphors, images, and symbols contained in this myth, one can through the process of amplification extract the psychological meaning of the myth that is pertinent to both
the collective understanding of myth, the collective unconscious, and
the process of individuation as formulated by C. G. Jung.

The *Popol Vuh* was established as a significant epic story of creation that arose in a sophisticated and important American culture
in Mesoamerica isolated from the rest of the developing world. It
deserves to take its rightful place alongside similar creation myths
from other prominent cultures of the world. From it, one can glean
a clearer understanding of the foundation of the Maya culture, their
conception of the greater cosmos, and the template laid out to cope
with the challenges of life and the beyond. Their cultural and spiritual challenges hold a memory that is crucial to us in our current age.
It is a pity to ignore it.

My interest in Mesoamerican mythology goes back to early dreams
I had as a child and more recent ones that contain images I could best
explain from an understanding of this mythology. One of my earliest
powerful dreams was of a black jaguar stalking me. Of course, it was
terrifying, but why a jaguar, an animal I had no relationship with nor
had ever seen? I wondered why my psyche would pick this particular
image. I had to think beyond the images and symbols I was accustomed to, and that led me to Mexico and the Mesoamerican culture
where the jaguar is an important figure in their mythology. I also had
dreams of double-headed snakes with bird and jaguar heads. As you
will see, these images play important roles in this mythology. Because
they were frightening and persistent, I had to make a relationship

1

with these animals and all they represented, which in part is the capacity to carry the opposites of light and dark, reason and instinct.

Growing up in Los Angeles provided the soil that was steeped in this mythology and these images. My psyche absorbed them and used them to grab my attention and guide me on my life journey. I developed an affinity for tolerating the extremes, including life and death, and with that I discovered the potential for rebirth—the third process that completes the cycle. Shadow, the unrecognized elements of our personality, is ever present, and the goal is to shine a light in the dark to bring forth the dawn of consciousness, an understanding of one's shadow, and new life itself. This spectacular myth, the *Popol Vuh*, speaks to this process of creation, how difficult it is, how many failures there are along the way, and finally with luck and a good day, success. I found these ideas mirrored the process of individuation (one's personal development) that is described in C. G. Jung's writings. While the *Popol Vuh* is a myth, and myths are discarded aspects of religions, they contain symbols and images that reflect the collective movement of the culture in the creation of a cohesive society with its rituals, ethics, and standards of behavior. C. G. Jung's theories can elucidate the personal as well as the collective.

I owe a debt of immense gratitude to the Maya for lending me their myths and symbols, which nudged me along my journey to establish a relationship to the greater Self and giving my life meaning.* It helped me put our world into a larger context, full of light and dark, strife and joy, and it also speaks to the need for a constant relationship with the gods and how that relationship is reciprocal—the face we turn to the gods, or the greater Self, is the face it turns to us. The Maya were a deeply religious people, and every aspect of their lives expressed their relationship to the cosmos. The gods demanded that they respect and honor them to maintain the balance between earth, sky, and the underworld—the *axis mundi* that reaches into all three dimensions.

The Maya still worship, although the religion has been Christianized. Their gods now express themselves as Christian saints. The old

*Jungian terms such as "Self" are defined in Appendix 1.

The main Preclassic sites in the Maya region.
Adapted by author from map by Krause and Pendergast in Grube (2001).

religions never disappear; they merely fall into the deeper layers of the unconscious and emerge as images and symbols in our dreams, in our behaviors, and frequently in our symptoms. Jung rediscovered this fact, that humans live with a repository of past symbols that press up from the unconscious striving for that light of awareness that creates wholeness and gives meaning to one's life. Soul resides between light and dark. One's consciousness is widened by an understanding and tolerance for what was previously intolerable, and in so doing one's ego is strengthened. Individuation is a tough process. This

Maya timeline

Preclassic	2000 BCE to 300 BCE
Middle Preclassic	1000 BCE to 300 BCE
Early Sedentary Occupation	1000 BCE to 800 BCE
Formal Stone Platforms	800 BCE to 600 BCE
Late Preclassic	300 BCE to 250 CE
Classic	250 CE to 900 CE
Terminal Classic	900 CE to 1000 CE
Postclassic	1000 CE to 1542 CE

myth shows the failures, missteps, and difficulties along the way. The hero twins have to die many times and be torn to pieces, just as we do in analysis as we strive to clear away our destructive emotions and behaviors. "Death, blackness, decomposition and guilt are essential prerequisites of the *opus*, which have to be affirmed and suffered" (Neumann 1969, 145). We witness the struggle in this myth where it shows that one has to persevere through great difficulty to reach the goal, to accept help from the animals around and within us. One has to be tricky to find the way and to finally trust the Self and accept that the ego with its arrogance and desire for power and control is not the center of the universe. We experience these same steps in analysis and through the alchemical process of transformation, which Jung recognized and formulated into his psychological theories.

This book begins with an overview, touching on some of the significant aspects of the Maya culture and its creation myth as we begin to spiral deeper and deeper into it in greater detail to finally descend into the underworld with the younger hero twins as they depotentiate the demons—representing the shadow world and those psychological complexes that disrupt and destroy. Only then will the dawn of the new world, the fourth world, arrive, and we will emerge from our journey to stand again together on the face of the earth.

CHAPTER 1

REVISITING THE WELL
AT THE DAWN OF LIFE

One thing we can count on is that life is ever-changing. We have ample evidence of this from evolution, extinctions, mutations, the rise and fall of cultures, and what we experience in our own process of individuation.* We never arrive at an end point but remain on a long trajectory that keeps challenging us to grow and expand our world-view. That's why we cannot say we are individuated. It is a process of continual growth and development that moves much like an upward spiral around and around, reaching points we have touched on before but at different levels of the trajectory. We would like to think this spiral generally moves upward toward greater consciousness as we as individuals and the world's cultures gain more insight and under-standing, but there are also times when it descends and we seemingly have forgotten what we have learned.

The descent in alchemy is into depression, the *nigredo*, where all is black and blue and the memory of other times is inaccessible. We are forced to retreat into the desert of our being away from the lush, fruitful creatively accessible parts of ourselves. The dry land is full of heat and sand, where nothing grows and nourishment is limited. We wait, suffering the loss of what was once there, what we took for granted, resources we misused without thought: thrown back on ourselves to find a way forward, waiting for some new spark of light, some knowing spirit within to guide us out of this perilous land, not to return to what we remember but to discover something new, a new way forward. We pray this spirit or soul spark will appear—tiny like a firefly grabbing our attention and then disappearing, becoming stronger as we trust and follow, allowing the psyche to lead the way.

*Excerpts of this text were originally published in Shalit (2018, 179–97). Permission from Chiron Publications was granted to use them here.

Remembering there is such a force as a psyche is important—remembering its purpose, its presence, how it has shaped past worlds and has the capacity to do so again. Yet psyche cannot do this alone. Its mysterious intention is intrinsically connected to each one of us as the physical being who is capable of implementing its creative design, or not. Do we move up the spiral or down? History has shown we do both. Whether we participate actively in the evolution of our cultures is up to us. Without our participation our dominance and culture recede while the natural process of change continues on its natural course as a never-ending spiral.

I remember once hearing a physicist remark that with the inhalation of our breath we might be breathing in atoms that once made up the philosopher who was Plato. This points to the fact that life recycles itself endlessly. The disturbing feature in this statement is the implication that we are not so very important. We are made up of many parts that will be remade after we as we know ourselves are gone.

There is so much we don't know about the workings of the cosmos even though we presume to control our world, supported by the limited belief in the supremacy of science and technology. We are not actually the ones in control, but we may just have the ability to influence the process and the ultimate outcome for our species and the many others on this shared planet.

We *Homo sapiens sapiens* are the result of an incredible experiment of nature that made us—animals capable of creative thinking, language, and consciousness. Yet many of us contain the hereditary marks of extinct Neanderthals or Denisovans. I contain 2.7 percent Neanderthal DNA, for example. We now know that we live in a careful balance, supported by a multitude of other extinct organisms, still living within our DNA and within our gut. The template for life seems to be a reciprocity between a multitude in symbiotic relationship that makes up the one.

I am mindfully aware of how easy it is for this careful reciprocity that balances nature to go wrong. A glaring example is the specter of global climate change, which we have all witnessed and experienced increasing in intensity over the past years.

We have ignored warnings, we have gone into denial—we have not wanted to change, to believe this is possible. How could the earth stop taking care of us? She is our Great Mother after all, isn't she? How can we psychologically understand our participation in this dramatic shift? To start, it always helps to go back in history, to past cultures, to mythology, and into our collective memory bank to see what happened in the past when consciousness approached a similar challenge on the grand spiral of time.

Our Western mode of belief sees life as linear—starting at a beginning point of creation and ending at some unknown apocalyptic point in the future. Being of this mindset, many frequently fear that the end-time is imminent, visited upon us from some greater force like the gods. We live with this fear while ignoring the very real prospect that it may not come from some cosmic catastrophe but instead from our own hands.

In fact, we humans are creating an environmental disaster like none other through our total disregard for a living relationship to the soul of nature, the *anima mundi*. From our worst characteristics as a species—being arrogant, aggressive, self-serving, fearful animals that we are—we have wandered far away from the path that bridges soul and spirit, the cosmos and nature. We, in our shortsightedness, are poisoning our environment; heating it up, causing droughts and floods, starvation, migration, loss of fertile land; reducing our rain forests that give us oxygen and fresh water; acidifying our oceans and killing them, too. All this puts pressure on our societies, and strife results. Wars break out for the remaining resources. We consider building walls to keep the inevitable flood of migrants out as more and more are forced to leave unforgiving, lifeless lands across the globe from Central America, Africa to Asia.

We were created with free will, as many creation myths point out, allowing us to make choices. Free will allows us to respect and honor our creators, those forces of many names, the archetypes that influence our behaviors, and the natural balance between all species of animals, plants, and minerals on our shared earth—or not. We seem to have lost our respect for the Great Mother, the *anima mundi* that cares for us, feeds us, holds us—and has done so since we evolved out of our exclusively animal selves. With our belief that we can take from her whatever we please, in any way, and pour into her toxins that both stifle her and her other creatures, we are unwittingly choking off our source of life.

Not only have we lost our relationship to the Great Mother along the way but to the Great Spirit as well. The natural balance between the spirit world, the earthly realm, and the underworld has been forgotten. We have become sophisticated, clever, and technologically adept, seemingly rational and superior to all else on our planet, but we have forgotten the importance of balance. As Jungian psychologist E. Neumann pointed out, "The further progress of mankind will in fact depend, to no small degree, on whether it proves possible to prevent the occurrence of [the] splitting process in the collective psyche" (1969, 58). It seems that is exactly where we are right now. We have forgotten our creation myths, our stories and the imperative to honor the gods—those forces greater than us. Even carrying the marks of extinct species in our own DNA, we forget this can also happen to *Homo sapiens sapiens*, leaving us not so "wise" as our name suggests.

FORGOTTEN WORLDS, MYTHIC STORIES

Returning to history and lessons from the past, I turn to the K'iche' Maya creation myth from Mesoamerica called the *Popol Vuh*, which is a striking example of a story that lays out a template for humanity to live in balance with spirit and nature. It is a forgotten, obscure piece of writing that was almost destroyed to intentionally leave no evidence of it or its civilization's existence. Thankfully it survived, sequestered away and preserved for us to reflect on and held in the memory of its people. This myth is significant because it represents the collective mindset of a very sophisticated civilization that evolved in America, uninfluenced by the rest of the world except through the shared objective psyche.

It is no easy task to work with this material because so much of the culture and writings was destroyed, and I am approaching it from a completely different perspective than most others. Previously this myth has been studied from the perspectives of anthropology, ethnography, art history, and socio-politics, but no one has undertaken a

Jungian psychological study of the myth. The purpose of examining the themes, metaphors, images, and symbols contained in this myth through a Jungian lens is to extract the psychological meaning of the myth that may be pertinent to both the collective understanding of myth and the individuals' process of what Jung described as "individuation." While most anthropologists, ethnologists, and art historians studying Mesoamerica describe the symbols and images, they do not speculate on their meaning. While extrapolating the name of a symbol from the context of the scene in which it is placed and the hieroglyphs naming it, the meaning for the most part remains elusive.

Previous studies found meaning in reference to other local sources such as neighboring cultures, later cultures, or current cultures of Mesoamerica. It was not their purpose or interest to think about this material from a psychological perspective. The prevailing view seems to be that "models of reality reified in religion, myth, ritual, and symbol systems (are) instruments of collective response to existing social conditions" (Freidel and Schele 1988, 88). Yet a few researchers strived for a deeper understanding by looking outside the bounds of this culture alone and by examining the work of "daykeepers,"* who still listen to the ancient murmurings that spring from the psyche through their interpretation of the calendars. They hold the belief that ancient whispers of the gods continue to speak through them, as the "lightning" rushes through their bodies as heated blood, giving them second sight, much like the visions and dream images received from the dream voice, which collectively emerge as myths.

From a Jungian standpoint, the metaphors and symbols of this myth are not only unique to the Maya world but carry within them an archetypal meaning, which is universal. While this archetypal perspective remains a contested standpoint in other fields, for our purposes, I present the Jungian argument. Conclusions are proposed

---

*Daykeepers are the shamanic priests who are "active practitioners of the indigenous religion who are initiated calendar diviners, dream interpreters, and curers" (B. Tedlock 1982, 42). They understand the sacred texts and calendars and read them for information about the nature of the days and future events. Each day represents a different archetypal energy, and it is the daykeepers' job to pay attention to the movement of the energies through the days.

from the amplification that has allowed better comparison to other creation myths throughout Mesoamerica and the world. Robicsek and Hales extended their work beyond the borders of Mesoamerica when they pointed out that "ancient Maya vase paintings can be arranged in a sequence and read as pages of a codex. These vases represent merely a fragment of a much larger mythological scenario that once must have been, as M. Coe has suggested, akin to *the Egyptian Book of the Dead* or its Tibetan counterpart" (1981, 274).

The *Popol Vuh* is a complete creation myth and is easily comparable to books of the dead. As will be discussed later in relation to the Jungian viewpoint, mythic material appears in individuals' dreams; therefore, the motifs from the *Popol Vuh* may appear in dreams as well. The presence of these analogues provides support for Jung's (1977a) concepts of the universality of archetypes and the collective unconscious. While I am not an anthropologist, archaeologist, or ethnographer, I am a Jungian analyst, and my interest focuses on the potential meaning of the myth, symbols, and images and how they impact development.

"The *Popol Vuh*, also known by other names—*The Book of Council, The Light That Came from across the Sea, Our Place in the Shadows,* and *The Dawn of Life*—is a metaphorical expression of the origins of the Quiché Maya culture" (D. Tedlock 1985, 23–24). From evidence of early murals and carvings it is clear that this myth was prevalent in Maya culture across Mesoamerica.

The Maya are an ancient group of people who have lived in southern Mexico, Guatemala, Honduras, Belize, and El Salvador from around 2000 BCE to the present. The Maya rose to the heights of an incredible civilization in Preclassic time, 800 BCE to 150 CE, in the Mirador-Calakmul Basin in the Petén lowland area in central Guatemala. To help locate where this is, you may be familiar with Tikal, one of the cities just outside this area that arose from 400 BCE to 200 CE and was primarily a Classic city-state. The Maya in El Mirador, a large well-established city-state in the Petén, were in constant conflict with the rulers of the city-state of Tikal, who later joined forces with the fierce warriors of Teotihuacan from central Mexico to inflict harm on their neighboring city-states.

"The Quiché Maya were a militaristic group originally from the Petén, the Maya lowlands, who migrated to western highland Guatemala sometime during the Early Postclassic period, between 900 CE and 1200 CE" (Christenson 2003, 27). There are currently about half a million Quiché Maya, now referred to as K'iche', still living in the region. Our focus is on these creative, hardworking Maya who took their culture to a state level of civilization. Fifteen hundred years before the Spanish conquest, the Maya developed a sophisticated hieroglyphic system of writing. It is a linguistic system consisting of symbols of thoughts and objects along with symbols representing sounds of words. In other words, it was partly phonetic and partly logographic. This combination results in a system of writing capable of complex literary compositions. This is roughly parallel to Greco-Roman development, yet it developed quite independently. There were and are many different languages in the Maya world. There is evidence of early writing in the Preclassic lowlands around 200 BCE and elsewhere even earlier.

In addition to their language and system of writing, the Maya developed a very sophisticated means of counting time. They conceived a calendar system that consisted of the intersection of two calendars: one was for telling the past and future, the lunar Tzolk'in; and the other, the solar Haab', was used for laying out the rituals necessary to ensure proper relationship to the gods and sufficient harvests. These two calendars combined to form what is called the Long Count, allowing calculations into the far distant past and well into the future.

The Maya were brilliant astronomers and mathematicians and developed an ability to calculate time unsurpassed by any other civilization in the world. It was they who developed the concept of zero, referring to the end or completeness, a fertile void, rather than absence as we conceive of zero, yet Arabs in India are usually given credit for this discovery. Zero, as a glyph in the K'iche' language, is seen as a head with a hand over the lower jaw. *Lub* is the place or the erect flat stone, where the traveler rests his pack at the crossroads.

The beginning date of their calendar and of this fourth and current world is August 11, 3114 BCE. You might remember December 21, 2012, when the Maya fourth world on their calendar came to an end and people were predicting an apocalypse. Of course, nothing happened except the end of that cycle rolled into the next cycle in its continuing circular fashion.

It has been estimated there were about eight million Maya living in the Preclassic period, and currently there are approximately six million Maya still living, the majority in Guatemala, which is 40 percent Maya. Many have immigrated to the United States. The Maya civilization thrived and was at its peak from 800 BCE to 150 CE before its sudden collapse and huge population migration to other areas. By 900 CE there was a second and final collapse of a small group that had reestablished itself in El Mirador, along with the collapse and decline of the rest of the Maya world. By that time the Maya culture, influenced by central Mexico, had shifted first from Tikal, Calakmul, and Copan to Chichén Itzá and Mayapán in the Yucatán Peninsula in Mexico.

The more familiar Aztecs were a late arrival, 1200 CE, and of short duration—three hundred years until the arrival of the Spaniards in 1519 CE. They assumed the mythology and customs of those groups around them as a way of giving themselves credibility through ancestry. Indeed, the different Mesoamerican peoples shared much of their mythology and customs. For them, being connected through time and mythology was crucial and created their reality.

As the Maya developed into an agricultural culture, their mythology reflects the interrelationship and dependence on the gods for healthy and productive functioning. The gods were personifications of the seasons, weather patterns, the movement of the sun, moon, and Venus across the sky. Through the movement of the celestial bodies, time was tracked and rituals were performed to keep the cycle moving through the passage of the days, years, seasons, and eons. It was the responsibility of the shaman-lords, the K'uhul Ajaws, and family elders to maintain a relationship with the gods and the veneration of the ancestors through rituals and bloodletting. Building large temples and plazas for ritual displays held the group together. As David Freidel clarifies, "Ancient Maya ideology were the interconnected, fundamental ideas held by elite and commoners alike about the order of the cosmos and everything in it" (2018, 87). Religion was the principal source of power for the ruling elite, who were not significantly involved with organizing and overseeing the practical issues of the state. Yet as the elite class grew and power and lineage challenges became more common, they expanded their temple construction to further cement their power. This required larger populations to build the structures and more people to feed. Wars and the need to defend themselves from neighboring city-states increased, as is seen by the addition of fortifications around many cities. This expansion altered their focus on healthy stewardship of the land and resulted in a breakdown of values—the balance between nature and spirit, humans and the gods.

The K'uhul Ajaws served the role of *axis mundi*, the personified axis of the universe. As A. Demarest points out:

> Auto-sacrifice was not the only source of blood offered to
> the ancestors and deities. Turkeys, macaws, and bats were
> offered up in ritual. While mass human sacrifice on the scale
> of the sixteenth-century Aztecs was not practiced . . . they did
> carry out sacrifices of captives through decapitation. Far more
> regularly auto-sacrifice, incense and prayers were a part of daily
> life. . . . Blood was conceived as a "holy essence," the sacred
> glue that bound together the universe, connecting humankind
> to the ancestors and deities. The various sacrificial rites and
> bloodletting released this sacred substance, creating portals
> for communication to the supernaturals, to the past, and to the
> future. (2004, 191, quoted in Freidel, Schele, and Parker 1993,
> 201–24)

"Their focus was on the cycle of life and death, providing the metaphor for the agricultural cycle and the annual rebirth of the crops" (Demarest 2004, 182). The survival of the group depended on knowing when to plant, when to cultivate, and when to harvest and having plenty of rich topsoil and water for the plants. As an agricultural society, they focused on the circularity of the seasons throughout the year. The movement of the sun across the horizon was traced from birth to death as it descended in the west at dusk. From there it went through the nine layers of the underworld, to struggle with the gods of the dead, vanquish them, and then rise above the horizon in the eastern dawn to welcome another day—a repetition of what the gods themselves, the Maize God, Sun, and Moon, had once done to start the world in motion.

Through the reenactment of the myth of creation, historical time is paused while sacred time allows it to begin anew, as Mircea Eliade so clearly explained:

> Sacred time appears under the paradoxical aspect of a circular time, reversible and recoverable, a sort of eternal mythical present that is periodically reintegrated by means of rites. . . . Sacred time does not live in the historical present. For the religious person, profane time can be periodically arrested. Cosmos is world. For the archaic cultures the world is renewed annually. The New Year comes from the sanctity of the creator's hand. The New Year is a time of purification—the expulsion of demons or scapegoats. Saturnalia is a return to chaos. . . . Life cannot be repaired, it can only be recreated through symbolic repetition of the cosmogony. . . . The origin myth was copied after the cosmogonic myth, for the latter is the paradigmatic model for all origins. (1957, 70–84)

The myths and development of culture move hand in hand, the one influencing the language and thought that is used to form the structure and guide the interactions of the people. Just as spirit and matter are inseparable, these two halves influence each other even when one side is forgotten and relegated to the shadows of unconsciousness. When this happens, the shadow takes on an uncontrollable power, forcing its recognition—usually in a destructive way.

The Maya were in decline in 1524 when a Spaniard named Pedro de Alvarado was peacefully invited to enter the K'iche' capital city, Cumarcah, or Utatlán in Nahua. Fearing a trap, he executed the Maya rulers and in so doing, along with the smallpox and measles he brought with him, completed the decimation of the civilization.

MYTH AND RITUAL

The Maya live according to a ritual calendar that sees time as cyclic, not linear. In the ever-changing movement from one moment to another, each moment reflects the unique quality of a different god, representing a specific archetypal energy. The Maya world was created and destroyed three times. We live in their fourth world, and according to their ritual calendar, it may again be destroyed and re-created as necessary in the constantly moving cycle of change. What form a new creation will take, we don't know, but we do know why the first three worlds were destroyed. The cause of the demise of each of the prior worlds was a loss of relationship between the created and the divine. The gods sacrificed themselves to bring humanity into existence and in return require respect and sacrifice in their honor. This is a potent, reciprocally beneficial psychological contract that was put in place through their mythology and informed every aspect of their lives and culture.

Their myth reflects the typical union of opposites in the early matrix of chaos before energies have been differentiated, then come together again at the end of the process when they reunite into wholeness represented symbolically by the birth of the new god, in this case the Maize God. The new symbol opens the way for the creation of a cohesive culture including spirit and nature, compassion and reason.

It is by no means an easy process because to achieve wholeness or the birth of the new god, mythic heroes had to first fight to domesticate the underworld gods—those demons we would say are the wild, out-of-control instinctual energies that reside in the unconscious. These demon instincts—power, arrogance, vanity, greed, hatred, lies—need to be defeated before culture can emerge with its new guiding symbol, laws, and collective behaviors.

For the Maya, words connected to nature such as "sowing," "dawning," "sprouting" are used to refer to the dawning of new life, light, and humanity. This is an agricultural metaphor related to the birth, death, and rebirth cycle of nature and all of the earth's inhabitants. Maize was used to create the humans in the fourth world.

The goal for the Maya gods is the creation of a race of beings that can contain and express consciousness and reflect it back to the gods in a more differentiated way. The gods want a race that can speak their names and worship them in the form of prayer and sacrifice:

> A fundamental aspect of indigenous highland Maya religion is the belief that human beings stand as essential mediators between this world and that of their patron deities and ancestors. Sacred ritual performed at the proper time and in a manner established by ancient precedent, is necessary to maintain this link or all creation runs the risk of collapse. (Christenson 2003, 71n66)

The Maya words used to describe what the gods desired from humans included "purity of being," "truth," "light," "clarity," "whiteness," and "brightness." The gods wanted their creation to honor them and make offerings and sacrifices, in other words, to be in relationship with them. This points to what was of highest value in the Maya culture. The creators were trying to create people who *ponder*, *consider*, and *have compassion*. Those who are alive have light, while those who are dead are hidden from the sun.

THE RAIN FOREST WEEPS

The Maya were strongly forewarned in the *Popol Vuh* about the wrong attitude that could lead to their civilization's decline in the story of Seven Macaw, the vainglorious bird who usurped power after the destruction of the third world, and in the destructive actions of the demons in the underworld. The correct attitude is one of humility and respect for the sacred. Sacrifice comes from the word *sacer*, meaning "holy or sacred." When humans fall out of relationship to the sacred, humility that comes with sacrifice is forgotten, soul is lost, and shadow escapes through an open door into our individual lives and into our cultures. We run the risk of embracing the material world as the only reality, which was Seven Macaw's mistake. Power and striving for wealth seem too great a seduction for humans even with all the warnings, and for the Maya this took the form of frequent wars with neighboring city-states and grandiose construction projects.

There are many theories about why the Preclassic Maya civilization collapsed. It might have been due to a series of droughts, epidemic disease, overpopulation, or severe conflicts with neighboring groups like those in Tikal. It is speculated that climate change drives the rise and fall of civilizations across the globe. Richard Hansen, the lead archaeologist in charge of the excavation in the Mirador-Calakmul Basin where there were 417 major cities and over 964 smaller communities (these figures may change when new evidence arises), has theorized that as their striving for power and desire to impress themselves and surrounding cities increased (or, in the words of the *Popol Vuh*, their vaingloriousness), the Maya sought to build larger and higher temples. Each one was covered with white plaster on which they vividly painted the buildings with mostly red paint. To make the plaster, they needed lime, which they removed from their limestone quarries, and to achieve a heat high enough to produce the white plaster, they burned an abundance of green trees. Therefore, the Maya clear-cut the trees in the rain forest, allowing plaster runoff into the water holes, the *bajos*, with dire consequences (Hansen 2018, 171–73).

To give an example of the scale of construction I am talking about at El Mirador, let me give some comparisons. The most massive pyramid in the world is La Danta, 236 feet high and 2.8 million cubic meters in volume, built during this Preclassic period. The second largest temple in El Mirador is called El Tigre and was constructed in about 600 BCE. It was eighteen stories high or 180 feet, six times the surface area of the largest pyramid at Palenque. All of the major pyramids, the acropolis, and the plaza at Tikal, the Classic Maya site, could fit inside El Tigre. It took five million man-days of labor to build, or one thousand men working for thirteen years, and required twelve men to carry each block, which weighed about one thousand pounds. It must be remembered that the Maya had no beasts of burden. Humans did all the heavy lifting.

At the top of El Tigre remains evidence of a bloody battleground, including hundreds of spear tips and arrowheads, bone fragments, and smashed pottery. The battle most likely took place between 400 and 300 BCE between the remnants of El Mirador's Kan Kingdom's royal family (Kan refers to snake, yellow, and precious) and warriors from Teotihuacan fighting with those from Tikal.

The Maya also built a series of raised causeways, or *sacbeob*, white roads of stone covered with lime plaster that rose above the rain forest floor. *Sac* means "white," and *be* means "road." These were 6 to 12 feet high and 90 to 120 feet wide with a thick layer of plaster covering them. The oldest date speculated for this construction was about twenty-four hundred years ago (Bawaya 2007, 22).

This early highway system allowed the Maya to connect to the many cities in the basin as well as to transport the rich topsoil from *bajos* and *civales*, swampy marshes, scattered through the Mirador-Calakmul Basin, to replenish the agricultural fields. Yet over five hundred years (300 BCE to 200 CE) the Maya increased the quantity of lime plaster used to cover their buildings, from a thin veneer of one-half to one inch thick to five to fifteen inches thick. With the heavy depletion of the forests and the runoff of plaster clay into the marshes containing the nutrient-rich muck used for topsoil, it was locked in like cement and no longer accessible for collection to replenish the fields. The Maya could no longer grow food. Conspicuous consumption caught up with them.

The rain forest is a very difficult environment to live in. It can be intermittently wet with rainfall from May to September and arid the rest of the year. While the Maya took great care in creating water systems to capture and direct the flow of water, it was the unique presence of the *civales* or *bajos* in the Mirador-Calakmul Basin that supplied the precious fertile topsoil that enabled vast food production on their terraced land to support the development of the Preclassic Maya civilization. They grew vegetables, including corn, peppers, squash, and beans. The soil was so fertile that it could yield two to three crops a year. It was a tenuous balance between water, agricultural fertility, and population growth.

The Maya system was built on growth and expansion that funneled wealth to the nobility, ruled by the divine king who oversaw ritual, religion, war, and temple construction. The economy itself was left to others. It was an inflexible system that could be thrown into imbalance easily by increased conflicts or sudden drought. With such a rigid social system it is difficult to change course when necessary. It is believed that human disruption of the balance in the Preclassic Maya natural world, droughts, the large population needed for building, and wars resulted in a disaster that led to the area's sudden collapse and abandonment in 150 CE. The unusual environment with ample water and fertile soil supported a population of well over two hundred thousand in some of the many cities in the basin, millions overall. After this collapse, only a small group remained. Most migrated to Calakmul and Uaxactun. Nearby Tikal, with influence from the warrior-like Toltecs of Teotihuacan, rose to power and became an important Classic period site around from 200 CE until its demise in 900 CE.

Teotihuacan's influence can be clearly seen in Yucatán at Chichén Itzá, which rose to power after the final Maya collapse in 900 CE. It is interesting to note that the people in the Late Preclassic period in the Mirador-Calakmul Basin ranged from an average height of five feet eight inches to six feet three inches. The Maya stature, though, began to decline thereafter along with their previously nutritious food supply (Richard Hansen, pers. comm., November 18–21, 2013).

"Natural catastrophes were also common in Mesoamerica and played a role in the demise of the Maya. Years later, from approximately 1447 to 1545, it is documented that the Maya experienced fifteen earthquakes, two famines, a snowstorm, five solar eclipses, one fertile year in 1455, one comet, one plague of rats, eight smoking stars, an epidemic, a windstorm, and a final series of devastating epidemics" (Keber 1995, 318–23). These were all foretold through their calendrical calculations and occurred before the Spaniards arrived on Maya soil.

A lyrical poem was spoken and written by a singer who was a daykeeper/diviner some years before the arrival of the Spaniards. It gives a clear example of not only the visionary clarity of thought but also the poetic sensibility of the Maya. (One can only imagine what it was like listening to the singer/diviner and hearing about the future of their culture.)

> On the day 13-Ahau,
> the *k'atun* [twenty-year period] will come to an end,
> in the time of the Itzá,
> in the time of Tancha, Lord of Mayapán.
> There is a sign of the one and only God.
> The sacred tree will come,
> it shall be manifest to all,
> so that the world shall be enlightened, oh father.
> It will be the beginning of strife,
> the beginning of rivalry,
> the man-priest will come,
> he will bring the sign of God
> in the time to come, oh father!
> Shouting from a distance,
> he will come and you will see the pheasant
> which flies over the tree of life.
> A new day shall dawn in the north,
> it will dawn in the west,
> Itzam will disappear . . .
> the bearded men,
> the men who come from the east,
> the bearers of the sign of God.
> Everything will change in a moment.
> (Roys 1973, 167–68; Maya Text, 106, quoted in
> León-Portillo 1969, 91)

The Spaniards made landfall in the Caribbean and from there sailed to Yucatán during a score of stones named 2 Lord, according to the Maya calendar date, beginning in 1500 and ending in 1520. (Stones refer to a period of time in the Maya calendar.) "Little by little a great darkness, a great night, came over our fathers, our grandfathers, oh my sons, when they were sickened by the pox" (D. Tedlock 2010, 369). The Spaniards brought with them smallpox and measles that decimated not only the Maya but eventually all indigenous societies across the Western Hemisphere. This was one of the worst pandemics in the history of the world, killing 85 percent of the indigenous people, yet it is rarely spoken of. This decimation of the population made it easy for the Spaniards to conquer the rest of the indigenous population.

During the Postclassic period, the Maya were heavily influenced by groups beyond their borders, particularly from central Mexico. The Maya nobility spoke not only K'iche' but also the Nahua language of central Mexico as their second language and Toltec as their third language. Not only were there trade and political interactions, but many of the ceremonial practices and belief systems were adopted. For example, Quetzalcoatl was featured prominently in the *Popol Vuh* and referred to by the name Kukulkan. The feathered serpent and the K'iche' god Tohil were equivalent to Quetzalcoatl. Much earlier, in 378 CE, warriors from Teotihuacan arrived in the lowland Maya center, Tikal, imparting their influence and control. The Maya rulers began to claim their authority from Toltec and central Mexican lineages without losing their fundamental Maya character.

The K'iche' consisted of a diverse group of people living in the highlands of Guatemala, the lowlands, and Yucatán. They originated in the lowlands during the early Preclassic period (1200–900 BCE). There is a plaster carved frieze, dated 300 BCE, in a water canal in El Mirador of Hunahpú, one of the hero twins carrying his father's head. This indicates the myth was alive at that time in that location. "The *Popol Vuh* was a book that opened clear vision to the past, present, and future for those daykeepers who read it. It was based on *ilb'al*, which means 'instrument of sight or vision'" (Christenson 2003, 34).

The remaining Maya hymns and poems are considered to have a refined aesthetic sensitivity, as in the previous lyric poem. This is roughly parallel to Greco-Roman development, yet it developed quite separately. Those in many fields of study find it interesting that civilizations have developed independently yet exhibit parallel patterns, suggesting the possibility of organic, developmental dimensions of social evolution.

Another example of their poetry was sung and written down after the arrival of the Spaniards with a more grounded view of the conquest.

The Foreigners made it different
when they arrived here.
They brought shameful things
when they came here. . . .
No fortunate days
were granted to us then. . . .
This was the cause of our sickness.
No more fortunate days for us
no more decisions.
And in the end we lost our vision,
it was our shame.
Everything was revealed!
(Leon-Portilla 1969, 91)

The *Popol Vuh*, written down sometime between 1554 and 1558, is an expression of the central myth that was passed down in both verbal and written form from much earlier traditions, perhaps as far back as the Olmec and early Maya, three thousand years ago. It comprises the K'iche' myth, legends, and history, but also it is a literary epic, a book that most closely parallels the Bible for the Middle Eastern and Western cultures, and like the Bible has survived to the present in Maya culture. This book or story was presented as a poem with rhyme and humor. Only four Maya codices survived the destruction by the Spaniards, who burned hundreds of books. Because it was transcribed after the conquest, some consider it to be colonial (Ochiai 1986, 83–84). However, with the absence of Christian images and themes and the discovery of the hero twin frieze in the Mirador-Calakmul Basin dating to 300 BCE, it is now confirmed to be precolonial:

> No known Precolumbian text contains the kind of long story-
> telling devices, descriptive detail, commentary, and extensive
> passages of dialogue found in the *Popol Vuh*. It is more likely
> to have been a compilation of oral traditions based to one
> degree or another on mythic and historical details outlined in a
> Precolumbian codex with their associated painted illustrations.
> (Christenson 2003, 35)

In the mid-sixteenth century, a copy of the *Popol Vuh* was found that had been transcribed from oral tradition using the Latin alphabet to depict K'iche' words. This text was copied and translated into Spanish at the end of the seventeenth century by Father Francisco Ximénez, parish priest of the village of Santo Tomás Chichicastenango, which is in the lowlands of Guatemala. Two European travelers interested in aboriginal cultures happened upon this book. Carl Scherzer subsequently published a Spanish version, and Abbé Charles-Étienne Brasseur de Bourbourg translated and published the book in French at the beginning of the eighteenth century. The version written by Father Ximénez contains 112 folio pages in two columns with K'iche' on one side and Spanish on the other. It was brought to Europe by de Bourbourg and later acquired by Edward E. Ayer, who included it in his linguistic collection preserved in the Newberry Library in Chicago. A scanned copy of the contents of the *Popol Vuh*, prepared by Brigham Young University, is available digitally on CD-ROM (Christenson 2007).

The *Popol Vuh* can also be compared to great epic poems such as the *Mahabharata* and *Ramayana* of India or the *Iliad* and *Odyssey* of Greece. In its original language, it was written as a poem with parallelisms of all kinds, including couplets and triplets with repetitions and redundancies. This form of structure encouraged embellishment through the use of metaphors, synonyms, and descriptions to more specifically express the ideas. It was written without grammatical conventions of sentences, punctuation, or paragraphs. The use of parallelism served to structure the ideas into understandable units. It is very difficult to bring a sense of the poetic nature of the text into translation, as it can sound odd to the Western ear, for example:

Left behind his head their father.
Merely he was left at Crushing Ballcourt
(Christenson 2003, 151)

While in other verses it is clearer, such as:

It being manifest
It being declared,

It being expressed as well,
(Christenson 2003, 45)

In addition to the parallelisms, the use of mnemonics to imitate sounds was common as well as the play on words. Because this story was orally presented, the delivery was up to the bard to elaborate and add all poetic expressions that would be theatrically presented to maintain the attention of the audience. When read in text form, the intent was to conjure up vivid images in the mind of the reader: "The text was to be read and pondered rather than skimmed over" (Christenson 2003, 5).

The *Popol Vuh* was also called the *Dawn of Life* because it told of the first rising of the morning star, sun, and moon. The Maya world encompassed many different groups, but there is evidence that a similar worldview among the groups existed; this consists of the concept of the fivefold structure of material and spiritual space with the four directions and the fifth at the center as the *axis mundi* or world tree; their strong belief in the importance of ancestors; cyclic time as a sacred entity; the belief in the one-in-many principle of divinity (that the one god has many different manifestations); complementary dualism; the reciprocal nature between sacrifice and nurturing that binds humanity to the gods; supernatural combat and secular conflict as creative and life-sustaining forces; the belief that humans were made from the divine and life-sustaining substance maize; and the extraordinary power of spoken and written language as a symbolic entity in itself (Gossen 1986, 6–7).

The myth itself describes the creation of three inadequate worlds and finally a fourth, which is inhabited by humanity, the current world. Through the story, the history of the creation of the world and its ancestors is preserved. The Maya creation myth was at the heart of everything they represented in their art and architecture, in the very structure and planning of their houses and cities, as well as their social structure, ritual calendars, way of behaving, and view of the world. Additionally, it informs the group in regard to how they are to live their lives and the nature of their relationship to their creator. All cultures have creation myths that act as fundamental ordering principles for not only the culture but also for the individual. Many of these creation myths have similar motifs.

This creation myth duplicates, in story form, the movement of the sun, moon, Milky Way, Venus, Mars, and the Pleiades. "The Maya viewed the Milky Way as the road to Xibalbá [the underworld] and saw in the seasonal movements of constellations along the ecliptic their fundamental creation story" (Miller and Taube 1993, 157). The sky itself replays the creation in its yearly movements. Sunset on August 13 reveals the death of the god and darkness, while February 5 was the day of renewal or rebirth. It is said that the gods wrote mythic actions in the sky so that every human could read them and affirm the truth of the myth. This story is written down in the *Popol Vuh*, describing the creation of the world and its inhabitants out of the primordial sea and sky. It is a book that gives clear insight into the past, present, and future with its actions and characters representing moments in time that, according to the sacred calendars, repeat in a cyclic fashion.

Each god in the Maya pantheon has its contra-sexual opposite, and many times it is difficult to know which manifestation a god/goddess is taking. Each god/goddess contains the potential for both the creative and destructive. The gods are dynamic, and their qualities can be seen as not only opposite but also complementary (Austin 1993, 126). Further, A. Austin pointed out that "binary opposites [which have a] universal or almost universal presence . . . are intrinsic to the process of human thought" (168). The masculine is the celestial force considered dry, hot, and luminous, while the opposite comes from the underworld and is dark, feminine, wet, and cold. Both reflect the nature of the gods as well as the human soul, half luminous and half dark. These dichotomies are expressed as sacred and profane, natural and supernatural, or light and heavy. These elements manifest in the world in cyclic patterns in the form of time, ordering the world in positive and destructive ways. The Maya conception of their gods is parallel to other cultures' views of the gods, where the gods are ambivalent, dark and light, containing all opposites much like Abraxas, the Gnostic god, a combination of Christ and Satan. The Western monotheisms, however, fell into the trap of one-sidedness and got stuck in the idea of a theodicy where God is seen as divine goodness separate from evil. For the Maya, death and decay are a part of the eternal return.

This myth reflects a union of opposites, which is commonly seen in myths as the early matrix of chaos before elements have been differentiated and at the end when energies reunite into wholeness. Creation myths are about the movement from the primary matrix of chaos in the unconscious to a further differentiation of those energies. Words such as "sowing," "dawning," "sprouting" are used to refer to the dawning of new life, light, and humanity. The birth, death, and rebirth cycle reflects the planting of corn, as the growing of corn was a fundamental symbol for the cycle of life.

DAYKEEPERS: KEEPERS OF THE VISION

The *Popol Vuh* is the book that opens clear vision to the past, present, and future for the daykeepers who read it. The daykeepers were and continue to be the shamanic priests trained to read the day using divinatory calendars, to interpret dreams, and to effect cures. They are the ones who clear away the foggy breath on the mirror to see beyond the world of immediate reality into the further dimensions that are the domain of the gods. They remain open to the world of spirit and contemplate the natural cyclic progression of the cosmos to help fellow travelers on this life's journey relate to the multiplicity of influences at play. Parents will ask about the day of birth of a child, for example, wondering if it is auspicious or not—in other words, which god carries that particular day and what archetypal energies represented by that god will be their child's burden because of that day.

We have no such book, but we do have the ability to be introspective and observant. We have our dreams that can guide our decisions and actions, if only we would pay attention to them. Through them we hear the whispering of the psyche, of the larger cosmos, offering warning and guidance, nudging us to follow our journey in balance with spirit and nature. Our inner dream voice—the Self—is our equivalent of a daykeeper. It behooves us to remain in close contact with our own inner wise figure. However, when this relationship ceases to function, as it frequently does for individuals and for cultures, we lose our connection not only to the psyche but to the natural world as well. Similarly, we can easily find ourselves in a world of materialism, power, and violence. Nature pays a heavy price for this imbalance. For the Maya, the Mirador-Calakmul Basin environment became stripped and degraded to such an unanticipated extent that it could not sustain them, and this just may prove to be true for us as well. The Maya rulers failed to respond effectively with solutions to the increasing problems in the infrastructure of the state.

In such times of chaos, we humans fall back on our basic survival instincts. Yet these are shortsighted, tribal, and culturally destructive, pushing us into inflexible ideologies, fearful, if not paranoid of others. Memory is easily lost, and humanity does not learn the lessons from history as we forge ahead with our clouded visions about the future.

The spirit expressed through myth and ritual that originally gave shape to our culture has fallen away, leaving us without a secure sense of containment, and our civilization is now vulnerable as it crumbles around us. Materialism, superficiality, empiricism, arrogance, and narcissism resulting from early relationship trauma are the mantras of our postmodern world, where the individual is alone without cultural/ritual guidance or even the knowledge of the presence of an inner compass. Many science- or science-fiction-minded people put their hopes on artificial intelligence and technological singularity—when humans transcend biology through robots—and plan to escape to Mars when our earth collapses or disappear into virtual reality. Do we ever stop to ask ourselves what kind of world we want? Do we try to clear the fog on our mirror to see down the road? A Native American proverb about our earth reminds us: "Treat the earth well. It was not given to you by your parents; it was loaned to you by your children."

There is a striking similarity between the lead-up to the Maya collapse in 150 CE and what we are facing today. While the impact on the Maya was limited to a region equivalent to one country and one rain forest, our current risk of collapse will affect the entire world and all living creatures, the very soul of the world, the *anima mundi*. We are not merely dealing with the effects of plaster runoff but with the runoff of chemicals and carbon that have grown far beyond our control, affecting every living organism on our precious earth.

CONCLUSION

The Maya gods came together in council to make decisions on the creation of the world. This is a good reminder to share the decision-making process with others—in honest relationship. It not only refers to outer real others but also to all the inner others in the unconscious whose voices influence the decisions we make on a daily basis. Sitting in council with all of them would help bring the multiplicity of viewpoints, complexes, desires, and affects into view to enable us to make the best possible decisions, even if it means we have a few abortive creations. We learn from those too. Yet we also have lost the ability to speak to each other. Our councils no longer work.

Myths speak with the loud as well as the soft voice. The *Popol Vuh* states that at the successful creation of humans and this world, the Maya gods were turned to stone when the sun's first light touched the face of the earth. Their voices became internal so that humans might remember their origin and connection to the living gods through their dreams and that soft inner voice of wisdom that whispers when they dare to listen.

The Maya see their creation myth, as laid out in their *Book of Council*, as the avenue back to their gods. Understanding it opens the door to the clarity of vision dimmed at the creation of humans. From another culture, another time, we can strive for that same clarity by understanding the ancient voices of wisdom—from our own ancestors, as well as from those of other cultures. The one voice speaks to all through metaphor from the archive of humanity's memories. By listening and reflecting, we can return to the well at the dawn of life for renewal. We need the courage to do this.

CHAPTER 2
DIFFICULTIES WORKING
WITH THE TEXT

This book uses an approach from analytical psychology and historical phenomenology to unveil the symbolic meaning of the myth. From a Jungian perspective, this is the most effective way to unlock an understanding of the symbols and themes in the myth. The *Popol Vuh* presents unique problems for the historian as well as for the psychologist. Because the Spaniards destroyed all but four original Maya codices, few examples of original text or other original preconquest documents exist. Vases, stelae, and murals are helpful but an incomplete source of information. This presents a difficult problem for the psychologist whose work is informed by history. How is the psychologist to understand what the symbols in the myth meant to the ancient K'iche' Maya themselves? There are, however, contemporary understandings of what certain symbols or images mean to the K'iche'. The meaning can be triangulated by using contemporary understandings. If one believes an image is used to mean a certain thing on a stele, for example, and it is found on other carvings or pottery used in the same way, one can assume that the image carries a specific meaning. The difficulty with triangulation of meaning is that the images in Maya artifacts and hieroglyphics carry multiple meanings. It is hard to pin them down.

One of the greatest difficulties for the researcher in studying this work is to suspend Western thinking. Nothing can be assumed. One must metaphorically move into the world of creation by suspending one's prior belief system and observing with new eyes. The Maya were isolated from the rest of the world, unable to share their culture or thinking with anyone not in the Western Hemisphere. While their thinking and sensibilities may be different from those of others, their human nature and instincts are the same. In this way, the psyche is the same for all humans yet reflects unique cultural differences. It is important to emphasize this last point, that Jungian thinking recognizes the differences in cultures:

> The archetypal motifs presumably derive from patterns of the human mind that are transmitted not only by tradition and migration but also by heredity. The latter hypothesis is indispensable, since even complicated archetypal images can be reproduced spontaneously without there being any possibility of direct tradition. (Jung 1989a, 50)

Jacobi ([1957] 1971) and D. Brown (1991) postulated that symbols have universal meanings, and there seems to be a growing interest in this idea in anthropology. Therefore, one way to approach Maya symbols and symbolic themes is to delve down into the collective or universal level of symbolic understanding. By including the universal meaning seen across both local and diverse cultures and comparing this meaning to what is known about the K'iche' symbols, the reasons for the particular thematic inclusions in this myth may become clear. One must remain aware that the method of using symbols from one culture to inform an understanding of another is questioned for its scientific validity. The concepts of archetypes and the collective unconscious, which lay out an understanding of the existence of universal patterns, themes, and symbols, is not widely accepted outside of the Jungian community because it is more of a phenomenological assertion that does not pass the strict empirical test required by standards of science. But, as more researchers are moving toward phenomenology, such concepts are becoming more credible, as seen in D. Brown's (1991) writings. The difficulty is asserting that a concept means the same thing in different cultures. Nevertheless, Jung (1977a, 1977b, 1977c) and Campbell (1982a, 1991a, 1991b) use this cross-referencing method in their understanding of symbols:

> Critics have contented themselves with asserting that no such archetypes exist. Certainly they do not exist, any more than a botanical system exists in nature! But will anyone deny the existence of natural plant-families on that account? Or will anyone deny the occurrence and continual repetition of certain

morphological and functional similarities? It is much the same thing in principle with the typical figures of the unconscious. They are forms existing *a priori*, or biological norms of psychic activity. (Jung 1977a, 183n)

Nevertheless, a number of Maya anthropologists and ethnologists have taken up the idea of archetypes as a way of understanding the themes and patterns that are similar in different myths throughout Mesoamerica and across the world. Austin (1993) went beyond a single focused viewpoint in studying myths and instead looked through multiple lenses, touching on religion and psychology as well. He brought in the concept of archetypes and the influence of the collective unconscious that he explains through his understanding of what he identified as the Maya "cosmovision":

> If each god is an individual type of force that characterized a species at the beginning of the world, that continues to form part of today's individuals, and that circulates in the form of time over the earth, then there must be an essential participation between the gods and their influences, their creations and infiltrations, their surroundings and garments, their possessions and powers, their field of operation, and their victim. . . .
> The god and the individual shared characteristics because the person's force was a portion of the god's force. . . . The transmission of a god's power extends beyond the observable effects of willful acts. That power is a unique substance that takes possession of whatever it impregnates. . . . The forces have their spheres, their times, their ways and reasons to act or to mitigate the results. All of this comes together when a body is possessed. The possessor and the possessed share the essence; the transfer itself is a form of possession. (Austin 1993, 123–24)

This view reflects an understanding of archetypes and the collective unconscious as understood by analytical psychology. Austin stepped into a process rather than remain an observer of a lost culture as an artifact. He imagined the intimate connection between the gods and humans, the reciprocal relationship that takes place during ritual sacrifice where the precious life force in the form of blood is shared between the two. In the process humans are transformed, but so are the gods through the circulation of this divine force. He and others (Austin 1993; León-Portilla 1988) pointed out that time is essentially the carrier of this force that emerged as the gods ordered the cosmos with the four directions, the four pillars, or cosmic bearers, holding up the sky and earth, with foundations in the underworld called the Bacabs. Through them and the central axis flows the divine force, setting time and the archetypes in motion.

The concept of the Maya cosmovision is not easy to grasp and requires thoughtful introspection into the connection with nature in a world that is quite different from any other. Stepping back into the Jungian understanding of the archetypes, personal experience working with those energies, and being familiar with the psychological impact they have on humans are helpful in grasping the perceived world the Maya constructed from these same forces. Although the archetypes may be different, the structure and laws governing them are universal, always leading back to the central archetype of wholeness or the essence of god, the unknowable.

THE FACT OF ISOLATION AND THE COLLECTIVE UNCONSCIOUS

America was isolated from the rest of the world until the fifteenth century and yet produced myths that are strikingly similar to those produced in other parts of the world. This is an interesting fact that to date has not been adequately explained except by way of the archetypal structuring process itself. There is little to no evidence of cultural transmission across the oceans from other continents to the Americas. Most research on the *Popol Vuh* creation myth has been done by anthropologists or ethnologists in their studies of the Maya culture and its concrete representations, and as a result, its religion tends to be looked at in concrete practical terms. There has been little speculation from a psychological point of view or in terms of how the myth informed the development of the culture and the psychology of the individuals within that culture, except from a few anthropologists. The prevailing viewpoint seems to focus on humans creating myth to explain their cosmos as opposed to mythic themes being an intrinsic part of human experience, in other words, emerging from the collective unconscious. Studies focus on the individual elements and their relationship to the culture rather than on a larger comparison with the rest of the world. This is understandable in light of the fact of the American continent's isolation. Yet an understanding of why this creation myth is so similar to those of other cultures not in America, such as Egypt, Assyria, Greece, and India, remains an interesting question, especially in light of the concept of the collective unconscious.

It is understood that Jung's (1977a) concept of the collective unconscious is a hypothesis that generally has not been accepted or understood within the academic community. It is not easy to pin down or quantify but can be studied qualitatively. Comparing myths and their common motifs to dream material is one way to demonstrate the common emergence from the unconscious. Jung saw archetypes as the organizing patterns in the unconscious, the images that emerge as expressions of basic human instincts. The motifs in myths are, therefore, archetypal. From Jung's viewpoint, these archetypal motifs are universal, which explains why there are frequent similarities in different cultures. The definition of the collective unconscious includes the idea of common motifs that emerge in all cultures. Assuming they are reflections of instinctual patterns of behavior, it is possible the individual will manifest these same patterns in dream material. This concept of the collective unconscious was one of the cornerstones of Jung's theory of psychology affecting individual as well as cultural development.

Von Franz (1972) brought this argument down to the personal level when she pointed out that an individual will often have creation myth dreams or dreams with motifs from creation myths after an emotional breakdown, or when emerging from a psychotic experience. These motifs indicate that consciousness is building up again with a new awareness of reality (108–9). From this example one can speculate on the importance and organizing function of the archetypal motifs, especially the Self as the archetype of meaning and wholeness that acts as the backdrop to individual and cultural mental health.

Another, yet contrary, explanation for this similarity in motifs and images is from the Marxist point of view. This focuses on the similar nature of all people and basic hierarchical power struggles in cultures leading to conflicts over space, resources, and survival. The political anthropologists look at the overarching structures of society, economy, and politics through mythology. From this point of view, therefore, the motifs and images reflect the economy, subsequent population density, and political structures (Johnson and Earle 2000). From this perspective, the myths can be understood without drawing on psychology or religious ideas.

Another explanation for the similarity of mythologies in the "old" and "new" world could be that migrating groups that crossed the Bering Strait retained the memory of early customs and myths, which were then included in their lives as they settled. This may, in fact, be true but is not necessarily the whole truth. Yet now we have evidence that the migration took place much earlier than previously thought into the Americas. It was believed people migrated in 13,000 BCE across the Bering Strait as the ice receded, but now there is evidence of footprints dating back to 30,000 BCE across the ice itself. So as more evidence is revealed, the facts change.

Further discussion is needed among psychologists, anthropologists, ethnologists, and art historians to understand the psychological point of view and to explore whether the concept of the collective unconscious contributes to the dialogue about the nature of cultures and mythic material.

CHAPTER 3
UNDERSTANDING MYTHS

Mythic expression began when humankind began to symbolize. This grand leap forward in consciousness took place approximately 40,000 BCE when *Homo sapiens* began to see their participation in their world as being larger than objective reality alone. Evidence for this dramatic shift comes from the prehistoric drawings of animal images on cave walls. Even the dates here are in flux as much earlier cave paintings are discovered, and there is now speculation that Neanderthals also participated in this larger viewpoint. For the first time, humans stepped into sacred relationship with the animals that participated in the process of offering themselves as sacrifice, not just as animals but as spirit animals connected to the gods. In return, humans accepted their part of a reciprocal relationship in honoring the gods through rituals and sacrificial offerings and, in effect, opened the door to the sacred (Campbell 1988a). This leap in consciousness commenced a pattern of human behavior that remains with us today. The pattern reflects the human need for the creation of myths, which is seen in all cultures. It can be described as an archetypal pattern (Jung 1977a) that is inherent in human nature, a human universal (D. Brown 1991), an elementary idea (Bastian 1895), or divine forces that manifest as archetypes in human time (Austin 1993). Whatever it is called, it seems to be a pattern that is integral to one's very being.

Myth is a narrative that emerges from the imagination of the shaman or priest who is the mytho-poet who gives voice to the collective unconscious of a particular group, expressing patterns that reflect their origin and their world. Each poet picks up the narration and adds or changes it along the way until it is finally written down. With this, however, it lacks the force and subtle inferences that go beyond the spoken word. It loses its connection to its environment, the special occasion for its telling, its audience that anticipates the drama, the emotional state of the narrator and listener. It loses much of its impact as it moves from the lived story to a relic of the past.

In terms of creation and continuing codification, the social and physical worlds conversely affect the narrative. The outer world is a reflection of the inner world, and vice versa. One cannot exist without the other, although many of those who study myth ignore the inner influence. Myth is not merely the remains of the past in the form of old narratives that are seen as fantasy but living processes that continue to change as humans and their cultures are influenced by new and different challenges. Creation myths capture moments in history from specific cultures, while at the same time they reflect the influence of the collective unconscious on the patterning of human lives and culture:

> Myth-belief is present in every area of social life, diluted, scattered, but doubtless having an enormous capacity to explain and guide. It is found in maxims, images, omens, rules for the most diverse techniques, governmental structures and actions, family relationships, invocations, rites, insults and curses, classifications, and jests. . . . The general picture shown by a tradition at a given historical moment is like a sampling of the different stages of development of mythical history: here an object to which a will is attributed, there a relationship underlying kinship, further on an episodic explanation of a natural cyclic phenomenon, all of them social acts that are parts of processes potentially forming mythical narratives. (Austin 1993, 184)

Archetypes are the patterns that influence human and cultural behavior. It is the expression of these patterns in the creation of the mythic narrative that is of interest in this research, as well as how myths and motifs translate into ritual and, finally, why myths are important for the individual and the culture.

To understand the human and social motivation behind this phenomenon, this book includes different viewpoints from disparate fields of study: psychology, anthropology, ethnology, art history, comparative religion, sociology, and economics. The central viewpoint is that of Jung (1967, 1974, 1976, 1977a, 1977b, 1977c, 1978, 1981, 1983, 1989a, 1989b, 1997), against whom others are compared and contrasted. One creation myth, the *Popol Vuh*, has been selected as an example. It contains creation, lunar, and solar motifs. It is a complicated myth similar to other creation myths in Mesoamerica and fundamental in its influence on all aspects of individual and cultural life there. Although most scholars prefer to limit comparisons to similar local cultures, the motifs can be compared to myths elsewhere on the American continent and throughout the world. Austin asserted that myth and power have gone hand in hand throughout history and in different traditions: "To the extent that social organizations resemble each other, their mythical productions and functions of their myths are similar" (1993, 283). Both myths and the institutions are part of the same dialectical exchange, which reciprocally reinforce each other, and from this material, a culture's view of reality is derived. For this reason, it is not surprising that some of the motifs in the *Popol Vuh* are similar to those in the Egyptian creation myth, for example. This supposition supports the concept of an underlying pattern that influences the development of myth as well as culture.

ORIGIN, FUNCTION, AND PURPOSE OF MYTHS
From the Jungian perspective, myths are manifestations of themes and motifs, that is, archetypes, in the collective unconscious that emerge into collective consciousness to guide and correct attitudes and behaviors, much like dreams do for the individual. They are important in that they connect individuals to the unconscious, to the Self, and to the sacred. All cultures have myths that evolve as consciousness changes, and there may be a number of myths influencing a culture at any time. It is not only the Judeo-Christian creation myth that influences Western culture. One additional example beyond the most commonly known creation myth in the West is the myth of the hero's journey. Here in America, this myth manifests in collective consciousness as a very individualistic journey: each individual can succeed through hard work and perseverance. An aspect of this myth that seems to be playing out now in our culture is pushing this myth to an extreme, with the defiant, independent individual aspiring to destroy the so-called dragon, representing rebellion against established authority and conformity. The focus is more on destruc-

tion than transformation. One additional example of a myth that influences Western culture is the myth of evolution. Even though it is thought of as scientific theory, it functions as a myth in its influence on individuals' lives. These myths form the basic construct of American culture and lives; they are the foundation for the development of American thought about its place in the world and its relationship to the cosmos. In explaining where such myths come from and why they are important to people individually, Jung said:

> The contents of the collective unconscious are, as I have pointed out, the results of the psychic functioning of our whole ancestry; in their totality, they compose a natural world-image, the condensation of millions of years of human experience. These images are mythological and therefore symbolical, for they express the harmony of the experiencing subject with the object experienced. All mythology and all revelation come from this matrix of experience, and all our future ideas about the world and man will come from it likewise. . . . They are only the raw material, which, in order to acquire a meaning, has first to be translated into the language of the present. . . . The historical, universal man in us joins hands with the newborn, individual man. This is the experience, which comes very close to that of the "primitive," who symbolically unites himself with the totem-ancestor by partaking of the ritual feast. (1981, 380)

Jung explained that human beings have a basic instinct built into their biology that causes them to make sense out of chaos and create meaning. He called this the religious instinct (344). It is primary in all human beings, and it is expressed through archetypes in the form of myth, fairy tales, and dreams.

Campbell listed four functions of mythology:

> The first function of a mythology is to waken and maintain in the individual a sense of wonder and participation in the mystery of this finally inscrutable universe. . . . The second function of a mythology, then, is to fill every particle and

quarter of the current cosmological image with its measure of this mystical import; and in this regard, mythologies differ as the horizons, landscapes, sciences, and technologies of their civilizations differ. . . . The third function, no less important, is the sociological one of validating and maintaining whatever moral system and manner of life-customs may be peculiar to the local culture. . . . A fourth, and final, essential function of mythologies, then, is the pedagogical one of conducting individuals in harmony through the passages of human life, from the stage of dependency in childhood to the responsibilities of maturity, and on to old age and the ultimate passage of the dark gate. (1988a, 8–9)

Eliade elaborated on the purpose of mythology:

The sum total of primordial revelations is constituted by his myths. . . . The myth, then, is the history of what took place *in illo tempore*, the recital of what the gods or the semidivine beings did at the beginning of time. . . . It is the irruption of the sacred into the world, an irruption narrated in the myths, that *establishes* the world as a reality. . . . Hence the supreme function of the myth is to "fix" the paradigmatic models for all rites and all significant human activities—eating, sexuality, work, education, and so on. . . . Man's religious behavior contributes to maintaining the sanctity of the world. (1987, 95–99)

From another school of thought altogether, called structuralism, Lévi-Strauss (1983) did not make the assumptions previously described about an existence of a human universal myth-making function. Instead, he limited his exploration to the study of language, believing that the specific domain of culture may be understood by means of a structure, that structure being language. To this way of thinking, the structure, type, and location of each element determine (1) the whole; (2) every system has a structure; (3) these structural laws have to do with coexistence, not change; and (4) the structures are the real elements underlying the apparent meaning. To him, myth is a system of

symbolic logic that functions through a concept of opposites fundamental to the mysteries of humans and the world.

Myths assign meaning according to the necessity and constraints
of a particular society. Lévi-Strauss stated: "Semantic symbolism
finds its space at the very top, in the zone where language, tran-
scended by myth, locks into external realities" (1983, 147). His theory
did not advocate social change; however, in contrast to this, Karl
Marx, another empirical thinker, developed a materialistic philosophy that advocated for change. Marx's materialistic philosophy saw
myth as a means to maintain a power structure and, hence, control
over the masses. Justice and morality were not absolute but instead
could be abused:

> Marx's philosophy of history is based on the idea that history
> can be interpreted by class struggle, and class struggle can itself
> be understood by the notion of an ideological superstructure
> superimposed upon a social substructure. . . . The ruling classes
> oppress the inferior ones; to that end, they impose their political
> systems and organizations. But the ruling class also created an
> "ideology," which includes religions, morals, and philosophy, and
> which is at the same time a reflection of the social structure and
> a means of oppressing the inferior classes. (Marx 1964, cited in
> Ellenberger 1970, 238)

The Marxist view places myth and religion at the center of a social
ideology that is used to support power and personal or class aims.
Myth becomes identical to ideology. This view has been taken up
by many cultural anthropologists to explain the reasons for social
control, conflict, and class stratification. One could say it is the polar
opposite of Jung (1981) and Campbell's (1988a) viewpoints, as well
as of those researching and studying comparative religions. The reasons why mythological and religious symbolism have been potent to
all populations is seldom if ever discussed. The difference between
the human instinct that desires participation with the sacred and
the dogma that is formulated to codify the idea of religion and use it
for purposes of power and control remains a subject not addressed.
Johnson and Earl in their book *The Evolution of Human Societies*

stand on the shoulders of Marx in their exploration of human societies from the perspective of evolutionary anthropology and ethnology and claimed:

> Religious institutions helped to consolidate the chief's control. Throughout the chiefdom were shrines used to house the gods and to accommodate ceremonies constructed by priests drawn from the ruling elite. At large shrines dedicated to Ku, the god of war, ceremonies initiated and supervised by the paramount himself built a consensus for military action among his supporting chiefs. More common were small community altars used during the annual Makahiki ceremonies. For these ceremonies, Lono, the god of land and fertility, traveled around the island accompanied by the paramount chief. Acting for the god, the chief performed rites at community shrines designated to maintain the fertility of the community's land. In return he received food, craft goods, and raw materials. The ritual obligations and significance of the paramount were made explicit by these rites, which embedded the financing of the governing chief in the ceremony to guarantee the land's productivity. (2000, 290–91)

Johnson and Earle reasoned:

> Nor was religion in any sense an independent institution. The state religion was represented at administrative settlements throughout the empire by temple mounds, or *ushnu*, that stood prominently in the main plaza and acted as a focus for ceremonial occasions, where they proclaimed the ruler's divinity and thus his legitimacy. The stability and fertility of the natural world, being dependent on the supernatural, were mediated by the ruling Inka . . . religious institutions serving as an important agent of social and political integration. (323)

Most anthropologists have followed this more empirically based sociopolitical and economic point of view as they have studied the rituals and religious beliefs. An exception is B. Tedlock, an ethnologist/anthropologist who takes a phenomenological approach to the study of myths and rituals of the Maya:

Linguistic knowledge is often held up as a measure of
professional seriousness in anthropology, but it is also a measure
of anthropological participation. What lies behind the belief
that "going" native is a real danger to the anthropologist is the
logical construction of the relationship between objectivity and
subjectivity, between self and other, between scientist and native,
as an analytical opposition. The implication is that the native way
of knowing is somehow incompatible with the scientific way of
knowing, and that the domain of objectivity is the sole property
of the outsider. . . . Human intersubjectivity distinguishes the
"social" from the "natural" sciences. (1982, 5)

Through language, B. Tedlock entered the experiential world of a
culture as a means to understand it from the inside out. She participated in a subjective experience and, therefore, did not merely look
at the materialistic social constructions but felt into the deeper meaning and importance of myth and religion in the culture. B. Tedlock
saw myths and ritual practices as representing an important living
relationship between humans and the greater cosmos that needs to
be reenacted regularly as a way of keeping the mutual relationship
intact. The creation myth, for example, is re-created in ritual as a way
to re-create the world, to move from temporal time into sacred time.
Eliade stated:

Sacred time appears under the paradoxical aspect of a circular
time, reversible and recoverable, as part of the eternal mythical
present that is periodically reintegrated by means of rites. . . . Life
cannot be repaired, it can only be recreated through symbolic
repetition of the cosmogony. (1987, 70–82)

B. Tedlock moved away from the traditional ethnologists and anthropologists, coming closer to Jung (1967, 1977a, 1977c, 1989b) and Eliade (1987) in her thinking. Austin was another anthropologist who
bridged the gap between science and the humanities through the
study of mythology:

Today, we consider mythology to be one of the great
achievements of humanity, but one that is obsolete. We

recognize the literary beauty of myths, their influence on the most divers artistic fields, their hermeneutical potential in the study of distant societies, their psychological depth, and the role they played in the ideological processes of the past. Yet nowadays we consider them to be anachronistic. We forget, in the false universalization of our scientific vision, that myth still performs its functions in the lives of a great many of the world's inhabitants. (1996, xv)

He reviewed different definitions of myth as story, a complex of beliefs, an expression of different kinds of reality, and a form of discourse. They are tales that reveal a universal and inner human sensibility and reflect the unitary energy of the human spirit. Myth, through the emergence of the sacred, supports the continuity of the social and cosmic orders by legitimizing both. On an opposing side, he pointed out that one of the most strident critics of the theory of myth, G. S. Kirk, "attacks the persistent and distorting effect of treating myth as a closed category that attributes the same characteristics to the myths of different cultures" (cited in Austin 1993, 26). Yet Austin added two clarifications to this. One is that, although similarities in mythic motifs allow comparison to other traditions, the comparability may not be due as much to human nature as to the fact that the forms that subsequently develop contribute similarly to the social structure. The second is that the distance in time between cultures makes it difficult to generalize (26–32).

He described six constant functions of myth and reminded the reader that myth still functions in the minds of most of the world's populations, even with the false universalism of the scientific vision:

1. Mythical narration keeps tradition alive. . . . 2. Myth teaches by binding generations together in its transmissions of values. . . . 3. Myth organizes knowledge by giving it structure and classifying the cosmos, and this knowledge reinforces knowledge. . . . 4. Myth explains because it is a synthesis of the explanations of society and nature. . . . Myth is mingled with ritual, festivals, and conjuring. . . . 5. Myth binds when, through the medium of belief and narration, it reaffirms the character of

the common knowledge and values of the group. . . . 6. Myth legitimizes. (Austin 1993, 283–84)

Biogenetic structuralism is a rather recent movement that attempts to understand mythology by bridging anthropology, psychology, and neuroscience. This view places the locus of all universal structures, such as language, culture, and human understanding of time and space, within the predisposed organization of the nervous system. According to this approach, due to a common physical structure, different individuals repeatedly re-create similar structures. This would offer an explanation for the commonality of mythic motifs across the world. Interestingly enough, it seems thinking in this area has moved full circle, back to Jung's viewpoint, which was based on the idea of archetypes: those imagistic, thematic representations of biologically based human instincts.

In *Tracking the Gods*, Hollis brought these threads together by describing four ways myths serve humans: they address "our relationship to the cosmos, to nature, to each other, and to ourselves" (1995, 13). He discussed motifs as being the universal patterns that are repeated not only in myths but in fairy tales and stories as well. These reflect the cultural symbols that direct people's lives individually and culturally. According to him, there are many ways to approach myth, not just psychologically. Hollis included antiquarian, sociological, proto-scientific, anthropological, linguistic, psychological, archetypal, phenomenological, symbolic, and historical or euhemeristic as other useful approaches (17–23). When studying myths, one moves through these categories of thought many times without being aware of the various lenses with which one is scrutinizing the material. Myths carry the imprint of past cultures and social values and consequently spark an interest in reading the stories or studying the people, culture, or language relating to it. Rulers and heroes have been memorialized through the imagination into myth. Events of significance become the material of mythic stories. Through oral tradition, archetypal themes emanating from the psyche containing the wholeness of what is conscious and unconscious creep in to offer lessons that are codified in the stories of myth. Just as science continues to test theories and hypotheses that are ever changing, myths change over time and among cultures to guide the relationship of individuals to their lives.

While still part of a living oral tradition, they have a living, independent life. Carried on from generation to generation in oral form, the content changes with each telling and changes with the development of the culture. At some point, the myths are written down when the stories are in peril of perishing. Someone decides to perpetuate them and transmit them more securely (Slochower 1970). There may be many reasons for this: loss of historical and cultural memory, decline in the culture, combat, or simply the erosion of time. What is held important as a living story of one's past, lineage, and religion becomes codified and is no longer reflective of the changes emanating from the unconscious or current social or environmental situations, but instead they become a snapshot in time. Because the myth in written form is a static view of an archetypal pattern, to achieve a larger view of the unconscious, it is necessary to compare myths from many cultures.

DIFFERENT TYPES OF MYTHS AND THEIR USEFULNESS

Having introduced the concept of myths and their relationship to archetypes and the collective unconscious, we can now focus on three categories of myths: creation, lunar, and solar. Mesoamerican mythology, both Aztec and Maya, is used as the primary source for examples, with the inclusion of myths from other cultures for comparison.

Although myths, fairy tales, and dreams all present archetypal material and depict, to varying degrees, the state of the collective unconscious, generally speaking, dreams are intended for the individual and fairy tales speak to concerns within local groups, while myths address the larger collective. Myths are a reflection of many minds creating a narrative. For that reason, the characters are generic and not personal. Myths have endings and reflect a whole process moving from the state of stillness, pre-creation, to the creation of a new world. Worlds may be created and destroyed and re-created a number of times, which is the case in Mesoamerican mythology. It follows the familiar path of renewal-destruction-renewal. The ending in fairy tales, on the other hand, is many times left unfinished because the tales show a piece of work and not the entire process. Dreams, being farthest away from the collective and the most personal, have recognizable characters and specific indications for the individual to help further wholeness. Because of their closeness to the collective unconscious, fairy tales and myths are a clear depiction of the complexes and difficulties humans have in common dealing with psychological material.

Myths deal with archetypal patterns that influenced ancestral peoples and continue to influence contemporary peoples. As cultures change, myths change. As groups of people lose sight of the early mythic material, it bubbles up again out of the collective unconscious in a new form but with similar themes. Because of this repetitive pattern, it is reasonable to compare mythic motifs of the past to those seen and experienced today. Myths that no longer carry potent symbols that are alive and meaningful to the culture indicate it is time for a new myth to emerge, with symbols that reflect the living connection between the worldly and the beyond. A reconnection to the creation myth is needed.

CREATION MYTHS

Creation myths are the most fundamental of all the myths, reflecting the human impulse to make sense of the world by explaining its origins. These myths directly connect the culture to the larger cosmos and to the gods. Through ritual reenactment of the myth, historical time is stopped as one moves into eternal time, where the culture has the opportunity to renew itself. All sins, transgressions, and weakness are burned or washed away as humans are metaphorically re-created in a purer form, better able to honor the gods and remain in relationship with them. Creation myths are more abstract than other types of myths because they depict the birth of the entire world. They may contain within them lunar and solar mythic sequences, as in the case of the K'iche' Maya and Egyptian creation myths. Von Franz said:

Creation myths are the deepest and most important of all myths. In many primitive religions the telling of the creation myth forms an essential teaching in the ritual of initiation. They are told to the young initiates as the most important part of the tribal tradition. In many other ways also . . . they refer to the most basic problems of human life, for they are concerned with the ultimate meaning, not only of our existence, but of the existence of the whole cosmos. (1972, 5)

Creation myths are the template for initiation rituals that help the young make the transition into adulthood. They serve the purpose of teaching them the valuable lessons passed down by the gods to humans about how to live and with what values. They offer a view from the temporal world into the larger spiritual realm, providing meaning to one's existence and to the cosmos. Many myths lay out specifics on how to behave, how and when to plant crops, when to harvest, how to perform ritual offerings to the gods to ensure plentiful harvests, or, for example, what to do if there is no rain. These offerings are called "sympathetic rituals," which often mimic acts designed to evoke a comparable act of the gods. For example, ritual intercourse in the fields is hoped to produce fecundity in the gods of earth and sky. There are ritually determined sacrifices and offerings made to ensure that the smooth and mutually advantageous relationship is maintained between humans and the gods:

Cosmogonic myths and mythology, in India for instance, are used every time a new house is built. At the moment one lays the foundation of a house, one (as it were) recreates the whole world once again. In the Middle Ages when the Vikings or the Anglo-Saxons first set foot in a new country, they built an altar and repeated the creation myth, meaning that this country had not formerly existed, and only now that they were there and it had entered their field of consciousness and they had set a conscious order in it, did they create it by coming into it and settling it. (Segal 1998, 250–51)

Within the K'iche' Maya creation myth, the *Popol Vuh*, is contained the story of hero twins who vanquish the vainglorious Macaw that has set itself up in a high tree as the god of the realm, although he is a false god. He has a jewel for an eye and the bright plumage that is typical for that bird. It is the duty of the hero twins to kill the bird because its attitude is wrong. In the Mesoamerican culture in general, it is wrong to be vain, arrogant, or greedy. In order for creation to continue, this bird has to be disempowered. A wrong attitude will not lead to a proper creation. This message is repeated later, when the hero twins have to deal with their arrogant older stepbrothers, who are eventually turned into monkey scribes. The third time in the story the heroes have to contend with this wrong attitude is in their encounter with the demons in the underworld that also need to be vanquished. This repetition of a moral theme shows its importance in the culture as a reminder and lesson for all.

There are usually a number of different creation myths in a culture, and in any given myth, different parts may be left out in its telling over time. For the Aztecs, the two great gods of duality, Quetzalcoatl and Tezcatlipoca, represent light and dark, good and evil, savior and trickster. They are opposites and complements of each other. In one myth, working in unison, they descend from the sky and see a large sea or earth monster striding on the sea in the form of a caiman. It is named Tlaltecuhtli, the earth lord, but it is considered both masculine and feminine. The two gods proceed to rip the monster apart, a common creation theme, and out of the pieces of his or her flesh, the world is created. Caiman skin is used in their language as a reference to the surface of the earth. In another version, these gods of duality carried Tlaltecuhtli down from heaven, and, while turning themselves into serpents, one grabbed a left hand and right foot, and the other took the right hand and left foot, and they pulled her apart:

> The upper portion of her body then becomes the earth, while the other half is thrown into the sky to create the heavens. The violent slaying and dismemberment of Tlaltecuhtli angers the other gods. To console the mutilated earth, they decree that all plants needed for human life will derive from her body. From her

hair are fashioned trees, flowers and herbs, and from her skin come the grasses and smaller flowers. Her eyes are the source of wells, springs and small caves; her mouth, the great rivers and caverns; and her nose, mountain ridges and valleys. At times, the earth goddess can still be heard screaming in the night for the blood and hearts of people. Ultimately, only sacrificial flesh and blood can soothe and quiet Tlaltecuhtli sufficiently to keep her producing the fruits needed for human life. (Taube 1993, 37)

This is the theme of the first victim. It is found, for instance, in the myth of the Assyrian first mother-goddess, Tiamat, the dragon monster who is slain by Marduk and out of whose body the world is created. It is found as well in India where "Purusha is cut up and each part of him becomes a part of the universe" (von Franz 1972, 98). Another myth, also mentioned by von Franz, tells that:

Out of Yamir's flesh was shaped the earth,
The mountains out of his bones,
The Heaven from the ice-cold giant's skull,
Out of his blood the boisterous sea. (97)

In these myths the world is created by a sacrificial act. This becomes the template for later ritual that is still practiced, although metaphorically, in the Catholic Mass today with the eating of the body and blood of Christ, through the process of transubstantiation. Sacrifice and the offering of oneself is the template for initiation ceremonies throughout the world. The *sparagmos* of Greek tragedy is the eating of the flesh of the scapegoat, now sanctified by the signification of ritual and belief. Then one eats the gods: here is my body, eat; here is my blood, drink. Eliade wrote:

Certain blood sacrifices find their justification in a primordial divine act; *in illo tempore* the god had slain the marine monster and dismembered its body in order to create the cosmos. Man repeats this blood sacrifice—sometimes even with human victims—when he has to build a village, a temple, or simply a house. What the consequences of this *imitatio dei* can be

is clearly shown by the mythologies and rituals of numerous
primitive people. To give only one example: according to the
myths of the earliest cultivators, man became what he is today—
mortal, sexualized, and condemned to work—in consequence of
a primordial murder; *in illo tempore* a divine being, quite often a
woman, or a maiden, sometimes a child or a man, allowed himself
to be immolated in order that tubers or fruit trees should grow
from his body. This first murder basically changed the mode of
being of human life. (1987, 101)

Initiations can be brutal, violent, and filled with torture, blood, and
sacrifice. It takes this brutality to open the veil between the temporal
and sacred worlds. One needs to metaphorically die to be reborn.
This level of violence shows the difficulty new ways and attitudes of
being have in crossing the threshold between the unconscious and
conscious realms. Many of these initiation rites are based on the examples offered by the gods themselves, although over time, the imita-
tion becomes less accurate, distorted, and even forgotten. Yet "it is
the periodical re-actualizations of the divine acts—in short, the religious festivals—that restore human knowledge of the sacrality of the
models" (Eliade 1987, 87).

One lives within the metaphor of the creation myth through ritual,
which in its cyclic repetition offers an understanding of awesome and
transcendent experiences. The New Year ceremonies, common in all
cultures, coincide with the first day of creation. Rituals in Mesoamerican cultures took place during the 5 "unlucky" days between the end
of one yearly calendar and the beginning of the next. The Maya solar
calendar consisted of 360 days with an extra 5 days during which the
demons of the underworld and other dangers were let loose upon the
world. Rituals were needed to keep them in check so that the world
could begin anew, that the sun would rise, and the mutual relationship between the gods and humans would continue. "It is by virtue
of this eternal return to the sources of the sacred and the real that
human existence appears to be saved from nothingness and death"
(Eliade 1987, 107).

The Maya lived with a calendar full of ritual days as a way to honor the many gods that represented the varying aspects of nature. Nature was constantly impinging on them in the form of rain, floods, volcanoes, droughts, and fires. The ritual sacrifices served the function of beseeching the gods for favors by paying tribute and honoring them with the hope of making life more tolerable. Yet for the Maya the relationship to the gods was not only that of father/son, for example, but it had a trickster element to it as well, where humans bargained with the gods and had to be quite clever in their approach. There was a playfulness not seen in the Judeo-Christian tradition. The Mesoamericans perceived their gods as capricious and unpredictable, just like their physical environment. This had a vitally important influence on their survival and consequently impacted the narrative of the creation myth.

In another version of the Aztec creation myth, the gods pondered together to create the world, which they destroyed and re-created four times:

> It is told that when yet (all) was in darkness, when yet not
> sun had shone and no dawn had broken—it is said—the gods
> gathered themselves together and took council among themselves
> there at Teotihuacan—the place where time began. (Sahagún
> [1577] 1953, 1)

Two gods prepared for the ritual; one was the rich, haughty god named Tecuciztecatl, and the other who was humble and diseased, was named Nanahuatzin. The two gods, after doing penance for four days, were dressed and made ready for their sacrifice. All the gods encircled the large hearth fire and asked who was going to throw himself into the sacrificial pyre first. "Who will carry the burden? Who will take it upon himself to be the sun, to bring the dawn" (Sahagún [1578] 1978, 4). Tecuciztecatl ran to the hearth four times but did not have courage enough to throw himself in:

> And Nanahuatzin, daring all at once, determined—resolved—
> hardened his heart, and shut firmly his eyes. He had no fear; he
> did not stop short; he did not falter in fright; he did not turn
> back. All at once he quickly threw and cast himself into the

fire; once and for all he went. Thereupon he burned; his body crackled and sizzled. (Sahagún [1577] 1953, 5–6)

Seeing that, Tecuciztecatl followed, and all the gods waited to see what would happen next. Slowly the sky reddened in all directions and Nanahuatzin appeared as Tonatiuh, the fiery sun god. Then Tecuciztecatl rose in the east just as brightly, but the gods worried that the two orbs would be equally bright, so they threw a rabbit in the face of the moon to dim it. Both the sun and moon hovered motionless in the sky. The two ruling gods needed the help of more life substance in the form of blood as the energy necessary to set the sun and moon in motion. The gods realized they had no other choice than to sacrifice themselves. Quetzalcoatl, in his form as Ecatl, the wind, then proceeded to cut each of the remaining god's hearts out and wrapped them in sacred bundles, in a form that could be worshipped by humans. "Just as the gods had to sacrifice themselves, so humans must supply their own hearts and blood to ensure that the fifth sun continues to move in its path" (Taube 1993, 43–44). The myth of the dying gods that is clearly laid out in the Aztec myth is also seen in the Egyptian myth of Osiris, the Mesopotamian myth of Tammuz, the Greek myth of Adonis, and the Christian myth of Christ. This mythic creation theme lays out the template for the reciprocal relationship between gods and humans. Even though this example is quite extreme, most creation myths contain the same message, including the *Popol Vuh*, as discussed in chapter 7 where mythic themes are compared.

Von Franz (1972), in her book *Creation Myths*, described typical creation motifs: creation by accident or as an awakening; creation from above or below; two creators or creation through sex; *Deus Faber*, or creation by crafting or making; creation from thought and emotion; the fourfold division of the world; something being killed and using the body to create the world (for example, a sea monster); creation from germs or eggs; abortive attempts at creation; and the heroes' journey. For example, the K'iche' Maya creation myth, the *Popol Vuh*, contains a number of these common motifs: creation from sex through the primordial Great Mother and Father; creation from thought and the importance of *the word*; creating the world from a great monster; the heroes' journey; and the fourfold division of the universe. Another typical motif is the abortive creation, of which there are three in the *Popol Vuh*.

The *Popol Vuh* is regarded as the most complete and sophisticated creation myth from the Americas and can be compared to those of Egypt, Assyria, and India. Not only does it contain a number of different creation themes, but it also contains the solar myth of the culture heroes as well as the lunar myth of the eternal return. It is infrequent to have a clear-cut myth depicting one theme. More frequently there is a mixture. Eliade explicated this tendency to mixture regarding the matriarchate:

> When the means of existence changed, that is, when men had learnt how to hunt big game, and women had found out how to cultivate plants, the *Urkultur* gave birth to two more complex and clearly distinct forms of society, the totemic society in which man was predominant, and on the other hand the matrilocal and matriarchal society where women were predominant. It was in the latter that the worship of the Earth-Mother originated and reached its highest development. . . . We do not know whether the matriarchate ever existed as an independent cycle of culture—in other words, whether a certain stage in the history of mankind was ever characterized by the absolute ascendency of woman and by an exclusively feminine religion. It is more prudent to say that matriarchal *tendencies* or *predispositions* are manifest in certain religions and social customs. It is true that certain social structures—for example, uterine descent, matrilocalism, the avunculate and gynaecocracy—show the social, juridical and religious importance of woman. But *importance* does not mean absolute *predominance*. (1960, 176–77)

In the *Popol Vuh* creation myth there are multiple sets of twins who do not represent opposites but oppose each other in complementary ways. Each set contains within it a duality. There are four segments constituting an overall creation of the world and humans, ending with a genealogy of the tribes and lords of the K'iche' Maya. It moves from the highest monotheistic god, who contains the duality of all opposites but eventually retreats, leaving the next layer of gods to do the actual creating, all the while keeping his eye on the process. The initial preconscious totality is actually a multiplicity containing all the archetypes, all the gods. The progression represents a differentiation of ego consciousness in much the same way as the twelve Olympians become also myriad lesser gods, the penates and lares, and so on. The consecutive gods are emanations of the original source and ultimately all aspects of the one. One can describe this either as the humanization of the gods or, alternately, the differentiation of aspects of the gods resulting from the process of humans' increased consciousness. In the *Popol Vuh* the story of the beginning of creation describes the primordial world where "all is still silent and placid. All is silent and calm. Hushed and empty is the womb of the sky" (Christenson 2003, 67). The sky and sea alone exist, nothing stirs, all is at rest, nothing stands erect. It is interesting that the word "erect" is chosen to describe a lack of creative potential while suggesting the potential for procreation through the phallus. From the phallus as from the word, the creative impulse emerges and takes form. All the gods mentioned in the opening scene, those of the sky and earth, and of the seas and lakes, spoke and pondered, bringing together their words and thoughts. In Mesoamerican mythology, creation is a communion of the elders. Through discussing, pondering, and arriving at a joint decision, the creations begin. Together they conceive the light and life. What is this but consciousness emerging out of the darkness? In this myth the light is inherent, present, and yet at rest within the darkness, unlike in the Genesis myth where darkness contains no kernel of light at all until light is later conceived. The original etymology of phallus was "the shining." The separating into opposites or differentiating one from the other is a movement into consciousness. This is a common beginning in creation myths, although in this myth there are two principal gods, sky and water, each containing multiple energies with different names and manifestations, including masculine and feminine—the multiplicity of wholeness—while in Genesis there is only one male creator god. It is clear that there are different cultural influences at work from the very beginning.

For the Mesoamericans, duality is inherent in everything; in the Judeo-Christian tradition the world is split into opposites from the beginning, with light remaining absent from darkness. According to von Franz (1972), cultures with a greater development have more differentiation between opposites, which results in a greater awareness of an ethical position. In the Maya myth, as seen later in the culture, in the hero's encounter with the demons, there is a clear differentiation between good and evil, while an awareness of evil in good and good in evil remains. This is not the case in Catholic theology, where evil is seen as the absence of good. Jung wrote his controversial book *Answer to Job* to clarify his position on the nature of evil (1989a, 355–470). He posited that evil existed in its own right and was not merely the absence of good, which is more in agreement with the Mesoamerican viewpoint.

The gods in the *Popol Vuh* attempt creation three times before they finally succeed. They began with the creation of animals, then mud beings, and then wooden beings. None of these creations could honor and worship the gods, so they were considered inadequate and destroyed. This theme of abortive attempts at creation is common in many cultures. For example, the Bible says in Genesis there were giants in the earth before the creation of humans, and these giants were destroyed by a great flood. The Babylonian epic *Gilgamesh* (2004) tells of a great flood that wipes out humanity. There are flood motifs in Hindu mythology. In Norse creation myths, as told in the *Edda*, giants were created before the gods, who then created the dwarfs before creating humans. In Greek mythology, the Titans were created first, then the Archons, and finally the gods who created humans. The Titans, giants, and dwarfs can be interpreted as representing those unconscious impulsive forces in humans that need to be made conscious and domesticated. These are the strong affects and wild behaviors that impinge on us from realms outside our humanity, from our instinctual layer, and do not further adapt to the collective or to others. This same struggle is undertaken in the myths of culture heroes through their descent into the underworld to face demons, as is the case in the *Popol Vuh*.

LUNAR AND SOLAR MYTHS

In the book *Tracking the Gods*, Hollis (1995) reminded the reader of two mythic motifs. The first motif, the myth of the eternal return or the great round, is a lunar myth associated with the Great Mother goddess and represents separation and return, hence the cycle of sacrifice, death, and rebirth. The second motif, the culture hero's journey, is a solar myth, representing separation from the Great Mother and eventually the Sky Father in "the journey out of the regressive powers of nature through the dark woods toward differentiation and individuation" (96). It is the development from innocence, naïveté, and identification to experience, wisdom, and individuation (53). Both motifs, however, retain their grounding in the mythos of masculine and feminine, even during separation and differentiation. These two cycles appear in the *Popol Vuh*: while the first section represents a typical creation myth, the next two sections involve two sets of hero twins, quite removed from the gods themselves, representing further attempts at the creation of consciousness and differentiation.

The first sequence, the lunar motif of the eternal return, is part of a process of development that is repeated over and over in the life of an individual and a culture. It takes its metaphorical expression from the agricultural cycle of planting, sowing, and harvesting of crops and the killing of animals for food. The individual descends into the maternal matrix of the unconscious as a way to change, grow, and find renewal. A sacrifice is always required for change to occur. This lunar myth brings the memory of temporality, mortality, and connection to the cycles of nature and the Great Round of life.

The second sequence is the solar motif of the hero's journey or quest. This journey begins with a *calling* and requires a heroic attempt to disengage from the grip of the maternal and the father/ruling authority in order to differentiate and individuate. The individual must leave the old life behind and embark on a journey to find new values, a renewed way of being individually and collectively. "This central myth seems to have three stages: departure, initiation and return" (Hollis 1995, 74). Again, sacrifice is required of the hero.

The hero's journey is a common theme in mythology, and in Jungian psychology it represents the confrontation with the shadow

(Campbell 1973), the dark chthonic forces of nature that prevent consciousness. It is symbolized as the fight with the dragon, the descent into the underworld, or the womb of the Great Mother. To advance beyond the matriarchal level of development both individually and culturally, the metaphorical dragon, symbolizing the Great Mother, must be slaughtered. The hero descends and endures trials and, if successful, arises with the "gift hard to attain," which is consciousness. Through this struggle, the hero separates himself from the primordial unconscious powers of the Great Mother and brings light or the new sun to the world. Culture is enhanced:

> The slaying of the mother and identification with the father-god go together. If, through active incest, the hero penetrates into the dark, maternal, chthonic side, he can only do so by virtue of his kinship with "heaven," his filiation to God. By hacking his way out of the darkness he is reborn as the hero in the image of God, but, at the same time, as the son of the god-impregnated virgin and of the regenerative Good Mother. (Neumann 1970, 165)

Seen from a sociological perspective, this shift from lunar to solar mythology represents the cultural development from a horticultural society, where the lunar, matriarchal sequence predominates, to an agrarian society, represented by the solar or patriarchal mythic sequence where maize is cultivated, allowing for the formation of culture. In a horticultural society, the men hunt while the women supplement the food source with a variety of foods, and perhaps supply the majority, from small planted plots of land. With the ability to domesticate maize, a society plants large fields of land to ensure a stable source of food. The men take over the fieldwork and become the suppliers of food.

Both sets of twins attempt to subdue the dark forces of nature. The first set, the father and uncle, the twin Maize Gods, fail and end up being sacrificed and reborn, never differentiating from the maternal. The second set, their sons, called the hero twins, successfully trick and overcome the powers of darkness, which leads to the differentiation of opposites and the creation of humans and culture. Many motifs within this part of the myth are common to both lunar and solar myths: blood and sacrifice, death and rebirth, a calling, descent, struggle, wounding, and return (Neumann 1970, 72). In the *Popol Vuh*, there is a shift from the matriarchal to the patriarchal culture. In the first shift the father and uncle in their journey into the underworld failed in their attempt to domesticate the forces of the underworld, something that is necessary if culture, with its rules and communal social development, is to develop. They did not have a sufficiently conscious relationship with nature to be able to draw on it for help, as did their sons, the second set of culture twins. When the father and uncle failed, the cut-off head of the father, One Hunahpú, was placed in a calabash tree, while the uncle, Seven Hunahpú, was cut up and buried under the ballcourt. Nature had control over them, not the other way around. The theme of the sacrificed god left in a tree is present in the Egyptian-Osiris, Assyrian-Adonis, Christian-Christ, and Nordic-Odin myths. This metaphor reflects the attempted transition from the earlier horticultural society to the more domesticated agrarian one. When one is in relationship with nature, one works with it, understands it, and cultivates it, and then one can domesticate the growth of plants to provide a sustainable food source, which for the Maya was maize. The twin Maize Gods represented the third stage of creation, which was inadequate. This first set of twins, the father and uncle, needed to die and be re-created for the final and successful fourth creation. For this reason, these twins were sacrificed and left in the tree and ground, waiting to sprout again, a reflection of the cyclic growth of the maize plant and the motif of the eternal return.

With the second set of twins, "this basic socioeconomic principle of American development is expressed in Hunahpú's [the son] declaration that 'we shall remain so as to feed you.' Thereby masculine preponderance is affirmed, and the man assumes responsibility from that time forward for the maintenance of the family" (Girard 1979, 158).

Yet the defeat of the forces of nature and the underworld is not the final step in the development of mythology. The next step requires overcoming the father through the hero's journey, overcoming the constraints and limitations imposed by the sun god, the father, an old cultural value, in order to become one's own person. Maya mythology does not take this last step. Its focus is on moving from the primordial, unconscious chaos into consciousness in the world in the form of the patriarchy, which conforms to the wishes of the gods by establishing the human race. Neumann refers to this process in general:

> The aim of this fight is to combine the phallic-chthonic with
> the spiritual-heavenly masculinity, and the creative union
> with the anima in the *hieros gamos* is symptomatic of this.
> But, since in the mystery religions the fight with the dragon is
> conceived only as the fight with the mother dragon, representing
> the unconscious chthonic aspect, the inevitable result is
> identification with the spiritual father, so far as the dragon-fight
> situation is reached at all in the mystery religions. The failure
> of the fight with the father-dragon, the overwhelming force
> of spirit, leads to patriarchal castration, inflation, loss of the
> body in the ecstasy of ascension, and so to a world-negating
> mysticism. . . . He remains hostile to the world, the body,
> materiality, and woman. (1970, 254)

The presence of twins in the myth is significant. Archetypally, twins represent a "twoness," which is a coming into the world, a reflection of opposites and inner contradictions that need to be overcome. They also represent an emerging consciousness. There is an archaic fear of twins, for they embody powerful, helpful, and destructive potentials (Chevalier and Gheerbrant 1996, 1047–50). There are many examples of twins and brothers in mythology, such as Cain and Abel, Esau and Jacob, Osiris and Set, Gilgamesh and Enkidu, and Romulus and Remus. Some twins or brothers are opposites that fight, while others contain both opposing characteristics within each individual. In the Maya myth, individual twins do not fight; instead, sets of twins oppose opposite sets of twins; the hero twins fight the twin gods of death and the monkey twins. This theme is also expressed in the overall union of masculine and feminine god figures, the twinning of opposites. Jung pointed out the inherent movement into opposition with the number 2. Opposition begets differentiation and reconciliation: "Two is the first number because, with it, separation and multiplication begin. . . . As soon as the number two appears, a unit is produced out of the original unity, and this unit is none other than that same unity split into two and turned into a 'number.' The one and the other form an opposition" (Jung 1989a, 118).

The *Popol Vuh*, which as mythic story could be one template for creation myths in general, begins with the stillness of the sky. A spawning of imagination in the hearts of the creator couple came forth with the word that began a process of greater and greater differentiation and consciousness. The spiritual emanation came into matter to create the world and all its creatures, including humans, who were capable of adequately honoring and respecting the gods, while the gods were capable of sustaining humans with a dependable food source in return. The journey through the underworld ends with death and rebirth, a process that is frequently seen as part of one's individuation. In the *Popol Vuh*, humans' other face is turned to the earthly world through the histories of the nations and tribes. This retelling of the story preserves the journey through the lineages connecting back to the creator gods and forward to the earthly lords, who were finally conquered by the Spaniards. The conquest was the end of their known world, yet it was not the end of their world according to their calendar. Their world was destroyed and re-created four times. They awaited the end and renewal of the fourth, a part of their never-ending cycle of life. This represents another mythic theme, the changing of the eons, found in the concept of the Tao in Chinese religion and yugas in Indian mythology.

Anthropologists and ethnologists have been most interested in the study of Mesoamerican mythology as a way to understand and explain the Maya culture. Few have gone further to explore the psychological and symbolic meaning of myth, much less the phenomenological experience one has with myth itself. This later approach is alive in the process of analysis, where an "analysand" metaphorically descends into the underworld through a depression and is faced with the inner demons and all the torments of his or her personally conceived hell. Myth is not examined for its relationship to living rituals. Today, young people tattoo and pierce themselves with no conscious understanding that this may be an impulse emerging from the patterns of initiation laid out in myths, much like bloodletting in Mesoamerica.

It is here that the psychological, archetypal, and symbolic approaches to myth become real. One finds oneself in what Jung (1981) referred to as the "psychoid" realm, where psyche and the world of matter meet and one lives the myth through the body. The outside observer becomes the dream ego and the protagonist. One enters the world of the universal mythic time; the individual's inner process takes on the journey that has been traveled many times before. It is here, in this realm and on this journey, that the symbol becomes alive again; the soul is recovered. One could say that the purpose of archetypal material is to further the individuation process. Understanding the symbolic meaning in this material helps foster understanding on the personal level. Eliade described this predicament so well:

> But modern man's "private mythologies"—his dreams, reveries, fantasies, and so on—never rise to the ontological status of myths, precisely because they are not experienced by the whole man and therefore do not transform a particular situation into a situation that is paradigmatic. . . . Symbol not only makes the world "open" but also helps religious man to attain to the universal. For it is through symbols that man finds his way out of his particular situation and "opens himself" to the general and the universal. Symbols awaken individual experience and transmute it into a spiritual act, into metaphysical comprehension of the world . . . for, by understanding the symbol, he succeeds in living the universal. (1987, 211–12)

The twins in the *Popol Vuh* were on a journey that was not of their own choosing, but the intention revealed through their actions, both failures and successes, led to the creation of the human race. Individually, this represents the birth of the ego and consciousness, and collectively it means the taming of the wild, destructive forces of nature and the creation of a cultural order that stands in relationship to the divine. The development was not complete, as it rarely is in cultures or individuals. It is an ongoing process requiring death-renewal-rebirth and the strength to pursue one's highest ethical values, to internalize both the mother and father within. While all the many previously discussed levels of mythic interpretation are culturally relevant, it becomes clear that the deeper, psychological, and religious nature of myths is a significant addition to the overall understanding of their meaning and function.

CHAPTER 4

TIME, SPACE, COSMOS, AND DIVINATION

Octavio Paz wrote, "Mesoamerican religions are an immense cosmic ballet of transformations, a grandiose dance of disguises in which each name is a date and a mask, a bundle of contradictory attributes" (cited in Ochiai 1986, 83). Mesoamerican creation mythology begins with sacrifices of the gods and of inadequate worlds. For these cultures it was common to offer sacrifices during rituals as a way to offer to the gods what was most precious to them, blood, the fundamental substance of life itself. The gods gave their blood to humans in their creation, and in return humans send their life force back to the gods as an offering. This elemental quid pro quo is found in all religions. The gift of life is purchased and then returned. The Aztecs were infamous for sacrificing many captives at the completion of a temple. Bodies have been found buried under the cornerstones of their buildings. Sacrifices were made for the inauguration of kings, for the death of kings, and for good or bad harvests.

The Mesoamerican 360-day solar ritual calendar demanded constant attention to the relationship between humans and the gods, while the lunar 260-day divinatory calendar consisted of days and numbers that represented the gods themselves. It is surmised that the number 260 came from the number of days of gestation of the human child as well as the number of days in the complete rotation of the planet Venus. It is also a multiple of 13, a sacred number for the Maya and the number of layers in their cosmic realm. It was multiplied by the 20 days of each month, 20 representing the number of fingers and toes on the human body. Every aspect of the Mesoamerican world was laid out in relation to the origin myth and their understanding of the cosmos. Their cities, temples, and homes in the temporal world mirrored the sacred world.

The idea of time in Mesoamerica was primary, and with the beginning of creation, it was set in motion by the divine energies. Each god represented a different archetypal energy; each moment represented a combination of divine forces that colored time for better or worse:

> Each instant of human time is a combination of divine forces that circulate in cycles of different dimensions. Through myth, humans seek to know the profound reality of daily life; but they must do it through a knowledge of the origin, because the archetypes exist in the origin, and the present is a combination of a group of archetypes that can be found in the different calendric cycles. (Austin 1993, 299)

The Maya developed a system of counting time into a sophisticated combination of two intersecting calendars, one for telling the past and future, the lunar Tzolk'in and the solar Haab', for laying out the rituals necessary to ensure proper relationship to the gods and sufficient harvests. These two calendars combined to form what is called the Long Count, allowing sophisticated mathematical and astronomical calculations into the far-distant past and well into the far future, in a never-ending cycle of beginnings and endings. Zero in their system denotes the balance between these two ever-present forces.

The oldest known calendar glyph, dating from the third century BCE, was recently discovered at the San Bartolo, Guatemala, archaeological site inside the ruins of the Las Pinturas pyramid. This glyph represents the calendar day name "7 Deer" and was found on mural fragments. This discovery points to the long history of calendar use and writing.

For the Mesoamericans, a king's lineage went back to the first humans and, therefore, the gods. Time was crucial and created their reality. Because they were an agricultural society, their mythology reflects the interrelationship and dependence on the gods for healthy functioning. The gods were personifications of the seasons, weather patterns, and the movement of the sun and moon across the sky. Through the movement of the celestial bodies, time was tracked and rituals were performed to keep the cycle moving through the passage of the seasons, days, years, and eons. The sun's movement traversed from birth to death across the horizon and then descended in the west at dusk. From there, it went through the nine layers of the underworld where it struggled with the gods of the dead to vanquish them, then rose above the horizon in the eastern dawn as the Maize God. It was preceded by the morning star, Venus. Now sun and moon were ready for another day, just as the gods themselves had once put them in place to start the world in motion. This process was not linear but cyclic, repeating itself endlessly. Here was the intersection of temporal and sacred time. Through the reenactment of the myth of creation, historical time is paused, while sacred time allows it to begin anew.

The 260-day lunar calendar, also called the *almanac* and *Tzolk'in*, the sacred divinatory calendar, is used for telling the future and understanding the life that awaited children according to the day they were born. *Tzolk'in* means "to order the days," "to read or clarify." The purpose of the Tzolk'in is to give meaning and reason to the day-to-day randomness of people's lives and the passage of time. There are twenty day signs, which are logographic signs that each represent a different god with different characteristics. The following are signs in the Tzolk'in calendar corresponding to the gods, with their Maya and English translations:

1. Imix: waterlily crocodile
2. Ik´: wind, breath, life, violence
3. Ak´b´al: darkness, night, early dawn, jaguar-sun
4. K´an: maize, net, sacrifice
5. Chicchan: snake
6. Kimi: death
7. Manik': deer
8. Lamat: rabbit, Venus, maize seed
9. Muluc: water, jade, rain, offering
10. Oc: dog who guides the night sun through the underworld
11. Chouen: howler monkey, craftsman, patron of the arts
12. Eb´: grass associated with rain and storms
13. B´en: reed, green/young maize, seed
14. Ix: jaguar, the night sun, maize, goddess Ixchel
15. Men: eagle, wise one, bird, moon

16. Cib: owl/vulture, death birds of night and day, wax, soul, insect
17. Cab´an: earthquake, formidable power, season, thought
18. Etz´nab´: flint knife, obsidian sacrificial blade
19. Cauak: rain, storm, celestial dragon serpents, chacs, gods of thunder and lightning
20. Ahau: lord, ruler, radiant sun god, Maya hero twins

Additionally there are 13 numerals, called the *trecena*, that correspond to other gods. Each of the twenty named day-gods is paired with a numeral from 1 to 13 and then rotate like a wheel containing two moving circles through the cycle of 260 days. It starts on 1 Imix and ends on 13 Ahau. The numerals for counting are based on 20, not 10 as in the decimal or denary system. Thirteen numerals multiplied by 20 days equals 260, the total days in the Tzolk'in calendar. Numerals are written with lines and dots. A single horizontal line is 5, while each dot placed above it counted as 1.

Kinh means "day" and "sun, supreme ruler." The twenty day deities listed above, and the deities that represent the numerals from 1 to 13 bear the attributes of the main deities of the Maya pantheon. The twentieth day name is *Ahau*, which means "lord or king." All calendar period endings and, therefore, the important festivals, fall on this day, both in the 260-day divinatory calendar and in the longer and more complex civic and agricultural calendar called the Haab'. "In computing periods of time, the priests endeavored to predict what would be the acts of the gods, to predict the nature of each deified moment" (León-Portilla 1988, 38).

The 365-day solar year called the Haab' gave the time frame for the agricultural calendar essential for planting and harvesting maize. It also dictated the timing of festivals and ceremonies. It was a type of civil calendar containing 18 months, each 20 days in length: 18 multiplied by 20 equals 360. There were an additional 5 days, called *Uayeb*, the unlucky days at the end of the year, which fall under the influence of the Lord of the Earth. Again, the months were deities that referred to food plants, seasons, or other characteristics of the year, for example, dry season, winter, harvest, or new moon. The following are their K'iche' names with English translations:

1. Pop: mat, community, marriage
2. Uo´: frog, black conjunction
3. Sip: red conjunction
4. Sotz´: bat
5. Sek: death
6. Xul: dog
7. Yaxk´in: new sun
8. Mol: water or jade
9. Ch´en: cave or well, black storm
10. Yax: green or first, green storm
11. Sac´: white storm
12. Keh: red storm or deer
13. Mac: to cover, enclose
14. K´ank´in: yellow sun, skeleton, rib cage of a dog
15. Muwan: falcon, owl
16. Pax: planting time
17. K´ayab´: turtle
18. Kumk´u: granary, ripe maize
19. Uayeb´: the last five unlucky or misfortunate days of the year

Although the Maya were aware of the incremental creep of time each year of 0.24 days that is seen in our Georgian calendar and accounted for with a leap year every four years, they chose to account for the creep by moving a day backward in their count every four years. Their conception of annual cycles is quite different from the modern one, but we arrive at the same point.

The number 13 is very important in Maya numerology, representing the 13 celestial levels and the number of turns in the 260-day calendar. It takes 52 years, or 18,980 days, for the *calendar round* to complete when the Tzolk'in and Haab' coincide. This represents the great cycle of the Long Count or the Great Round that places the date of creation of this world at 13.0.0.0.0, or August 13, 3114 BCE. The end of this cycle is the date that came around again on December 21, 2012, when it was feared the world would come to an end. It was a pause before it began anew. The Long Count is based on a grand cycle of very long time periods that are measured in large units called *b'ak'tuns* (144,000 days), *k'atuns* (7,200 days), *tuns* (360 days), *winal* (20 days), and *k'in* (1 day). The Long Count and the Great Round document and connect the material world to cosmic events, both historical and in the far-distant future. The fact that the earth was created and destroyed four times shows that the gods have carried the burden of time over and over again, through periods of growth and decline, passing it on from one to the next in this continuous, unending circular cycle. Events repeat themselves when the days are arrived at again and again:

> It becomes clear the Maya conceived of time in close association with the solar deity, something divine in itself, limitless and ubiquitous. . . . They had a continuous obsession for knowledge and pre-vision of the ever-changing reality of *kinh*, the divine sun-day-time. All the moments of time—the days, months, and years—are arrivals and presences of divine faces. They all successively come and go, letting their influences be felt, unceasingly determining life and death in the universe. Each moment is not only the presence of one god but the sum total of many presences. The deities of the numbers, those of the days, months, years, and other time measurements, come together in different points of arrival throughout the cycles. . . . The mysteries of *kinh*, whose essence consisted of the divine countenances, were bearers of good and evil. At the precise moment in which one of these periods comes to its completion, another deity takes up the burden and anew directs the flow of *kinh*. (León-Portilla 1988, 42–51)

The word *ilb'al* was used in the *Popol Vuh* to describe the original Precolumbian text as an instrument of sight, a means of seeing. "When humans were made, they had clear vision and could see to all four corners of the world and universe; in other words, they saw with the clarity of the gods" (Christenson 2003, 304). This disturbed the gods because humans were to propagate and honor the gods, not be as gods. So their vision was fogged, allowing them to see only what was near them, not the wisdom of the totality. The *Popol Vuh* was the instrument that revealed the original clear vision when it was read by a diviner or daykeeper. It opened a view into the past, present, and future. Each action and character in the text was associated with the planets, constellations, and the movement of the cosmos. Each carried an archetypal energy represented as a day, month, or year sign that had a predictable behavior. As the calendars cycled through time, so did the changing archetypal energies determining actions and events in the world. Knowing what was approaching, the Maya could appease the gods with ritual sacrifices and countermeasures, or not. For this reason, the *Popol Vuh* was much more than a mythic or historic retelling of the past but was instead a living experience that opened a door into the many dimensions of their cosmos, giving them a means of understanding and perhaps a bit of control over the fate that was handed to them daily:

> *Kinh*, sun-day-time, is a primary reality, divine and limitless. *Kinh* embraces all cycles and all the cosmic ages. The *Popol Vuh* speaks of the "suns" or ages, past and present. . . . Among the faces appearing in the diverse periods are those of the solar deity in all its forms and those of the gods and goddesses of rain, earth, corn, death, sacrifice, the great star, the moon, and hunting. These faces constitute the most significant nucleus of the Maya pantheon. . . . The Maya strove, by means of their computations, to foresee the nature of these presences and the result of their various influences at specified moments. Since *kinh* is essentially cyclic, it is most important to know the past in order to understand the present and predict the future. . . . The faces of time determined and governed all activities, the norms for agricultural labors, cycles of festivals, everything in life. The priests register the symbols and effigy of the time-gods as they arrive. They erect stelae, compose their books, and set the *katun* stones in place. . . . There was an essential relationship between the Maya and time and the world of the gods. (León-Portilla 1988, 54–55)

The Maya special image of the universe had great similarities with the conceptions existing among other cultures in Central America. The earth was a horizontal universe, and its symbol is shown either as the figure of a monster, fangs and claws of a crocodile, or with the form and head of a fantastic saurian. Their idea of directions was based on the fourfold plan, four corners, four angles, with the four cosmic segments that converge in the center to form the fifth direction of the world. The great crocodile is turned into four beings, each assigned a world direction—four monsters, known as the four Itzamnás (dew from the heavens or crocodile of the house), which are both terrestrial and celestial. They are related to the colors, the waters, the winds, and the sacred stones, the birds, the seeds, the cosmic *ceiba*, and the beings corresponding to each quadrant. In each sector grow the primeval *ceiba* with the corresponding cosmic bird. Also in each sector reside the Pahuatúns (gods of the wind), Chacs (lords of rain), Balams (protectors of the fields), and Bacabs (the supporters of heaven). The other deities that maintain a close relationship with the earth are the young Maize God (the father twin, One Hunahpú, resurrected from the underworld), the jaguar, the god of death, and others associated with different temporal periods (Roys 1973, 62–65). South is to the right, north is to the left, west is below, and east is above. The Maya did not conceive of the four directions as contemporary people do, nor did they have maps. Everything traversed on the plane of the movement of the sun (*kinh*) across the horizon from east to west with the north and south along the sides.

There are three realms: earth, the upper realm, and underworld. The deities of the upper realm are counterparts of the earthly reality, but the serpent deities are always in couples, connoting a certain dualistic idea of the deity—the Moan birds and the celestial "dragons." The upper world consists of thirteen levels, each with its own ruling deity. The *Popol Vuh* lists twelve demons in the nine levels of the regions of darkness. The thirteen gods of the upper world are associated with the thirteen day gods, while the night is ruled by the gods of the underworld (Villacorta and Villacorta 1930, 74). As mentioned in the *Chilam Balam of Chumayel* (Roys 1973), the various planes of the universe went through an upheaval. Prophecies of a *k´atun* date, 11

Ahau, was the struggle between the thirteen gods of the upper world and the nine gods of the lower world. The burden of this *k´atun* provoked a cataclysm involving the three planes of the universe. In the end, the primogenital *ceibas* are reborn in the five regions of the earth as a sign and in memory of the violent encounter of divine forces that destroy and then re-create the universe through the various suns that are also the great cycles of time.

The horizontal space appears surrounded in its turn by the twenty day signs. The Pahuatúns dwell in the underworlds; the Bacabs, or supporters of the work, dwell on earth; the Chacs reside in the clouds. All correspond to cardinal points and the color for the different years. The burden of the years becomes manifest in each quadrant of the world when a cycle is concluded. *Kinh* is conceived as deified time and space:

> Thus, the spatial universe exists, changes, dies, and is reborn in each of the "suns" or ages as a consequence of the actions of the gods or countenances of time. Space is not static. . . . Isolated from time, space becomes inconceivable. In the absence of time-cycles, there is no life, nothing happens, not even death. (León-Portilla 1988, 86)

Time and space are intertwined, and their mythology was interwoven into cylindrical computation:

> The temporal universe, created again and again by the ancient face of the solar deity, makes possible through its cycles the arrival of all the other god-periods. These, with their own rhythm and measure, bring with them diverse forms of burdens, good and bad fates, with which all reality is tinted and permeated in a succession that never terminates. The deities of the numbers, the days, the months, the *katuns* and *baktuns* make their entrances and are acting until their journeys are done. Then they pass their burdens to the other time-gods as they arrive. (León-Portilla 1988, 94)

To know a *kinh*'s past burden leads to a prediction of its future recurrences. Each child's birthday was looked at in terms of positive and negative qualities or influences by the ruling god of that day. By understanding the meaning of the number, day, and month and the archetypal energy they represent, one has the ability to remedy what is perceived to be negative through sacrifices and rites that neutralize the negative fate and instead bring forth a favorable destiny. This escape valve prevents a belief in absolute fatalism (León-Portilla 1988, 106).

The Aztecs much later used these same calendars and incorporated much of this fundamental belief system into their worldview. In Mesoamerica it became the foundation for belief, having been developed earlier than other systems of counting time, although it was not unique in the world, for example, in India:

> Cosmic cycles are called *yugas*. A complete cycle was called *mahāyuga* and comprised 12,000 years. It ends with a dissolution, a *pralaya*, which is repeated more drastically (*mahāpralaya*, the Great Dissolution) at the end of the thousandth cycle. For the paradigmatic schema "creation-destruction-creation-etc." is reproduced ad infinitum. The 12,000 years of a *mahāyuga* were regarded as divine years, each with a duration of 360 years, which gives a total of 4,320,000 years for a single cosmic cycle. A thousand such *mahāyugas* make up a *kalpa* (form); 14 *kalpas* make up a *manvantāra* (so named because each *manvantāra* is supposed to be ruled by Manu, the mythical Ancestor-King). A *kalpa* is equivalent to a day in the life of Brahma; a second *kalpa* to a night. One hundred of these "years" of Brahma, in other words 311,000 milliards of human years, constitute the life of Brahma. But even this duration of the god's life does not exhaust time, for the gods are not eternal and the cosmic creations and destructions succeed one another forever. (Eliade 1987, 108)

Karma is the force for the eternal return to life, the law of the universe. The only hope was the abolition of karma, resulting in the non-return-to-existence—the final deliverance, or *moksha*, the transcendence of the cosmos.

In the Greek world, the people lived by the myth of the eternal return:

> An infinite succession of cycles in the course of which the same reality was made, unmade, and remade in conformity with an immutable law and immutable alternative. The Pythagoreans, Stoics, Platonists—reached the point of admitting that within each of these cycles of duration, of these *aiones*, these *aeva*, the same situations are reproduced that have already been produced in previous cycles and will be reproduced in subsequent cycles— *ad infinitum*. No event is unique, occurs once and for all, but it has occurred, occurs, and will occur, perpetually; the same individuals have appeared, appear, and will appear at every return of the cycle upon itself. Cosmic duration is repetition, and *anakuklosis*, eternal return. (Eliade 1987, 110)

"The Greeks identified time with the divine river Oceanos, which surrounded the earth in a circle and which also encompassed the universe in the form of a circular stream or a tail-eating serpent with the Zodiac on its back. It was also called Chronos (time) and later identified with Kronos, the father of Zeus, and also with the god Aion" (von Franz 1978, 5). Aion, the god of time, was an image of the dynamic nature of life and all its opposites, which are included in this cosmic principle. These views are quite different from the current Western view of time, which is seen as linear, having a starting point and a potential ending point rather than being seen as circular and repeating.

CHAPTER 5

A SYNOPSIS OF THE
Popol Vuh CREATION
MYTH

This chapter provides an overview of the entire myth so that it is clear in the reader's mind before the study delves into the amplification of a specific section in chapter 6.

The *Popol Vuh* runs on with no punctuation or section breaks, but the translators break up the text in different ways to make it more manageable to the reader. I follow D. Tedlock's (1985) formula of breaking the *Popol Vuh* into five sections, which include creating the world and its contents four times, the unacceptable beings, and finally, humans. The myth ends with a genealogy of the tribes and lords of the K'iche' Maya. The *Popol Vuh*, therefore, moves from the realm of the gods before creation, through the creation of humans, and into the temporal world of noble lineages, right up to the time of the Spanish conquest. The text shifts from the mythological to the historical and from the cosmos into the realities of everyday life.

The myth sequence as written in the *Popol Vuh* is not complete. There are other mythic segments that appear on vases that are not included in the *Popol Vuh*, for example, the presence of the supreme god Itzamná, connected with the Principal Bird Deity (Taube 1992, 40). This deity was significant in the Preclassic period but evidently lost favor later. It was incorporated into the section in the *Popol Vuh* dealing with the vainglorious Seven Macaw. This may be an example of how mythologically the old gods die and are replaced. The Principal Bird Deity dies as the sun sets and rises reborn as Itzamná. Also excluded are details about the three hearthstones. Early construction of the Maya temple buildings was in an E-Group layout focusing on an east-west axis with large plazas for ritual ceremonies that included everyone, not just the elite. Being triadic, it represented the three hearthstones. Richard Hansen (pers. comm., November 21, 2013)

A section of the larger Preclassic frieze from the Tigre pyramid in the
Mirador-Calakmul Basin, showing Hunahpú with a jaguar headdress,
carrying One Hunahpú on his back.

suggested that the absence of these motifs indicates lost segments
of the myth that had been omitted over time. Additionally, there are
actually two beginnings to the *Popol Vuh* myth, just as there are in
Genesis.

Recent excavations in the Mirador-Calakmul Basin in Guatemala
revealed a carved frieze of the culture hero twins flowing along in a
stream of water. Hunahpú carries the head of his father, One Hunahpú, on his back while facing Xbalanqué, but they are separated
by serpents. The frieze is situated at the base of the Tigre pyramid.
What is most revealing about this frieze is that it is Preclassic, dating
to around 300 BCE. This is highly significant in that it dates the story
in the *Popol Vuh* farther back than ever thought (previously, some had
believed it to be post-conquest).

On the upper register of the frieze is the bird god Itzamná, and to
its left is a cormorant feeding a fish. In later carvings, the bird is eat-

Preclassic frieze from the Tigre pyramid in the Mirador-Calakmul Basin, showing Hunahpú and Xbalanqué in a river channel, with Itzamná in the center top surrounded by serpents. The cormorant feeding the fish is to the far left.

ing the fish rather than feeding it (Hansen, pers. comm., November 12–18, 2013). This difference is also significant juxtaposed to alchemical symbolism. In alchemy there is the image of the pelican feeding its young, which refers to the concept of bringing the new, young life forth. This would refer to the new ideas, attitudes, and behaviors that are emerging into consciousness. Jung's (1978) book, *Aion*, suggests that the fish is a symbol for Christ, who in this case represents the Christ image as an inner representation. This is the savior and archetype of wisdom and wholeness that manifests in individuals' dreams and certainly did culturally with the birth of Christ. The bird feeding the fish, therefore, may represent the spiritual deity, perhaps connected to the Principal Bird Deity nourishing the new impulse emerging from the unconscious.

There are also murals at another Preclassic Maya city-state, San Bartolo, that depict illustrations on a grand scale of themes from the *Popol Vuh*. Many ceramic vases from the Classic period in Maya history depict images from the *Popol Vuh* as well. These can be seen in the five volumes of Justin Kerr's (2000) Maya vase books and on his website.*

THE BEGINNING OF THE ANCIENT WORD

The narrative begins by saying that what will be written is the ancient K'iche' word, which tells the traditions, the stories of the beginning, the recounting of their origin. K'iche' means "many trees or forest." It is the account of the sowing and dawning by the creator gods. The world had nothing but a dark, empty sky and a calm sea below; absent was the earth.

The gods who resided in the primordial sea were named the Heart of Sea, Heart of Lake, Sovereign and Quetzal Serpent, Framer and Shaper. The process began when the gods of the sky called Heart of Sky, Heart of Earth, Newborn Thunderbolt, Raw Thunderbolt, and Huracán joined the gods of the primordial sea. The word *"hurricane"* derives from the word *Huracán*, meaning "flash of a leg or lightning." It was used to describe the Maya creation god and the god of the powerful, swirling wind among the Carib Indians of the West Indies. The god Heart of Sky, or Huracán, is like "the eye of the hurricane forming the divine axis around which time and creation revolve in endless repetitive cycles of birth and destruction" (Christenson 2003, 70n62).

Then came the *word* that emerged from the minds of the gods. They came together and talked, thought, and pondered. Together they possessed great knowledge. Arriving at accord, they conceived of light and life, the emergence of the earth from the sea and everything that was to inhabit it. This was the word of Heart of Sky

*See Maya Vase Date Base, http://www.famsi.org/research/kerr/articles/rollout/.

The genealogy of the gods that appear in the *Popol Vuh*

Heart of Sky/Heart of Earth—Sovereign Plumed Serpent—Xpiyacoc (m) and Xmucané (f)

Huracán	Heart of Lake	Framer and Shaper
Youngest Thunderbolt	Heart of Sea	Grandmother and
Raw Thunderbolt		Grandfather
Sudden Thunderbolt		He Who Has Begotten Sons
		She Who Has Borne Children
Falcon		Maker of the Blue-Green
Turtle Dove		Plate
		Maker of the Blue-Green
		Bowl
		Midwife and Matchmaker
		Hunahpú Opossum and
		Grandfather
		Hunahpú Coyote (f)
		Coati and Grandmother
		Great Peccary (m) and
		Great Tapir (f)

and Heart of Earth, Heart of Sea and Quetzal Serpent, Framer and Shaper, Xpiyacoc and Xmucané. These last two gods were called on to do the actual creating and were also referred to as She Who Has Borne Children and He Who Has Begotten Sons, Patriarch and Midwife, Grandfather and Grandmother. Both were diviners and were the divine masculine and feminine, now differentiated from the original wholeness. Together they brought the creation of the earth, mountains, valleys, trees, and waterways. Then the animals were conceived: deer, birds, pumas, jaguars, serpents. This was all before the dawn arrived.

The Framer and Shaper asked the animals to speak, and they could not. They only "squawked, chattered, and roared" (Christenson 2003, 76). The gods wanted "beings who will walk, work, and talk in an articulate and measured way, visiting shrines, giving offerings, and calling upon their makers by name, all according to the rhythms of a calendar" (D. Tedlock 1985, 34). The animals were left to serve and be eaten.

Creations that appear in the *Popol Vuh*

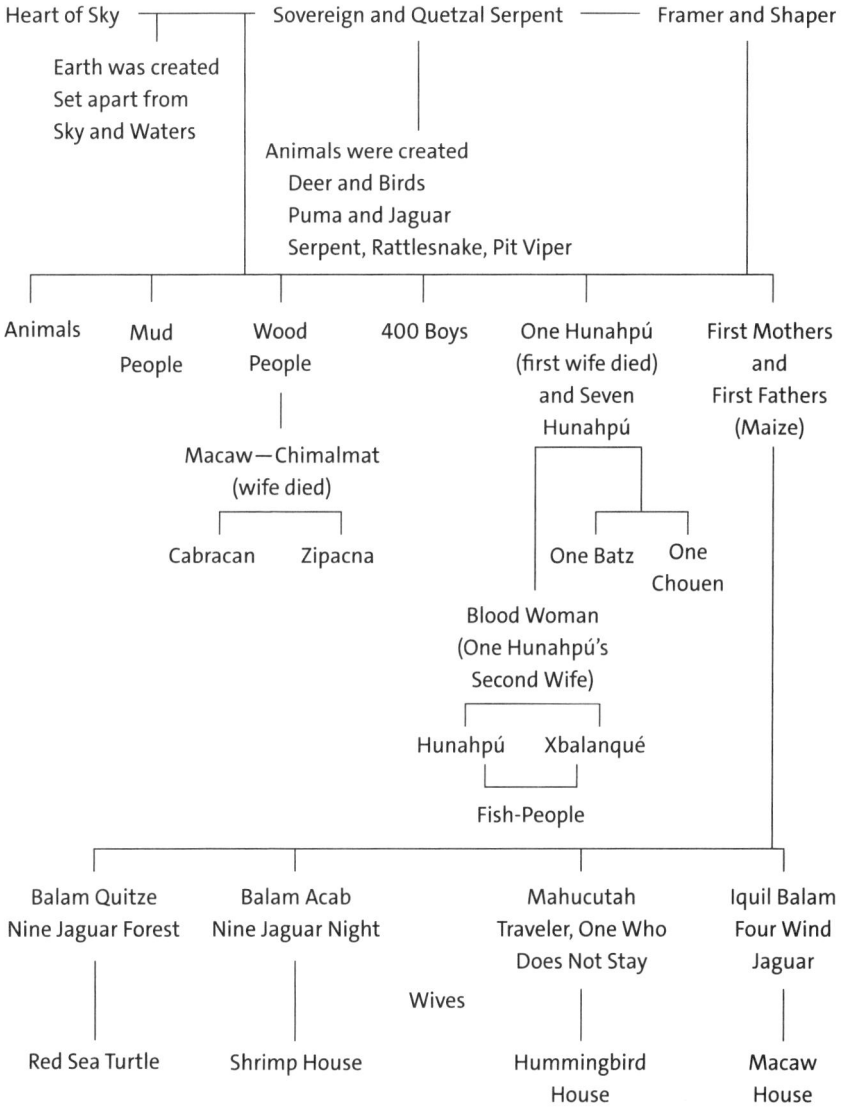

Heart of Sky ——————— Sovereign and Quetzal Serpent ——————— Framer and Shaper

Earth was created
Set apart from
Sky and Waters

Animals were created
Deer and Birds
Puma and Jaguar
Serpent, Rattlesnake, Pit Viper

| Animals | Mud People | Wood People | 400 Boys | One Hunahpú (first wife died) and Seven Hunahpú | First Mothers and First Fathers (Maize) |

Macaw—Chimalmat
(wife died)

Cabracan   Zipacna

One Batz   One Chouen

Blood Woman
(One Hunahpú's
Second Wife)

Hunahpú   Xbalanqué

Fish-People

| Balam Quitze Nine Jaguar Forest | Balam Acab Nine Jaguar Night | Mahucutah Traveler, One Who Does Not Stay | Iquil Balam Four Wind Jaguar |

Wives

| Red Sea Turtle | Shrimp House | Hummingbird House | Macaw House |

The gods tried again and created beings of earth and mud, but these merely fell apart and dissolved in water. It was another mistake, but the gods asked the Framer and Shaper to try again. Next they carved beings from wood, but the wooden beings did not have hearts or minds either. The gods then sent a great flood to destroy them, and they were crushed and torn to pieces. The animals and instruments they had misused all rose up in anger against them to destroy them. The wooden effigies that were not destroyed in the flood and the uprising turned into monkeys.

THE BEGINNING OF THE DEFEAT AND DESTRUCTION OF SEVEN MACAW AND HIS SONS

At this point in the myth during the world of the wooden beings, before there were the sun and moon, there was just a little light on the face of the earth. Sitting high up in a tree, pretending to be a god, was a vainglorious Macaw who survived the flood. He was called Seven Macaw, and he was enchanted with his own power because of the light that shone from his eyes, beak, teeth, and face, which were covered with gold, silver, and jewels. From these, light was reflected to show the way to the inhabitants of this world. Seven Macaw sparkled, but he did not have the clear vision of a god. He saw only what was in front of himself.

Opposing Seven Macaw were the hero twins, Hunahpú and Xbalanqué, who are featured later in the myth. Hunahpú means "one blowgun hunter," while Xbalanqué carries the letter "X," referring to young or feminine and also to jaguar and sun. Xbalanqué could mean "young, hidden jaguar sun." Hunahpú and Xbalanqué are gods, and they know that people will not be able to live on the earth with Seven Macaw high in a tree posing as a god. He must be destroyed, for vanity and pride are evil and cannot be tolerated. Seven Macaw had two sons: Zipacna, who created mountains, and Cabracan, who destroyed mountains with earthquakes—a pair with opposing energies. These sons had the pride of their father and also had to be destroyed.

While Seven Macaw was at the top of the nance tree eating fruit, Hunahpú and Xbalanqué approached and shot him, wounding his jaw and eye and causing him to fall to the ground. They tried to grab him, but instead Seven Macaw tore off Hunahpú's arm and flew home to his wife, in terrible pain from his dislocated jaw.

The boys then consulted with the Grandfather and Grandmother and came up with a plan for how to kill Seven Macaw and retrieve Hunahpú's arm. They decided to approach Seven Macaw and offer their services to pull the tooth that was causing the bird's pain, which was so bad by that time that the bird immediately agreed. They told the bird he had a worm in his tooth, which was the cause of his pain. They also told Seven Macaw that they could heal his eyes. Both the tooth and eye were the bird's finery, but the boys told Seven Macaw that both would have to come out; so out they came. With that, Seven Macaw lost his face and fell dead, and his wife died as well.

At this point in the story, it was time to deal with the vainglorious sons of Seven Macaw. One by one the boys set traps for them, but not before Zipacna, a monstrous crocodile, killed four hundred boys who were trying to carry a heavy tree trunk they hoped to use as a supporting lintel for a hut and were struggling under its weight. They asked Zipacna to carry it for them. The huge crocodile agreed to help and easily carried the tree trunk to its location. The boys knew that the beam held a great power of the sacred and that any being who did not observe the proper ritual or have the proper authority to carry the beam would be going against the gods. So the boys plotted to kill Zipacna by having him dig a deep pit, and while he was inside, the boys dropped the lintel on top of him. Clever as he was and suspecting a plot, he had dug a side passage in the pit where he hid from the boys' view. After three days, when the boys saw ants carrying fingernails and hair out of the pit, they believed the croc was dead and rejoiced at their success. They then proceeded to get drunk. This was when Zipacna made the hut collapse, and it fell on their heads, killing them all. The four hundred boys then arose into the sky and became the Pleiades.

The twins then came up with a scheme to kill the crocodile. Zipacna was famished from his time waiting in the pit, and he was not finding any crabs to eat. The twins conjured up a huge crab and told him that it was hiding in a cave at the base of a mountain. Zipacna immediately went to catch it. He was trying this way and that to get into the small opening so he could reach the crab when he finally became stuck on his back. The mountain collapsed on top of him, and Zipacna was turned to stone.

Now it was time to defeat Zipacna's brother, Cabracan, the destroyer of mountains. Huracán told the boys to lure him to the east where the sun rises. The boys told Cabracan of a mountain that kept rising higher and higher, and of course, Cabracan wanted to destroy it. On the way the twins said if they saw any birds, they would shoot them and cook them for the earth shaker, who was sure to be hungry. Hunahpú and Xbalanqué then transformed a great bird out of a tropical flower and stone and cooked it. Cabracan smelled the bird cooking and was drooling with desire and hunger. The twins gave him the bird to eat and that was his downfall. As they marched along toward the large mountain, he became increasingly tired, so tired that he could not destroy the mountains. The boys then tied him up and threw him down into the earth and buried him. Cabracan was defeated like his brother and his father.

THE STORY OF THE TWO SETS OF TWINS AND THEIR FATEFUL JOURNEYS

The tale then moves into the mythic story of these Macaw-killing heroes' father and uncle, another set of twins named One Hunahpú and Seven Hunahpú. They were sons of Xpiyacoc and Xmucané, the male and female creator deities, who were the oldest of the gods, the Grandfather and Grandmother earth, planting deities associated with the forces of creation and destruction. One Hunahpú and Seven Hunahpú were born in the night.

One Hunahpú was married to Xbaquiyalo, which means "yielding lady bone water." They had two sons, One Batz, or Howler Monkey, and One Chouen, which also means "howler monkey" as well as "artisan." They were clever scribes, "flautists and singers, writers and sculptors, jade workers and precious metal smiths" (Christensen 2003, 113). They derived talent from their father to become writers (scribes), singers, and artists.

One Hunahpú and Seven Hunahpú loved to play dice and ball with their sons every day, and when they were at the ballcourt, Hura-

Demons that appear in the *Popol Vuh*

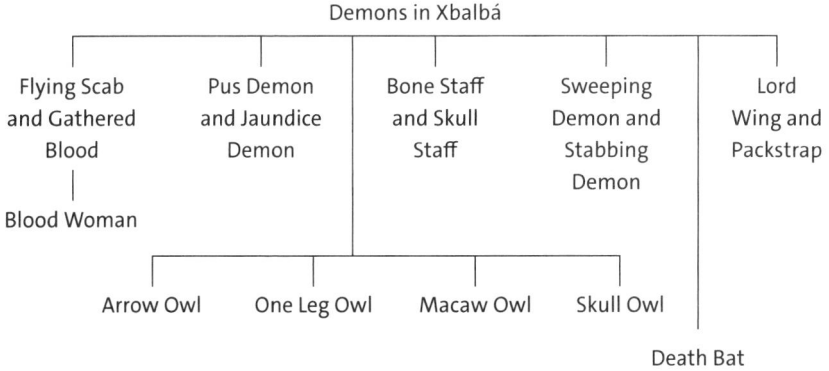

Demons in Xbalbá

Flying Scab and Gathered Blood	Pus Demon and Jaundice Demon	Bone Staff and Skull Staff	Sweeping Demon and Stabbing Demon	Lord Wing and Packstrap

Blood Woman

Arrow Owl	One Leg Owl	Macaw Owl	Skull Owl

Death Bat

cán's Falcon would go and watch over them. Then the wife of One Hunahpú died. The ballcourt, named Honor and Respect, was conveniently located on the path to the dead, called Xibalbá. The lords of the underworld, One Death and Seven Death, become furious with all the stomping and shouting from above, and conferring with each other, they decided to invite the Hunahpú twins down for a ball game. The gods of death were upset because the noise reflected dishonor and arrogance, the same theme that appeared in the killing of the vainglorious Seven Macaw. It was these elder twins' second set of twin sons, Hunahpú and Xbalanqué, who killed the bird and its sons. At this point in the myth, their father and uncle were called down to meet their own challenge.

This descent is the myth's first journey into the underworld. In this myth, the ballcourt is located at the entry point into the underworld. The underworld holds twelve demons, and each one has a task. The lords of the underworld are named One Death and Seven Death; Flying Scab and Gathered Blood, whose job was to sicken the blood; Pus Demon and Jaundice Demon, who swelled people up, causing pus and jaundice; Bone Staff and Skull Staff, who skeletonized people through starvation; Sweeping Demon and Stabbing Demon, who stabbed people if they stopped sweeping their homes; and Lord Wing and Packstrap, who would kill people on the road while carrying heavy loads.

The demons from Xibalbá sent their war councilors, the four owls named Arrow Owl, One Leg Owl, Macaw Owl, and Skull Owl, to invite the twins to the underworld to play ball. The twins were told to bring their ball game gear. The twins accepted the offer but first left instructions with their mother—as their father was dead. They took all of their equipment but left their rubber ball behind because they believed they would use it again. They told their sons to play the flute and sing, to write and carve to keep their grandmother joyful in their absence. But she wept with sadness even though they told her they would not die.

Guided by the messengers, the twins descended the long path to Xibalbá. They passed by Trembling Canyon, Murmuring Canyon, Scorpion River, and Blood River to arrive at the crossroads where the Red, Black, White, and Yellow Roads intersected. The Black Road spoke to them, telling them to take its path, the lord's road, so they did. As they arrived at the council place, they were to correctly address the demons seated on a bench, but the twins didn't realize that the seated demons were just manikins. The lords roared with laughter at this failure, because they knew the twins were already defeated. Then the demons welcomed the twins and offered them a bench to sit on. Because the bench was very hot, the twins burned themselves, another failure that caused shrieks of laughter from the lords of the underworld. One Hunahpú and Seven Hunahpú were directed to proceed through the next set of trials, which consisted of surviving a night in each of a series of houses, the House of Darkness, Shivering House, Jaguar House, Bat House, and Blade House.

In the House of Darkness, they were given a cigar and a torch and told to keep them lit until the morning, which they failed to do. Thus, they were sacrificed and buried at a place called Crushing Ballcourt. The head of One Hunahpú was cut off, while the rest of his body was buried along with his brother. The head was placed in a tree by the road, and after that the tree bore fruit for the first time. From then on, it was called the calabash tree.

The lords gave an order that no one should visit the tree, but Blood Woman, the daughter of the demon Gathered Blood, was curious about the calabash and decided to visit anyway. When she did, the skull fruit began to speak to her, asking her what she wanted. She said that she wanted to see the skull. So the skull fruit asked Blood Woman to put out her right hand, and the skull proceeded to spit into her palm. The spittle immediately disappeared but not before it had impregnated her. The skull told her that spittle is like the seeds of potential life, like one's essence that carries one on to become complete again through progeny. In this way ancestors never die but reemerge in future generations. Blood Woman was then told by the calabash to go up to earth to live with his grandmother.

When Blood Woman's father discovered she was pregnant, he was furious, and not taking fornication lightly, he asked her if she had seen the face of a man. She had not and told him so, but her father did not believe her and ordered the Owls to take her to the forest to sacrifice her and bring her heart to him. She explained to the Owls what she had done and convinced them not to sacrifice her but instead to collect red sap from a tree as a substitute for her heart. In return, she allowed the Owls to travel up to earth. They accepted this arrangement and offered the sap as a substitute to the demons to burn in offering to the gods. The deceit was not discovered, and they relished the smell of the burning sap as its smoke rose to the gods. The demons were defeated because Blood Woman had tricked them.

Blood Woman was not well received by the grandmother or the twins' sons, soon to become monkeys. She was told by the grandmother to collect corn in the field as a test to see if she were truly her son's wife. Lamenting not knowing how she would be able to do this with only one ear of corn in the field, she begged for help from the guardians of food, and they provided her with a net full of corn. The animals helped Blood Woman by carrying the net full of corn back to the grandmother, who was shocked at the quantity, thinking it had been stolen. She went to the cornfield to see for herself and immediately realized that her daughter-in-law was enchanted and, therefore, indeed was her relative.

Blood Woman gave birth to the third set of twins, Hunahpú and Xbalanqué, the hero twins. They were loud babies and upset their grandmother, who demanded they sleep outside on an anthill, where they slept blissfully. Their older half brothers, One Batz and One

Chouen, wanting them to die, moved them to a thorn bush. One Batz and One Chouen were jealous and treacherous. While being great singers and flautists, excelling in everything they did and being born with great vision, nothing came of their talents because of their envy. Their abuses of others merely fell back onto them. The hero twins ignored them and went on with their hunting. Their envious older brothers ate all the food, but "they tolerated it, for they knew their own nature, and this was a light by which they could see" (Christenson 2003, 142). One day the heroes did not bring home birds to eat, and their grandmother became enraged. The boys told her the birds were stuck at the top of a tree, and they needed their brothers to climb up and retrieve them. The older brothers agreed to go at dawn. This plan was really a plot to "overturn their nature" (142).

At dawn the four boys went to the Yellow Tree, which was filled with birds. The heroes shot their blowguns, but none of the birds fell down. The older brothers then agreed to climb up, and as they did, the tree grew larger, swelling in size. When they tried to come down, they couldn't. The twins suggested they loosen the ends of their loincloths and tie them around their bellies to make it easier to climb down. As they did that, they transformed into howler monkeys, and the loincloths became tails. They clambered off into the forest. The twins returned home and told their grandmother that their older brothers had changed. The twins called their older brothers home to sing and admonished the grandmother to refrain from laughing. She was given four tries not to laugh at them, but in the end she was not able to contain herself; they were too hilarious with their red, silly, puckered-looking faces and their paunchy bellies. They had been turned into howler monkeys because of their pride.

The twins were now substitutes for their brothers and responsible for clearing the fields. In the morning they took their axes and hoes and swung them into the ground, but the instruments then took over and did all the work on their own while the boys sat there giving instructions. In this way the boys deceived their grandmother, pretending to cultivate the field while really hunting with their blowguns. However, on the second day, they arrived and discovered that all the work that had been done had been reversed. They wondered who was playing tricks on them, and they suspected the animals: the puma and jaguar, the deer and rabbit, the fox and coyote, the peccary and the coati, and the small and great birds. This time, they felled all the trees and stayed hidden to see what would happen. Sure enough, all the animals emerged and began their work. One by one the animals passed by the boys while the boys tried to grab them, but without luck.

Finally the boys caught the deer and rabbit by their tails and broke the tails off. This is why their tails are short to this day. The last animal to pass by was the rat, and the boys snared the rat in a net. They strangled it and burned its tail in the fire. That is why rats do not have hair on their tails. The rat told them that he must not die at their hands, that he had a message for them in his belly. The boys' job was not to cultivate maize in the field. The animals had another job for them. The rat told them that there was something hidden in the rafters of their grandmother's roof that belonged to them. The rat would not speak further without being given food. The boys gave food to the rat and also gave it the right from then on to all the trash that was swept out of the houses. They then discovered what had been hidden under their grandmother's roof—a rubber gaming ball of their father's, along with the yoke and arm protectors.

The boys conferred all night with each other and finally enlisted the rat's help in retrieving the equipment. They arrived home at midday and asked their grandmother to prepare a meal and to fetch water because they were thirsty. While she was gone, the rat clawed through the rope securing the prize in the roof, but the grandmother was returning more quickly than expected. To delay the grandmother, a mosquito drilled a hole in the water jug to make it leak. The grandmother and mother took their time trying to stop the leak while the boys hid the ball game equipment in the ballcourt. Then they took their blowguns and went to the river, where they saw the duo sealing the water jug.

The boys rejoiced and spent a lot of time sweeping out the ballcourt before playing. The lords of Xibalbá again heard the stomping about and were enraged as before. "Have they no shame. . . . Did not One Hunahpú and Seven Hunahpú die when they tried to puff themselves up before us?" (Christenson 2003, 154). The demons again sent the messenger Owls to tell the boys to come in seven days to play ball. The messengers arrived at the house before the boys returned and delivered the message to the grandmother, Xmucané, who was heartbroken by this news. These were the same messengers who delivered the invitation for her sons that led to their deaths. Suddenly a louse fell down on her. She picked it up, then asked it if it would like to deliver this message to her grandsons. The louse left, as the summoner with the message. As it went along, it came to a toad who asked where it was going, and the story was told. The toad offered to eat the louse so it could get there faster, and it did. As the toad with the louse inside went along, it came across a great snake named White Life, and the same thing happened. Now the message was in the stomach of the louse, in the stomach of the toad, in the stomach of the snake. A falcon swallowed the snake, and the falcon and its contents arrived at the ballcourt and perched on the edge crying out, "Wak-ko! Wak-ko!" This caught the boys' attention, and they shot him down, wounding him in the eye. The falcon disclosed that he had a message in his belly but told the boys that first they must cure his eye, which they did by patching the hole with a small ball of rubber. Then the falcon vomited up the snake, which vomited up the toad. The toad did not vomit up the louse, and the boys beat him, squashing his rear end and crushing the bones of his backside with their feet, trying to get him to release the message, but he did not. Finally, the boys opened the toad's mouth and found the louse stuck in front of his teeth. So, because of his behavior, there was no food for the toad. Instead, the toad became food for the snake. Finally, the louse delivered the message, saying that their grandmother insisted that they must go to the underworld, Xibalbá, and play ball with the demons.

Returning home, the boys decided to leave behind a sign of themselves and their word in the form of maize plants, which they planted in the center of the attic of their grandmother's house. The boys explained to their grandmother that, when the maize plants were healthy, so were the boys, but when the maize plants died, the boys had also died. Then they left on their journey, taking the same road their father and uncle had taken before them, but when they arrived at the crossroads, this time the roads were black, white, red, and blue-green. They were suspicious and sent a mosquito ahead to bite each of the demons and obtain their names. From then on, mosquitoes sucked the blood of people on the roads.

Taking the Black Road as their father and uncle had, the twins finally arrived at Xibalbá. The boys saw the wooden effigies of the demons, passed them by, and went on to name each one of the demons with his proper name. It wasn't really a mosquito but a hair plucked from the front of Hunahpú's knee that had bitten the lords of the underworld. When offered the bench to sit on, the boys refused, knowing it was a hot slab instead of a bench. So they finally were led to the House of Darkness and again told to preserve the cigar and torch until morning. The boys succeeded in placing a red tail feather in the place of the torch flame and a firefly in the tip of the cigar, thereby foiling the lords. They were surprised and wanted to know where the boys came from and who gave birth to them because they seemed to be unique. Without answers they went to play ball.

The demons threw out their ball to play, and the boys thought it had a skull hidden inside when it was merely a drawing of a skull. They refused to play. The Xibalbans' ball was actually hiding within it the knife used for sacrifice, White Dagger. Since the twins threatened to go home because of foul play, it was agreed that the first game would be with the boys' rubber ball. The prize for winning was three bowls of red, white, and yellow flower blossoms and one bowl of whole flowers. The two sides played very well, and finally the boys gave themselves up as defeated to the cheers of the Xibalbans. Then the boys were led into Blade House, the second trial, where blades cut and sliced those who entered. The boys told the blades they would from then on cut the flesh of animals, and the blades then lowered their points. While passing the night, the twins called out for cutting ants to help gather flowers for the four bowls, which they did from the Xibalbans' own flower tree, behind the backs of the two bird guards stationed there. As punishment for the guards' failure, the lords split their mouths open, and to this day whippoorwills have a gaping mouth. The ball was dropped into play again, but the play ended in a tie, so they agreed to play again at dawn.

Hunahpú and Xbalanqué spent this night in the House of Cold, and freezing it was until the boys ruined the cold—they were tricksters. They were fine in the morning when summoned to play ball once again. Next, they spent the night in the House of Jaguars, and when they were approached to be eaten, the boys gave the jaguars what they wanted to eat instead, scattering bones in front of them. The fourth challenge was the House of Fire, but they were not burned. The Xibalbans were dispirited as a result of these failures.

Yet the House of Bats was a challenge. The boys spent the night inside their blowguns until morning, when Hunahpú decided to peek out to see if morning had come. At that moment, Death Bat swooped down and cut his head off. One Death and Seven Death placed the head on the ballcourt and rejoiced at their success. Xbalanqué, in his shame, summoned all the animals, asking them to bring their food. After much food arrived, the coati rolled along a squash, which was transformed into the head of Hunahpú. Heart of Sky—Huracán, arrived because it was about to dawn, and he did not want dawn to arrive, so he asked the opossum to blacken the sky with soot, which he, Grandfather, did four times. As the sky appeared, it turned red, then blue. Hunahpú's squash head was functional, and he spoke in council with the others to plan the next step. They instructed the rabbit to wait in the tomato patch at the end of the ballcourt for the real head of Hunahpú to roll near, then dash away to grab the attention of the Xibalbans while Xbalanqué switched the squash for the real head. This is what happened, and Hunahpú's head was replaced on his body while the seeds of the squash were scattered.

Now the boys saw it was time for them to die, and they summoned two seers, sages named Descended and Ascended (Christenson 2003, 177). They discussed what to tell the Xibalbans when they asked the seers what to do with the twins' bones. It was decided it would be best to finely grind the bones up, like maize, and throw them into the river, not scatter them in a canyon or hang them in the top of a tree.

The boys were invited to a bonfire of heated stones in a pit oven and asked to play a game of jumping over it. Instead, the boys jumped in together and died. Then, as planned, the Xibalbans summoned the seers and asked what to do with the bones, following the instructions to grind them up and throw them into the river. The ground bones did not scatter but sank down, and then the boys appeared again on the fifth day. People saw them, looking like catfish or people-fish in the river. Then the boys became orphans or vagabonds and danced many dances. They set fire to a house and immediately re-created it. They then sacrificed and revived themselves while the Xibalbans admired the tricks. Word spread to One Death and Seven Death, who wanted to know who these two boys were, so they sent a message for the boys to come to them. The boys refused, saying they were too timid and too ashamed to enter such a lordly house. But they were threatened and pestered, so finally they went.

When they arrived, the boys humbled themselves, stooping and bowing, and the lords asked who they were, without receiving a response. So the lords merely asked the boys to do the dance of sacrifice, then to burn down a house, and to do all they knew, and they would be paid. So they did many of the sacred dances; then they were asked to sacrifice their dog, which they did, and afterward they revived him. The dog was very happy with this. Then they burned down the lords' house and restored it again. The lords rejoiced and marveled at all this as well. At this point, the lords told the boys to kill a person, so the boys did, extracting his heart from his chest and then reviving him. Next they were asked to sacrifice themselves, and Xbalanqué killed his brother; then the murdering boy revived his brother. Each arm and leg was severed, and his head was cut off and rolled away. His heart was cut out as the lords went on dancing with great joy. But Hunahpú was immediately brought back to life, and in the lords' great enthusiasm, the lords asked to be sacrificed themselves. Xbalanqué and Hunahpú then chose One Death to die and then also grabbed Seven Death, but the boys did not revive them. In the confusion, the Xibalbans realized what was happening and begged for pity. They all fled into the canyon to hide, herded together and crammed like ants. When the boys went to retrieve them in their newly humbled state, the boys finally revealed their names and the names of their fathers.

The demons have caused trouble, and the boys and their father and uncle have suffered because of them. The demons will no longer be great but will be left with useless broken pieces, and only the worthless will come to them, the wretched and the afflicted, those who have sinned:

> Their glory was not great in the past for they wanted only
> conflict with people of ancient times. Surely they were not true
> gods. Their names merely inspired fear, for their faces were
> evil. They were strife makers, traitors, and tempters to sin and
> violence. They were also masters of deception, of the black
> view and the white view. They were called masters of harm
> and vexation. Fundamentally their faces were hidden. Thus
> their greatness and glory were destroyed. Never again would
> their dominion become great. This was the accomplishment of
> Hunahpú and Xbalanqué. (Christenson 2003, 188)

Meanwhile, back home, the boys' grandmother had watched the maize plants die and revive over and over again. When the plants died, she was beside herself with confusion and grief, but she was filled with joy as they came to life again, and she named them "Middle of the House, Middle of the Harvest, Living Corn, Earthen Floor" (D. Tedlock 1985, 185). The first to die a long time before had been their father and uncle, and when they saw their father's face again, they spoke to him. Xbalanqué and Hunahpú put Seven Hunahpú back together again and then asked him to name his body parts. Because he could only name his mouth and nothing above or below, they had to leave him in the Place of Ball Game Sacrifice. Here, he was told he would be prayed to first and would not be forgotten. "You will be the first to have your day kept by those who will be born in the light, begotten in the light. Your name will not be lost" (D. Tedlock 1985, 159). Thus, their deaths were avenged. The two boys, Hunahpú and Xbalanqué, then ascended into the middle of the light as the central lights, straight up into the sky, becoming the sun and the moon. Light shown across the sky and on the face of the earth while the four hundred boys killed by Zipacna ascended to become a constellation of stars. (One Hunahpú, the head in the calabash tree, became the god of maize.)*

*This is not in the *Popol Vuh* but known from other sources.

THE CONCEPTION AND
CREATION OF HUMANITY

The myth continues to describe the beginning of the conception of humanity that took place just before the appearance of the sun, moon, and stars. She Who Has Borne Children and He Who Has Begotten Sons, the Framer and Shaper, and Sovereign and Quetzal Serpent reconvened once again to ponder and join their thoughts in the darkness before the creation of humans. Maize was discovered as the important essence used to create the flesh of humankind. Yellow and white corn came from two mountains, Paxil and Cayala, or Broken Place and Bitter Water, and the four animals that pointed the way to the corn were the fox, coyote, parrot, and crow.

Maize became the flesh of humanity, while water became the blood. She Who Has Borne Children, Xmucané, ground the maize nine times to form the first mother-fathers. The first four men were modeled and named Balam Quitze (Jaguar Forest), Balam Acab (Jaguar Night), Mahucutah (Traveler, One Who Does Not Stay), and Iqui Balam (Wind Jaguar). They were good, wise people and had clear vision. They saw perfectly across the earth and sky above and below, and their knowledge was complete, seeing the four corners and four sides of the cosmos. The gods were not pleased with this, not wanting them to be like gods, so the gods took back their knowledge and clouded their vision—like breath on a mirror. They could now see only what was near, where they were. The wisdom of the first four people was lost right at the beginning.

Then their wives came into being by the thoughts of the gods. They were named Cahapaluna (Red Sea Turtle), Chomiha (Shrimp House), Tzununiha (Hummingbird House), and Caquixaha (Macaw House). This is the root of the K'iche' people, who gave birth to all the future tribes with different names. Some became bloodletters and sacrificers. They came from the east. It was still dark, in the shadow, for the dawn had not yet come. They watched closely for the morning star that would precede the sun. They decided to find a god to protect them, to be their guardian, and headed to Tulan Zuyua, or Seven Caves, Seven Canyons to receive their gods, who were named Tohil, Auilix, and Hacauitz, placed at Rotten Cane. The gods were representatives of their makers and were carried and cared for by the mother-fathers. It was here the tribes began to speak different languages, and after that they could no longer understand each other.

Tohil was the god that possessed fire, and because of a messenger from Xibalbá who had the wings of a bat, it was suggested he receive something in exchange for the fire, but he only agreed to give it in exchange for human sacrifice. One tribe, however, stole it and did not have to pay tribute. When they left Tulan, the tribes' journey began as they wandered to find a safe place to hide their gods. They settled in canyons and on mountains. Patohil was the mountain place of Tohil, where they waited for the appearance of the great star. Finally, it arrived, and they burned their *copal* incense in the direction of the dawn, as they saw the birth of the sun. As it rose, everyone was happy, and all the animals cried out, overjoyed. When the sunlight hit the earth, it dried everything out. It had been muddy before. With the arrival of the sun, moon, and stars, the gods became stone, along with the sacred images of the puma, jaguar, rattlesnake, and yellowbite (guardian of the bushes). Now the gods spoke only through their genius, which was heard in the inner ears of humans.

The mother-fathers would anoint the mouths of the idols with blood and bring many offerings to the gods. But Tohil demanded human sacrifice, so abductions of travelers began for this purpose. The tribes that lost members were furious and decided to do something against the gods. They knew the gods went to bathe at a certain place in the river every day, transforming into young men, so they selected three young women to go to seduce the three gods. It did not work, but the gods gave the girls three coats with drawings done by three mother-fathers to take back to their lords as a sign. Each of the lords put on the cloak: the first having the image of a jaguar; the second, an image of an eagle; and the third, yellowjackets, which came alive and stung the lord, causing horrible pain. That was their defeat. Yet the tribes plotted once again. The tribes armed themselves and headed for an attack on Tohil, but Tohil and the mother-fathers already knew about this, so they were ready. When the attackers arrived, they all fell asleep on the road and had their eyebrows and beards plucked out and their metal stolen. The warriors awoke and decided to go ahead and storm the citadel of the mother-fathers, who were ready with four large gourds full of yellowjackets and wasps to use as weapons against the intruders. The citadel was surrounded by thirty times eight hundred people, but the penitents and sacrificers were not afraid; they let loose the insects and fought successfully. The tribes were conquered, and from then on, the failed attackers had to pay tribute.

THE ACQUISITION OF AUTHORITY
AND GENEALOGY

The first mother-fathers knew it was time for them to die, to return from where they came, their own tribal place. Each of them, Balam Quitze, Balam Acab, and Mahucutah, had sons, while Iqui Balam did not. They were true sacrificers, and with them instructions were left. It was the proper day of Lord Deer that indicated it was the day they should leave. Their work was done. Balam Quitze left a Bundle of Flames, sign of his being, for making requests of him. These were the first people to come from the east, to come across the sea. The tribes went east from where their fathers came, to receive their authority, the sign of their lordship from Nacxit and Kukulkan. With them, they brought writings. They built cities and pyramids covered with white plaster. They sacrificed to their gods and built war defenses. Many people were afraid of them, while their gods increased in greatness. In reading and understanding the *Popol Vuh*, they had a great instrument of sight. They were able to determine if there would be war, death, or hunger. There were nine generations of lords who were great in their essence.

The final pages of the *Popol Vuh* describe the genealogy of the three K'iche' lineages down to the Spanish conquest in 1524. The original book with the ancient writing is now lost, so there is no longer a way of seeing. But all is now complete concerning the K'iche', now called Santa Cruz.

To summarize, the mythic story begins with the stillness of the sky and sea. A spawning of imagination in the hearts of the creator couple came forth with the word that began a process of greater and greater differentiation and consciousness. The spiritual emanation came into matter to create the world and all its creatures, including humans, who were capable of adequately honoring and respecting the gods. The journey through the underworld ends with death and rebirth. In the *Popol Vuh*, humans' other face is turned to the temporal world through the histories of the nations and tribes. It preserves a journey through the lineages, connecting back to the creator gods and forward to the earthly lords eventually conquered by the Spanish. That subjugation was certainly an ending of their known world, yet it was not the ending of their world according to their calendar. Their world was destroyed and re-created four times. The fifth ending in 2012 just passed.

CHAPTER 6

AMPLIFICATION OF A
SECTION OF THE MYTH

Only one section of the myth of the *Popol Vuh* will be amplified, the part having to do with the descent into the underworld by the two sets of hero twins, the fathers and sons. The rest of the myth was described in the synopsis chapter but without the detailed amplification of this selected section. This allowed the demonstration of the myth's rich imagery, arriving at a meaning from the Jungian psychological point of view and placing it in the context of world mythology without having to amplify the entire myth.

THOUGHTS ON THE CREATION OF THE
FIRST THREE WORLDS

The cosmos begins in primordial stillness. The sky and sea alone exist. There is no earth. This describes unconsciousness, complete darkness until the spark of thought arises from a desire within. The opposites are split and in need of the creation of the third, an earth to sit between them and receive their creative attention. All begins with the "sowing and the dawning" (Christenson 2003, 60). There are three sets of gods representing the council who actively participate in the creation: Heart of Sky, Newborn or Youngest Thunderbolt, Raw or Sudden Thunderbolt, and Huricán, who come from the sky; Sovereign and Quetzal Serpent, Heart of Sea, Heart of Lake, who come from the sea; and the Framer and Shaper Grandmother and Grandfather, the diviners who do the actual work. After a dialogue among the gods, they conceive of the idea of the earth emerging from the sea and on the earth being plants, animals, and people. The sowing and sprouting of the seeds on the earth will be their dawning. The sowing of the sun, moon, and stars will begin beneath the earth and after a difficult passage will be their dawning. Human beings' sowing will begin in the womb to then emerge into the light at birth. At death, their body will be sowed in the earth, followed by the dawning, when their souls turn into sparks of light in the darkness.

The gods desired that human beings walk, work, and talk in a clear, measured way and that they visit the shrines of their gods, giving offerings and calling them by their names, all according to the rhythms of the calendar. The gods attempted this creation three times but each time failed. So the gods then called upon the elderly husband and wife, divine matchmaker and midwife named Mother and Father, or She Who Has Borne Children and He Who Has Begotten Sons, or Xmucané and Xpiyacoc, as they are later known. They are daykeepers, diviners who know how to interpret the ritual calendars, gods who are older than all others, the grandparents of all. These are important gods who play a continuing role in the narrative. It is interesting that Xpiyacoc, the masculine god, is passive, while Xmucané, the lunar-earth goddess, plays a prominent role. The cycles they follow in their divination and creation closely connect the stars' movements with the action that takes place in the story.

The idea of sex is never mentioned, but it is implicit in the myth. There is a relationship between sexual desire and creative thought (von Franz 1972, 128). Desire is an emotion. According to von Franz, emotion is the essential factor in all creation myths. What is emotion but the stirring of libido in the psyche? Libido is life energy, the fire that is activated by the Self in the form of a thought or desire. There is then a longing for something; in the case of creation, it is the presence of the other to be seen. This is the moment of illumination, and the person realizes he or she exists: the first awakening of consciousness. It can be seen in young children when they first realize they are an "I." Libido is desire, passion, yearning, emotion, energy, and an inner fire that is also expressed as gold and blood. Blood was the equivalent of gold to the Maya: a life-sustaining precious substance. "Fire's nonphysical and non-chemical aspect, namely as the intelligent substance of the world . . . contains and brings intelligent order into all things" (von Franz 1972, 139).

In Maya mythology, each masculine god has its feminine counterpart. Many times, it is difficult to know if the god in question is masculine, feminine, or both. Mother and Father jointly carried out the creation of the world, and they are not described as enacting separate roles but as acting together with one voice. This union of opposites is carried into their cultural and political life as well. There is a very important position supporting the king that is described in male-female terms. The priests were called mother-father, and the priest had to include his wife in his initiation ceremonies even if she had no interest. Only a married man was considered complete. Psychologically, this is so different from the Judeo-Christian myth. The absence of splitting the masculine and feminine into opposites and adversaries sheds light on the nature of this culture. Because of the destruction of the manuscripts and loss of historical accounts, many of the subtleties of the ancient Maya sensibility are missing. It is possible, however, to get a flavor of this sensibility from the myth because it provides a template of their relationships and psychology.

Heart of Sky, Heart of Earth, Newborn Thunderbolt, Raw Thunderbolt, and Huracán join the gods of the primordial sea: Maker, Modeler, Begetter, Heart of Sea, and Sovereign Plumed Serpent. Together their thoughts and ponderings form the word that sets the creation in motion. The god of the heaven with its many names is also the god of the earth. Heart of Sky presides over the creation and appears in many forms. As Huracán, containing Thunderbolt energy, it appears as three forms of lightning. Lightning is what starts fire; it is the flash of energy from the heavens that brings light and the creative spark. Huracán is a one-legged god, pointing to the concept of monotheist theogony where the gods are all parts of one single deity, a part divided off from another (Girard 1979, 68). Huracán is sky and earth and refers to vital spirit, soul, that which gives something life, the center of thought, imagination, and intuition. It is the deity that conceives of what is to be formed in the four creations. The other deities carry out that decision.

Out of stillness came the *word*. "The divine word implies instantaneous creation" (Girard 1979, 33). This is not the only creation story that begins in this way. Another example is the book of Genesis in the Bible. The Maya deities brought together their words and thoughts. This focus on the word and the fact that Huracán refers to intuition suggest that the Maya were a culture based on thinking and intuition.

Von Franz clarified this supposition and added introversion as an attitude: "It is striking that creation by thought is found mostly in Gnostic creation myths, in North American Indian creation myths, and in some Far East Indian creation myths, which to me shows that it exists predominantly in the realm of introverted civilizations" (1972, 129). This reflects the inner process of the godhead and the inner potentialities of man. Now there is a hypothesis that involves introverted, intuitive thinking. In this composite, sensation would be the inferior extraverted function. This might explain the highly developed rituals of mortification of the body, sacrifices, and bloodletting, as well as the colorful and imaginative, at times disgusting, descriptions of gods and demons that will be examined in the text. According to Jung (1974), the inferior function is projected out into the real world onto the body and objects. Christenson, in his translation of the *Popol Vuh*, said that the modern Maya "priests take note of sensations within their bodies, which they call 'lightning in the blood'" (2003, 71). Intuition would be introverted, which reflects the initial flash of desire, the thought to create. Thinking would be extraverted, as reflected in their acting on the intuition; feeling would be introverted, which is reflected in their poetry. This grouping provides a clue about the nature of the Maya and how they functioned psychologically.

To continue with the myth, the sky was set apart. The earth was set apart from the waters. Then the deities thought and pondered. Solely by the word the gods called forth mountains, valleys, groves, and forests out of the primordial water so that the earth could be created. This same pattern of thinking first created animals. They wanted the animals to speak so that they could worship the gods, but instead, they would only squawk, chatter, and roar. First the gods brought forth pure instinct, without the ability to think. However, this was not good; so the purpose of the animals was that they were there for the humans to eat them, as in the Bible, where animals are here to serve humans. The next attempt to create a race that would be able to worship the gods was the mud people, but they melted with rain. The mud people were made out of the earth itself, but the substance was wrong, and they melted back into the earth. Eventually, but much later, it was discovered that maize was the correct substance to use for creation, but not until after the third attempt: effigies carved of wood that did not possess hearts or minds. Because the wood people could not remember the gods, they could not worship them properly, and the gods sent a great flood to destroy them, to cleanse away the past and begin anew. In an alternate version of the *Popol Vuh* story, the effigies are crushed and ground up, much as maize is ground on a rock slab. Both of these operations are seen in alchemy, *solutio* and *mortificatio*. The descendants of the race of wooden people are monkeys. In other words, this creation myth begins with animals and moves to mud and wood, reversing the process of evolution, which began with the minerals and plants and then moved to the animals.

These first attempts at creation psychologically reflect attempts to change and grow. As children grow into teenagers and then into adulthood, they try on various personas as a way of finding, seeking, or approaching their true self. Many do not find it because it is not a locus; it is a process. Along the way they have to learn to control their animal instincts. Like mud that washes away, they have to contain their emotions and firm up their inner authority. Finally, the overbearing rigidity of wood can wound other people, just as in the myth when the household instruments were furious with the wooden effigies for misusing them. There was a lack of related compassion. These are good lessons for the growing youngster on how to behave and how not to behave in the search for one's face and heart. The growing demands of the culture required less selfishness and more relationship to the other, including the gods, as a collective spirit came into being.

After the great flood at the destruction of the third world, four monstrous demons came to dwell on the earth, and the greatest of all was an arrogant and vainglorious bird called Seven Macaw, who, along with his wife and two sons, appears on the scene at this point in the *Popol Vuh*. The text digresses from the creation story to discuss the mythic plight of the vainglorious Macaw, named after the beautiful and highly colorful bird that sets himself up in a tree as the ruler of the world. At this time, the earth was only dimly illuminated because the sun and moon had not yet risen. Seven Macaw had jewels for teeth and eyes that shone with the reflected light of those jewels, making him believe that he was the sun itself. He was arrogant, proud, and boastful, cultural traits the Maya found to be the most evil attitudes of all. Seven Macaw was considered a false sun and had to be brought down, which he was by the second set of hero twins, Hunahpú and Xbalanqué.

There are three sets of twins in this myth, and the set that is introduced at this point in the story are the children of the father twins. This is an example of psychic time, the mixing up of time, the nonlinear time seen in dreams. The son may be the same age as the father or may be the father of the father. This is mythic time. The son hero twins are Xbalanqué, meaning "jaguar," though the "X" makes it feminine, and Hunahpú, meaning "one blowgun hunter." Again there is the example of the mixing up of masculine and feminine. Huracán instructs these hero twins to slay the arrogant imposter, which they do by shooting out his gold tooth and his eye of black mirror. The Sky God oversees the creation, just as the Self oversees the process of individuation.

The black mirror in Maya mythology refers to divination or looking into the unconscious. There is a connection to unconsciousness and a lack of knowledge or clarity here, since a clear mirror would allow clarity. When Seven Macaw loses his teeth and eyes, he loses his power and glory and dies. This is a good example of how inflation and arrogance are dealt with culturally and psychically. The bird's loss of what represented his narcissism was too devastating and he died, much like the death in the water of Narcissus himself. Seven Macaw's wife died at the same time, showing the death of his contrasexual side as well. Seven Macaw was seen as the Big Dipper, part of the north. That an entire chapter was allotted to the hero killing the prideful bird is a powerful warning to the Maya people. The gods want humility, respect, and hard work. The whole process of creation circles around this attitude and around how to find a healthy balance between spirit and nature. Jung repeatedly warned about the dangers of inflation:

> He himself did not create spirit, rather spirit makes him creative, always spurring him on, giving him lucky ideas, staying power,

"enthusiasm" and "inspiration." . . . Spirit threatens naïve-minded man with inflation. . . . The danger becomes all the greater the more our interest fastens upon external objects and the more we forget that the differentiation of our relation to nature should go hand in hand with a correspondingly differentiated relation to the spirit, so as to establish the necessary balance. If the outer object is not offset by an inner, unbridled materialism results, coupled with maniacal arrogance or else the extinction of the autonomous personality. (1977a, 213)

The story continues with the twins killing Seven Macaw's two evil sons, Zipacna and Cabracan, who represent opposite energies: one creates mountains and the other destroys them. These represent giant, opposing energies that swing from creation to destruction with no way to find a moderate, mediating, or in-between force. Zipacna and Cabracan were both drawn into their deaths by their appetite for food, indicating being stuck at an undeveloped oral stage where affects are as large, wild, and uncontained as an earth builder and destroyer would be. One myth states that from the destruction of these two primordial yet proud giants the world is fashioned. "Later on, the four giants, having been defeated by Hunahpú, would become the four heavenly bearers, placed in the corners of the cosmos" (Girard 1979, 68). The four giants are Seven Macaw; his wife, Chimalmat; and their two children, Zipacna and Cabracan. It is these huge affects, swinging wildly from extreme to extreme, that need to be tamed as individuals grow up and become socialized.

Life emerging from the body of the defeated monster, representing the unconscious itself, is a typical creation theme. And indeed, this theme became part of the Maya cultural belief that the place for renewal and rebirth was the underworld. Individuals must confront their own demons, affects, and complexes to become healthy and whole. In this myth, that confrontation would be represented by confronting and transforming one's animal nature; one's muddy, watery feelings; one's cold, rigid nature; and the wild, giant-size affects and appetites. In that way, the opposites are bridged and consciousness increased. Out of that can emerge the new way of being, much like the raising of the Maize God into the sky, a bridge between the earthly and solar realms. A prominent image of the Maize God looks a lot like images of Buddha with its downward, inward gaze and hands in mudra positions. The similarities are remarkable.

AMPLIFICATION OF THE CREATION
OF THE FOURTH WORLD

Now the world was ready for the creation of humans in the fourth world. This is the part of the story that will be approached from a Jungian perspective using the process of amplification to expand the meaning of the image, to understand what the psyche is trying to tell us in its metaphorical language. The images are chosen for a specific reason. Deciphering the messages in dreams is precious information for our individuation process in helping us live a more conscious life. In myths, amplification shows us what is important to establish a functional, well-balanced culture. The meaning of each image is expanded from what is known from Maya iconography, from imagery reflecting the experience of psychological development, as well as from cultures across the globe. This is a journey that requires curiosity and imagination, while suspending our current worldview of reality to perceive another.

The text of the story is boldface, and the amplification follows.

This part of the myth describes the activities of three sets of twins—the father and uncle and two sets of sons, this time correctly ordered by age. It starts with the travails of the first set, One Hunahpú, the father, and Seven Hunahpú, the uncle.

The name *Hunahpú* means "*master of the blowgun hunter*." The name was also connected to the birth of the world from the primordial sea, as well as fragrant flower, and calabash. "Hunahpú is a day on the traditional Maya calendar referring to the memory of the ancestors" (Christenson 2003, 113).

The blowgun they use operates magically by blowing breath through the tube, therefore, representing a solar instrument (Girard 1979, 83). It seems that solar energy, representing greater consciousness, is what is needed now as the myth heads toward the fourth creation.

The number 1 means unique wholeness, referring to the divine couple, the moment before creation and the separation of the sky and sea, when all remains calm. It is the meeting of the gods representing the center of the *axis mundi* at the heart of the cosmic tree. It also referred to the Moon Goddess.

The number 7 referred to the jaguar god of the underworld, with the symbol of the night (León-Portilla 1988, 42–43). It is a number carrying religious significance. For example, the Maya's final destination after creation was the seven caves, and there were seven original tribes. Seven is also one of four numbers that corresponds to the year bearers, in other words, the beginning of one of the 4 days of the 365-day solar calendar (Stuart 2011, 145). It is the number of stars making up the Pleiades constellation, which was important to the Maya. It refers to the aggregate of the creator god or god seven, Huracán or Heart of Heaven. The *Book of Chilam Balam of Chumayel* declares:

> The one that is the Divinity and the Power, brought into being the Great Stone of Grace, there, where before was no heaven, and from it were born seven sacred stones, Seven warriors suspended in the spirit of the wind, Seven elected flames, and then seven times were lit the seven measure of night. . . . The seven gods were spoken of in the singular as "the Descendent of seven generation," produced by the Eternal. (Girard 1979, 31)

In psychological terms, the number 1 refers to the wholeness before separation and differentiation, the undifferentiated beginning of the analytical work as well as the end, when elements of the personality have been consciously examined and reunited, represented in alchemy by the image of the sacred marriage. It is here that the opposites are brought together and are held in conscious balance. The two opposites—light-dark, good-evil, sky-earth—become one again, one in consciousness and in totality. One represents the center of the individual and of the world, the world tree traversing the dimensions of the cosmos, vertically and horizontally. The beginning of the individuation process reflects the beginning of creation. Both individuation and myth reflect the influence of the psyche and its process in moving the individual and the culture toward greater awareness and balance.

In general symbolism, the number 7 represents a completed cycle and its regeneration as seen in the seven days of the week, seven petals of the rose, and seven planets. As a prime number it commonly depicts wholeness in many theologies: Christian, Buddhist, Muslim, Hindu, Sumerian, Plains Indian, and Pueblo Indian (Chevalier and Gheerbrant 1996, 859–66). *The I Ching* states in hexagram 24, called The Turning Point or Return:

> All movements are accomplished in six stages, and the seventh brings return. Thus the winter solstice, with which the decline of the year begins, comes in the seventh month after the summer solstice; so too sunrise comes in the seventh double hour after sunset. Therefore seven is the number of the young light, and it arises when six, the number of the great darkness, is increased by one. In this way the state of rest gives place to movement.
> (1970, 98)

This set of twins gives birth to two more sets of twins: One Batz and One Chouen, and Xbalanqué and Hunahpú. The names Batz and Chouen mean "howler monkey." They are called Masters of the Scribal Arts and were trained as great sculptors, jade workers, precious metalsmiths, singers, and performers.

There is a constant doubling in this myth, which refers to the parallelism in the K'iche' language itself, as well as the uniting of opposite and complementary elements or natures; hence, the pair of father-uncle and the two sets of twin sons appear. The doubling signifies the emergence of consciousness and relationship. Rather than have one representation of the archetype, we have two complementary aspects. The sets of sons oppose each other, so in this case it is not the opposition within the set of twins but between one set and the other. Similarly, there are two actual creator gods acting as one, and above them are even-number multiples of supreme gods acting in concert as one. It is a multiplicity of god and hero energies acting with a purposeful intention following fate that was set in motion by divine inspiration and council.

Chouen refers to the eleventh day of the ritual calendar, connected to the North Star and protecting scribes and mathematicians. Sometimes it is shown as a monkey and at other times as the sun. For the Aztecs it meant monkey and was associated with the west and the flower god called Xochipilli (Longhena 1999, 120). Both Batz and Chouen mean "howler monkey," and sometimes Chouen refers to artisan. Nevertheless, they seem to be two parts of the scribal archetype. Howler monkeys are spry, aggressive little creatures that screech loudly in the trees of Guatemala, skirting from one limb to another, protecting their territory. If one walks beneath a howler monkey, one runs the risk of being urinated on and having to choose between running and getting soaked. "And yet swinging in the shadows of humanity's ancestral tree, monkeys speak to the ambivalent fantasies and images of our animal origins—to both their romanticized pristine perfection, and to the ridiculous untutored hilarity of the instincts and antics of our monkey mind" (Ronnberg and Martin 2010, 262). Monkeys were the creatures to survive the destruction of the second world of wooden effigies. As scribes in Mesoamerica, they also resonate symbolically with the scribal and wise god Thoth in Egypt. In India, in the *Rāmāyana* the royal monkey god was called Hanuman, the unarmed and perfect warrior and son of the wind who moved mountains and was quick-witted and imaginative. Monkeys were frequently seen as clever tricksters in the older cultures, the fools carrying a natural wisdom, while in more current times, including today, they are seen as primitive and devilish. Discussing the psychological development of the trickster in a chapter in Radin's book *The Trickster: A Study in American Indian Mythology*, the author explained what Jung said:

The civilizing process begins within the framework of the trickster cycle itself, and this is a clear indication that the original state has been overcome. At any rate the marks of deepest unconsciousness fall away from him; instead of acting in a brutal, savage, stupid and senseless fashion the trickster's behavior towards the end of the cycle becomes quite useful and sensible. (1972, 206)

The name *Xbalanqué* is difficult to translate. The *"X"* refers to diminutive as well as feminine. *B'alam* refers to jaguar, known for ferocity and cunning. It was also associated with ritual powers of transformation, prophecy, sorcery, war, and the sun. So Xbalanqué could be called Young Hidden-Jaguar Sun. The jaguar was the animal totem, or *nahual*, of shamans and nobility alike, thought to be the embodiment of the sun god in the underworld. This god represented the sun when it descended at dusk, falling below the horizon into the underworld, and remained when the sun dawned into the new day.

Hunahpú, as described previously, refers to blowgun hunter and also to the last day in the ritual calendar, Ahau, referring to lord, power, sun, and flower. The ritual on the day of Ahau, the twentieth day in the Tzolk'in calendar, served the memory of the ancestors. The twins can also be related to trickster gods in other closely related mythologies:

> Hunahpú is characterized by prominent spots on his cheeks and
> body and frequently wears an *Ahau* diadem on his headband. . . .
> As for Xbalanqué, his face and body are invariably marked with
> a jaguar pelage, and occasionally wears a cut shell *yax*, (meaning
> blue-green or first) jewel on his headband or in his hair. (Stone
> and Zender 2011, 8)

Hunahpú also acts as a personification of the number 9 (Schele and Freidel 1990, 411). The hero twins are depicted from Preclassic times onward representing a model of reality:

> We argue that the central vision of the Classic-period Maya
> was their descent from hero twin brothers who had been
> apotheosized as Venus and the Sun. This mythological twin
> complex is preserved in transformed version in the K'iche' Maya
> *Popol Vuh* [wherein the twins are G1 and G111 of the Palenque
> Triad of hero ancestors]. G11, the third member of the Triad,
> is God K, the personified obsidian mirror of seers. . . . G11
> represents the blood bond between the Twins, a concept that will
> prove to be the central mystery of Maya religion. (Freidel and
> Schele 1988, 90–91)

In the night, One and Seven Hunahpú are born to two of the oldest creator gods, Xpiyacoc and Xmucané, the Grandfather and Grandmother earth and planting deities. Since the "X" refers to the feminine, the creator gods are feminine or contain the feminine within them. The daykeepers were considered feminine on their left side and masculine on their right. They were also referred to as He Who Has Begotten Sons and She Who Has Borne Children, Maker of the Blue-Green Plate, Maker of the Blue-Green Bowl, Great White Peccary and Great White Tapir, Midwife and Matchmaker (D. Tedlock 1985, 369–70):

> Because Xmucane and Xpiyacoc assisted in the creation of the universe at the beginning of time, thus setting in motion the endless cycles of day and night, birth and death, sowing and harvest, they stand as the ideal interpreters through divination of these cycles. (Christenson 2003, 80)

They were the divine grandparents, older than the other gods:

> The gods of the Mesoamerican pantheon were sets of linked metaphoric-metonymic transformations, taking identifying symbols from different codes derived from empirical observation and the dissection of the continuous flow of reality. Thus every god was built of a set of symbols made up, for example, of a vegetable code symbol, an animal or zoological code symbol, a planetary symbol, and many others. . . . These levels were ordered hierarchically, with some symbols dominating over others as distinct markers of each god. . . . God was both the one and the many. . . . Since the divine reality was multiple, fluid, encompassing the whole, its aspects were changing images . . . constantly being recreated, redefined. (Sosa 1986, 193)

One Hunahpú had two children, One Batz or One Monkey and One Chouen or One Artisan, who are writers, artisans, and smiths, talented and wise. Seven Hunahpú had no children, perhaps a servant companion only. Remaining consistent with the Maya concept of the blending of opposites in one figure, these two may actually be two aspects of the one, as all the protagonists were different emanations of the one. It is interesting that one twin does not have children. This is a theme that shows up again in the myth when one of the first four human mother-fathers does not have children, so his lineage is not carried on. It creates an imbalance of sorts, something is off, but that is life.

One Batz and One Chouen are said to be great thinkers and full of knowledge. They see into the past and future, having clear vision, and are described as inheriting these good qualities from their father.

Yet, having only good in their being points to a lack of "darkness" or "shadow," a Jungian term that refers to all that is not conscious in the psyche. The shadow is always present; it may merely be split off into the unconscious or the underworld, here called Xibalbá, or projected onto others. Psychologically, when there is a splitting of light and dark, it will result in a battle between these opposing forces as a way of bringing the conflict into awareness to find balance. The two monkeys contained all the talents and wisdom of gods, but it was their choice how they used it.

One Hunahpú and Seven Hunahpú are great gamesters who love to throw dice and play ball in their masonry ballcourt with One Hunahpú's sons, One Batz and One Chouen.

Dice is a game of fate, and it seems clear that a fateful game is set in motion, watched over by the gods. The two would pair off and oppose each other, in preparation for a larger battle, the confrontation with the shadow. Although it was on the earth, this ballcourt was also the path to the gloomy netherworld realm of Xibalbá and was called Great Abyss of Carchah and Honor and Respect (Christenson 2003, 119). The court was created by two parallel structures that formed a fairly narrow shape of an "I" (Miller and Taube 1993, 42–43). The two or four ball players met in the center of the rectangular court with their heavily padded protective gear and hit a heavy, solid rubber ball about six inches in diameter with their hips, never touching it with their hands, feet, or heads. Points were scored when the ball hit markers or stone rings along either side of the center of the court walls. The court ran east to west, displaying the symbolism of the birth and death of the sun. For the Maya, east and west were moments or special references, not points frozen in space (León-Portilla 1988, 197). As the ball followed the trajectory of the sun into the underworld, it emphasized the process of life, death, and rebirth, similar to the psychological process of the hero's journey and the growth cycle of the maize plant. "The ball itself may have been understood as the sun journeying in and out of the underworld" (Miller and Taube 1993, 43). As with all games, it is a conflict of opposites, two opposing teams competing for success.

The ball is round like a mandala and a symbol for the Self. In following the ball and attempting to get it into a hole, especially at the entrance to the underworld—at this crossroads—the ball game becomes a metaphor for the individuation process, the striving for wholeness. The ball was made out of latex rubber, which was frequently burned as an offering to the gods. For the Maya, rubber was associated with blood, and latex is called the Blood of Trees (Stone and Zender 2011, 68).

The four protagonists were engaged in the movement of fate set in motion by the gods. They gambled and played with little idea of the seriousness of their task. This is typical of the naïve youth who stumbles onto his journey without experience or forethought and without understanding the seriousness of what may await him. Like Perceval in the grail legend, these four were challenged in ways that attempted to lead to greater consciousness but failed. Just as Perceval failed to answer the important question the first time he was asked, their youthful *puer*, or "eternal youth characteristics," were overcome only with a second attempt. This is similar to dealing with one's emotionally based complexes that are repeated over and over again until one gains enough awareness and ego strength to recognize them. The myth shows that one will struggle and fail before creation and success are achieved. Old attitudes will be retired while the new ones will take their place. Resilience, perseverance, and hard work are required for the correct outcome.

During the game, the great Falcon of Huracán, Youngest Thunderbolt, and Sudden Thunderbolt, literally called "flash of leg," "small flash," and "green flash," the three aspects of the principal creator god, Heart of Sky, would watch over them.

The falcon is related to the principle of light, the Roman Jupiter, and the ruling principle, just as it is in Maya symbolism related to Huracán. It is the embodiment of the Egyptian Horus, the all-seeing eye, as well as Ra, the symbol of the rising sun. To the Incas, the falcon was a solar symbol (Chevalier and Gheerbrant 1996, 370). Fate is set in motion as Huracán, in the form of a falcon, oversaw and directed the process from above. Huracán is a symbol of the Self in this myth that unleashes the libido to begin the process of creation. For the individual, a spark erupts from the Self, perhaps as an image in a dream, a vision, or a symptom in the body, commencing the difficult process of individuation. It follows a similar path to what is seen in this myth.

Lightning is like a flash, the electrical charge of thought and inspiration. It is spirit touching down on earth in the form of fate, setting in motion the hero's task, just like a game of fate. It symbolizes the spark of life and fertilization. "Lightning for the Maya was a powerful form of creation and enlightenment—engendering divine force called ch'uel" (Gillette 1997, 222). The contemporary Maya daykeepers or shamans use the perception of lightning flashing through their limbs as a way of knowing what answers to offer the client (D. Tedlock 1993). The ever-present snake is a "widespread symbol of lightning in Mesoamerica and even in the American Southwest" (Hanks and Rice 1989, 358).

One Hunahpú's wife, the mother of One Chouen and One Batz, was called Xbaquiyalo, which means "yielding lady bone water," but she died.

The only female remaining at this point was Xmucané, the mother to Hunahpú and the grandmother to his sons. The loss of his wife and their mother points to a state of disconnection or distancing from the feminine, from nature, and from the instincts. The twins were heroes who took up the call to move from a matriarchal, agrarian stage of cultural development, where men had time to play dice and ball, to a patriarchal stage of consciousness, where they were put to work (Girard 1979, 138). They were summoned to the task of bridging two cultural stages but were presently at a disadvantage in having an inadequate relationship to the feminine. The old feminine had to die for a new relationship to the feminine to develop. It was the development from a lunar to solar consciousness.

This shift was important not only for the culture but also for the individual. This is seen as a stage of development in the individuation process. An individual moves away from the mother, represented by the containing womb of the matriarchy, the waters of chaos, to begin to differentiate and bring in consciousness that allows for the development of an observing, discriminating mind. "By submitting to heroic incest and entering into the devouring maw of the unconscious, the ego is changed in its essential nature and is reborn 'another'" (Neumann 1970, 149). This is replicated in the so-called second birth of baptism. As in this myth, the mother had to die so the heroes could develop independently. The grandmother remained as the overseeing creator goddess, but the grandmother is more of an archetypal figure than the mother. Archetypes do not die; their influence remains consciously or unconsciously.

As stated previously, Xibalbá was the Maya underworld, called the Place of Fear, inhabited by demons who cause sickness (Christenson 2003, 114).

The principal lords of Xibalbá, One Came and Seven Came (or One Death and Seven Death), become enraged at the thundering noise from the ball game above: "What is happening on the face of the earth? They're just stomping about and shouting. They shall come to play ball here, and we will defeat them. They have failed to honor us. They have neither honor nor respect. Certainly, they act arrogantly here over our heads" (Christenson 2003, 115). The gods of death are upset because the noise reflects dishonor and arrogance. They call together all the gods and demons of death and disease to decide how to defeat and kill the twins. One Death and Seven Death are called great judges and lawgivers. They give dominion to the other demons, named Flying Scab and Gathered Blood, whose job was to sicken the blood; Pus Demon and Jaundice Demon, who swelled people up, causing pus and jaundice; Bone Staff and Skull Staff, who skeletonized people through starvation; Sweeping Demon and Stabbing Demon, who stabbed people if they neglected to sweep their homes; and Lord Wing and

Packstrap, who would kill people on the road from carrying heavy loads.

It is interesting that the demons were called great judges or lawgivers. It may refer to the fact that the demons represented the old ruling principle that has fallen into the shadow and manifests now as complexes, as cultural and psychological consciousness moves to a new level. The old gods do not die but instead fall into the unconscious. Here, they had their own laws; in other words, they lived by their own rules, which were the rules of the complex, not the rules of the ego. They were severe and one-sided. They were not gods or immortals but were of false heart—hypocrites, envious, and tyrants. "We fear these complexes and archetypes for good reason. They usually try to kill our joys, our hopes, our plans, our loves and relationships" (Gillette 1997, 45). These demons represented the law of the negative Great Mother in the underworld that does not want change or light but instead brings sickness and death. The underworld contains the destructive, shadow aspects of nature. The negative Great Mother archetype fights against the creation of culture and individual separation from her. Of course, it is the hero's destiny to fight against her and bring consciousness and culture to life.

There were twelve lords of the underworld altogether. They appear in the codices in relation to rituals and oracles and were associated with special deities and animals (Longhena 1999, 77). The number 12 is important, representing completion in Western culture, much like 13 is for the Maya. In the Maya worldview, 12 remains incomplete except insofar that it is a multiple of 2, 3, and 4. There were nine levels to the underworld and thirteen in the upper world. Twelve referred to a youthful-faced god with the heaven sign, closely associated with Venus. It breaks down into 3 times 4, with four referring to the old man and sun, which is related to the last day sign in the Maya calendar and the four parts of the universe. It also referred to the four creations. Three referred to the god of rain and wind (León-Portilla 1988, 43). It indicated the three levels of the cosmos and the three hearthstones laid out at creation. The number 12, as a multiple of 4, reflected the universe. It seems that the archetypal energy for the demons was energy of the old way, although it held the possibility of refructification and renewal. The number 13, in Maya tradition, pointed to spilling of the old over into the new. It is a prime number like 7 and cannot be divided; it, therefore, represents completion and wholeness.

To clarify the manner of play at the ballcourt, Edmonson quoted Sahagún's description of the Aztec ball game:

At other times (the Lord) played ball to amuse himself and for this purpose they had their rubber balls laid aside. These balls were the size of large bowling balls. They were solid, of a certain resin or gum which is called *ulli* which is very light and bounces like an inflated ball. And he also brought with him good ball players who played in his presence, with other leading men in opposition, and they won gold and jade and gold and turquoise beads and slaves and rich mantles and rich kilts and cornfields and houses, etc. . . . In the middle of the court was a line made especially for the game; and in the middle of the walls, halfway down the playing stretch, were two stones like millstones perforated in the middle, facing each other, and they each had holes wide enough that the ball could fit into each of them. And whoever placed the ball there won the game. They did not play with their hands but hit the ball with their flanks. For playing they wore gloves on their hands and a leather apron on their flanks to hit the ball. (1971, 114)

From the noise in the ballcourt on the face of the earth, a challenge was knocking on the door to the underworld; fate was approaching. The death gods were upset about being disturbed, once again, and complained about a lack of consideration and arrogance, a lack of honor and respect. This is a continuing theme in the *Popol Vuh*. But to change an attitude or behavior, the old has to be disturbed and broken up. This is true for the culture as well as the individual. The names as designations of the demons reflected things that go wrong or cause people to fall into destruction away from the creative, life-sustaining path. These demons as archetypes represent the destructive, negative side of the psyche. It is quite humorous that they were now the ones disturbed, instead of doing the disturbing, naïvely initiating a conflict:

> The archetype, according to Jung's definition, is the accompanying inward aspect of the pattern of behavior, namely emotions, feelings, and inner representation, including even abstract concepts; that would be the archetypal disposition and those archetypal dispositions collide and fight exactly as instincts or patterns of behavior do. That is why in so many mythologies one finds a war of the Gods, or a war of the Titans. . . . Innumerable myths all over the world show the gods warring with each other. . . . The collision of different archetypal patterns probably stands at the origin of consciousness. (von Franz 1972, 103–4)

The demons send four owl messengers called Arrow Owl, One Leg Owl, Macaw Owl, and Skull Owl up to the surface to invite One Hunahpú and Seven Hunahpú to play ball with them in Xibalbá and told them to bring their ball equipment. Although their mother, Xmucané, tries to persuade them not to go, the two agree to follow the owls into the deadly underworld.

Owls were the war councilors in the underworld and were regarded as the heralds of sickness and death by the K'iche'. They were associated with Venus as the morning star, which represented war and was, therefore, inauspicious. In Western symbolism, owls are wise seers frequently associated with the feminine, while they embody darkness, rain, and storms as they rule the night. We could now say the owls are loose upon the world with the pandemic and changing climate.

The twins' father was also dead, so there was no ruling masculine principle. The boys had to leave the mother and go on their heroes' journey, which began with being challenged to a ball game in the underworld. Yet, thoughtlessly, they left their rubber ball behind, tied up in the rafters of the roof, disconnected from the earth or ground. As the object with which one plays ball, without it, they were starting out badly. One Hunahpú and Seven Hunahpú vowed to come back for it to play again, suggesting this would not be the only game played. Their monkey sons were told to play and sing, while the seriousness of the journey was treated lightly, and this wrong attitude without proper planning portended failure.

The path to Xibalbá is long and treacherous, and the twins descend and must pass by turbulent canyon rivers called Trembling Canyon and Murmuring Canyon. They pass through dangerous rivers named Scorpion River, Blood River, and Pus River. All these were successfully overcome until they reached a crossroads with four roads of different colors: black, red, white, and yellow. The Black Road spoke to them, telling them it was the lord's road and was the one to take, which they wrongly did, and it marks the beginning of their undoing.

Taking the Black Road represents listening to the shadow and complexes, not using their own judgment, not being discerning of the negative intentions of the unconscious voices. This foreshadows that the outcome will not be successful. On the other hand, it seems necessary to take this road, because the order of fate here is to descend into the dark realm to confront the lords of darkness. Only in so doing can the twins neutralize the dark forces enough to prepare the world for the creation of humanity. The old rulers need to be contained for the new age to dawn. This dilemma is a familiar theme in myths and an individual's journey, extending from Oedipus, driven by fate, to a dreamer presented with an untenable choice where there is both a negative and positive outcome, negative in the short run but positive overall. In the Greek-Roman mythology it is Hermes or Mercurius, a trickster god, who stands at the crossroads and forces whoever encounters him to make a choice that inevitably changes forever his or her life's course. This challenge for the twins was such a moment.

These four colors appear in creation myths frequently and also appear as the main colors in alchemy. "The philosophy in everything separates the basic substance of nature into four, so that we have first the *Nigredo* or Blackness, second the *Albedo* [or whiteness], third the *Citrinitas* or Yellowing, and fourth the *Rubedo* or reddening of the substance" (von Franz 1972, 224). They also represented the four directions in Maya cosmology: west was black; east was red; north was white; south was yellow. Black was the way to the setting of the sun and its entry into the underworld, representing death and war. "Heading Westward" was always a metaphor for death and dying in early European imagery. For the Maya, the crossroads was a traditional place of danger and decision. It was the focal point for the unseen powers of the directions. Each color and direction carried its own unique archetypal energy, both good and bad. Sins were ceremonially collected and abandoned at the crossroads. This seems to be similar in concept to sending the sins off on the back of the scapegoat in Jewish tradition, and the *Agnus Dei*, the Lamb of God who is sacrificed for the "blackness" of all.

Red represented the east, which is where the sun rises, initiating light and life:

> Red . . . had many references: the sun, blood, fire, the sap of the sacred ceiba tree, and roasted corn. All these symbols expressed vital force. Blood—which was a divine element—was abundantly shed during sacrifices and self-mutilations, for it was believed it would nourish the earth and the gods. . . . Even the water that flowed in the river of the netherworld, the Xibalbá, was full of blood. (Longhena 1999, 66)

Many of the sacred buildings in Maya cities were first covered with white plaster, then painted red. East is a very important direction in the *Popol Vuh*, as it is where Tulan, the place of creation, was located and where the first humans were instructed to go to gain their authority. Venus as the morning star carried the sun on its back to bring in the new day and the beginning of consciousness.

The direction associated with white was north, which represents purity and lack of color while being pure and sacred. It was the left side of the sun. The North Star and the Milky Way were attributes of white, with the latter leading to Xibalbá. The cold winter rains fertilized the maize and other crops. Soul was called the white-flower-thing (Freidel, Schele, and Parker 1993, 183).

Yellow was associated with the south and the precious ripe maize, precious jewels, water lilies, the background of the jaguar's skin, and death. A symbol for strength and life, it was the sun's large or right side. In Aztec symbolism, however, blue represented the south, so yellow implying the direction south was not universal throughout Mesoamerica. Blue-green is one of the four roads mentioned later in the story when the hero twins arrive at the crossroads. Yellow represented the maize plant, around which ritual and sacrifice revolved. Its abundance represented the health of the culture and life. The god associated with maize was the jaguar on its night journey, young jaguar sun or Xbalanqué.

It is important to know that the Maya did not think in terms of four directions. The sun traversed east to west while north and south were to the sides of the main line of travel, not distinct locations of their own. The following quotation shows the interrelationship between the drama playing out in the sky and the significance of the southern direction as associated with the water lily and maize plant:

> At the zenith conjunction the ecliptic divides the Milky Way into a water lily plant to the south. This is the body of water that the canoe of the east-west form of the Milky Way floats upon and sinks into. The Maize Tree is above, emerging from the blossom of the water lily, a slight expansion in the Milky Way at this point. The root "cord" may be related to the umbilicus stories of post-Conquest Maya in which the sky umbilicus of the created world is identified with the Milky Way. Ichnographically, the water lily plant resembles the umbilicus attached to the placenta in a human birth. (Freidel, Schele, and Parker 1993, 425)

The four colors are similarly important in Western symbolism, with black representing death, darkness, unconsciousness, and the *nigredo* in alchemy. White is its opposite, representing light, life, purity, and consciousness. Yellow is light and in alchemy represents a distinct stage in the transformation process, moving from the darkness to the light. Red represents blood, passion, heat, fire, and affect and in alchemy represents the stage of embodiment, *rubedo*, or bringing the light of consciousness into one's real manifest life. This myth shows that the Black Road or the alchemical stage called *nigredo*, indicating depression and lack of consciousness, represents the first stage of the work. Alchemy follows the same course of development seen in mythology. Later the hero twins again take the Black Road; in other words, they start in depression but are not defeated by their darkness. Instead, they are transformed by the experience and gain clarity.

When One Hunahpú and Seven Hunahpú arrived at Xibalbá, they greeted the underworld lords, but in fact these were only wooden manikins dressed like the gods of death. They did not recognize their true adversaries, which was their second mistake. The denizens of Xibalbá roared with laughter, now certain of their victory, because they saw how naïve the twins were.

This point is similar to the naïve attitude of Perceval in the grail quest. He did not know the correct question to ask and, hence, failed. Naming is significant to the Maya, as will be seen later when Seven Hunahpú cannot name his body parts and, therefore, had to remain buried in the ballcourt. The act of naming the other gives possession and magical dominion over the other. The motif of the wooden manikins is replicated here, having originated from the earlier failed attempt at creation. This portends another failed attempt.

They then invite One Hunahpú and Seven Hunahpú to sit on a bench, which is not an ordinary seat but a searing hot slab of stone.

D. Tedlock's translation of this part shows the humor in the original text:

> **So now they were burned on the bench; they really jumped around on the bench now, but they got no relief. They really got up fast, having burned their butts. At this the Xibalbans laughed again, they began to shriek with laughter, the laughter rose up like a serpent in their very cores. (1985, 111)**

Their third mistake was not recognizing the hot slab.

For the final set of tests, the lords of Xibalbá first gave the twins cigars and torches that had to remain lit and intact all night while in the Dark House.

Smoking tobacco was an ancient Maya tradition carrying religious significance. It was used as a bridge from the conscious to the unconscious realm, a way to convene with the gods and the ancestors. At dawn, the gods of death found that the twins failed this impossible task, as the cigars and torches burned away. The twins, unable to keep the light burning, remained in the dark, unconscious, without the instinct to know how to survive.

Because One Hunahpú and Seven Hunahpú failed, they did not have to spend the night in the four other houses: Shivering House, filled with a deep chill; Jaguar House, with jaguar's gnashing teeth; Bat House, filled with deadly bats; and Blade House, with blades moving back and forth. Tricked and overpowered by the lords of Xibalbá, the twins were sacrificed and buried at Crushing Ballcourt.

Crush refers to human sacrifice, while the blades in the houses refer to the instruments of sacrifice and bloodletting. As a token of their victory, the netherworld gods placed the head of One Hunahpú in the fork of a barren tree that stands by a road called the Place of Ball Game Sacrifice. Jung emphasized the archetypal significance of the figure of the divine sacrifice, who

> corresponds feature for feature to the empirical modes of manifestation of the archetype that lies at the root of almost all known conceptions of God. This archetype is not merely a static image, but dynamic, full of movement. It is always a drama, whether in heaven, on earth, or in hell. (1989a, 265)

The twins lost their encounter with the demons because they did not have the right attitude or relationship to the psyche. These twins were too light, naïve, one-sided, with a lack of connection to their shadow sides. They were sacrificed as a consequence. They did not have the skills to fight the complexes in the form of the underworld tasks and the demons that arose to defeat them. This is the theme of the primordial sacrifice; there is no creation without sacrifice. Heading down into the underworld means descending into a depression where one is challenged and eventually torn apart—hoping to survive wiser and more conscious. The twins did not make it far enough to pass into the houses of torture. Torture is the first stage of the work on the *prima materia* in alchemy, where the body is tortured and separated into its parts before it is reconstituted in a new way, emerging transformed. The analogue is the suffering, which, sometimes, brings people to therapy. The twins took the wrong road. In many fairy tales, the first attempt involves taking the wrong road. One learns from the suffering that ensues and then, hopefully, takes the right road the next time. It is suffering that transforms (Jung 1997, 426).

The head is put in the fork of the tree, in the middle ground between two opposites. The heroes have not become sufficiently conscious of the opposing forces within themselves, so they hang between the opposites. They relied on their thinking only and were disconnected from their instinct and from nature; such a connection might have provided them the ability to know how to survive the underworld forces. This set of twins represented the first attempt to subdue the dark forces and effect the transition from matriarchy to patriarchy to prepare the earth for the creation of humanity and culture:

> We use the word "patriarchate" in Bachofen's sense, to signify the predominantly masculine world of spirit, sun, consciousness, and ego. In the matriarchate, on the other hand, the unconscious reigns supreme, and the predominant feature here is a preconscious, prelogical, and pre-individual way of thinking and feeling. (Neumann 1970, 168)

This is another failed attempt at the creation of the world. The gods must try again if they are to defeat the demons of the underworld. Nevertheless, here there has been a sacrifice; the first step has been taken and offered. The next steps will be built on this one. By leaving the ball behind, it seems that the twins were aware of their limited participation:

> The motif of the first being to die . . . the idea that if one thing comes into reality something else has to go beyond the threshold to the other side . . . that creation is essentially connected with something dying or being destroyed will come up in many other tales. (von Franz 1972, 33–34)

Instantly, this tree becomes laden with calabash gourds for the first time, with the head becoming one of the many round fruits. Calabash is a round squash, much like the shape of a head.

Hunahpú literally means "calabash." At this stage in the myth, there is a symbolic regression back to the vegetative layer of the psyche in order to be renewed and transformed. This image is frequently seen in dreams. Hunahpú is a vegetative god, much like Christ, Osiris, Attis, Dionysus, and Odin. They are sacrificed and hung on a tree, and from there, they are reborn. Both twins die to bring forth light to the earth. Light is a metaphor for birth. There is mythological precedence for the severed head as seen in Egyptian Osiris and the Hebrew Teraphim, as an oracle head (Jung 1989a, 240–41). The head was thought to be the star Venus in the underworld, according to D. Tedlock (1985, 119). This tree had never borne fruit until the head was placed in its trunk. It is out of the process of death and destruction that the new beginning and the creative can emerge. This is the beginning of differentiation. Here the head representing thoughts, intuitions, and spirit was separated from the body. One now splits into two—thought and instinct—and is now ripe for the arrival of the real other with whom one can relate. This is an important step in analysis, when the *massa confusa* is differentiated, broken apart, and there are now opposing views. From here, dialogue can lead to the understanding of two or more different viewpoints.

The failure of One Hunahpú and Seven Hunahpú points to the state of cultural development of the Maya at the time. Symbolically, the culture had now created a tree sprouting fruit, indicating the beginning movement from a horticultural to an agricultural level of development. While the culture hero was not successful and the development of the culture remained on a vegetative level, the new potential was present, just as the buried body in the ballcourt represents the soul of the dead god waiting to fertilize the new life. The Maya had an association between fruit trees and ancestors. "Behind each ancestor is a fruit-bearing tree, indicating that they are rising from their graves in a fashion parallel to the sprouting of world trees" (Christenson 2003, 127).

The underworld maiden Xquic or Blood Woman, daughter of Gathered Blood, hears of this miraculous gourd tree and goes to see for herself. Blood Woman disobeys her father out of curiosity.

She stepped outside of convention and law, represented by the father as the prevailing authority, in order to think independently. This curious and rebellious attitude represented the instinct that was missing in the twins that was now introduced into the myth as a counterpoint to thought and intuition. All previous creation attempts began with the word. It has taken this long in the story to introduce feeling into their cosmology as well as a working relationship to instinct and the world of nature. As the daughter of One Death, Blood Woman acted as the bridge from the unconscious to potential consciousness as she engaged One Hunahpú in the calabash tree. This motif is similar to the snake in the Garden of Eden, who winds itself around the tree of knowledge, offering the temptation of something new. These steps ultimately bring greater choice to humanity. Blood Woman as an underworld goddess was the moon aspect of the First Mother. It was the maiden's desire and feeling that led her to the calabash tree. For the first time in the story feeling was introduced, and that resulted in her having an immaculate conception. The spark that begins the change in attitude is frequently curiosity and imagination, which Blood Woman possessed.

Blood was a significant symbol in Mesoamerican mythology as it represented a divine substance. Christenson explained the significance of blood:

> In Maya society, Blood is the most precious substance because it bears within itself the spirit or essence of the ancestors and thus, by extension, of the founding deities from whom they descended. It is therefore the repository of life which transcends individuals to include the ancestral dead. It is consistent with this view that "Lady Blood" [Blood Woman], daughter of an underworld lord, is the means by which the skull of One Hunahpú is able to produce life out of death. (2003, 128n274)

By offering blood in sacrifice, humans return the precious substance to the gods to maintain the important cycle of relationship between the gods and humankind. The demons in the underworld were also fed blood to sustain the shadow that is ever present and also in need of relationship:

Consciousness without the connection with the shadow means a violation of the blood; then people live beyond their means, they live in an unnatural imaginary way, above their own heads, which is an offense against the earth. If one lives close to the earth, if one lives with the blood, there are some things, which one simply cannot do or imagine. (Jung 1997, 237)

Psychologically, blood is very important. It represents the life force and libido that give people the strength and power to acknowledge their own authority to stand as the bridge between the inner and outer forces of life. It is also a symbol for lineage, as in the bloodline. The Maya believed in the replacement of souls from generation to generation, where children replace their parents and grandparents and those children who are named after the ancestor actually become the reborn person, with their personality, soul, and all other aspects of the individual (Freidel, Schele, and Parker 1993, 285). *Ch'ulel* is the activating soul substance in the form of blood that moves between humans and gods reanimating life, and it lives in the many sacred objects and places in the Maya world. According to Evon Z. Vogt:

Although subject to temporary damage, the ch'ulel is eternal. When a person dies, this soul hangs around the grave for some time, then becomes part of a pool of such souls in the care of the Father-Mothers, the ancestral gods, who may decide to plant it again in the body of a newborn baby. Parents have to be especially careful with these babies: "A small child is especially susceptible to *soul loss*, as the soul is not yet accustomed to its new receptacle." Ch'ulelob can move around outside the body, in dreams, during sleep, and visit the ancestors. The real power of the experience of soul, however, is revealed in its universality. (quoted in Freidel, Schele, and Parker 1993, 182)

Itz was a magic substance, the equivalent of *ch'ulel*, in the form of tree sap, dew, semen, and other secretions, just as maize dough and gruel were seen as sustenance.

The skull or bone speaks to her and asks what she wants. She stretches out her right hand before the face of the skull, and it

spits some white saliva into her hand. The spittle immediately disappears and impregnates her.

"In Maya, the word for bone is the same as the word for seed," says Gillette (1997, 198). The skull told her that the saliva was the essence of his son, who would go on and become complete. She received the spittle in her right hand, representing maleness and the possibility of having a male child. The Quiché (K'iche') associated right with male and left with female, which is also a universal representation (Chevalier and Gheerbrant 1996, 801). Spitting is a common creation motif, and saliva can either heal or inflict illness. She took the saliva into her body, which here is the seed of the new potential. Here it may have represented *itz* carrying the soul substance. The Maya believed that they lived on as ancestors if their children worshipped and remembered them through honor and offerings. To communicate with the precious ancestors, the Maya would perform auto-sacrifices: drawing spiny cords through their penises, tongues, or calves, as a way of achieving an altered state of consciousness. In this state, the veil between this world and the world beyond lifted, and they were able to communicate with their ancestors and conjure the gods. Hallucinogenic substances were also frequently used for this purpose. The ancestors offered advice and wisdom to the living. For the dead relatives to be reborn, the children had to have a metaphysical knowledge of the journey through the underworld to bring their relatives back to life, much like Hunahpú and Xbalanqué, who later successfully defeated the underworld demons and resurrected their father and uncle.

In the cleft of the calabash tree, One Hunahpú remained alone, in the dark, a head disconnected from the body. It was Blood Woman who introduced the relationship to the body. She became impregnated with the white saliva and, out of the mix of the head and body, produced another set of twins who were able to complete the culture hero's journey. For One Hunahpú, Blood Woman was the anima, a representation of his inner feminine, his soul who appeared and brought to him what he lacked: blood, passion, anger, emotions, earthy life, instinct, and cunning. She was the solution to the fork in the tree, the third transformative element. For her, One Hunahpú was the animus, a reflection of her inner masculine that offers the creative substance she herself needs to find wholeness. The birth of the hero twins reflected the union of the opposites and the third transformative element that emerged from the union to create greater consciousness. Christenson discussed this important part of the myth:

> The cycle of birth, death, and rebirth is one of the most prominent motifs in ancient Mesoamerican art and literature. The Maya saw death as a necessary part of life. For maize to grow and produce, a seed must first die and be buried in the earth. It was thus necessary for One Hunahpú to descend into the underworld to die before a new generation could appear and be capable of overcoming death. The maiden, Lady Blood [Blood Woman], stood as the intermediary. As the daughter of one of the principal lords of death, she belonged to the darkness of the underworld. As the consort of One Hunahpú, she had the potential to create new life from death. (2003, 130n278)

The skull tells Blood Woman to go up to the face of the earth, assuring her that she will not die because she has entered into a promise by accepting the saliva, which is a creative substance.

In other words, Blood Woman entered into the renewal drama. The Maya concept of face is very important to them and means honor, esteem, value, morality, worth, life, and soul. To know one's face is to know a person intimately. When one loses one's face, one loses one's character and substance and is stripped of all worth. She would not die because she was a contributing participant in the drama of creation. She was the new feminine who knew evil and darkness and chose independent action, leading to her own journey toward consciousness, up to the surface of the earth.

The skull says that the thoughts and words of Huracán, Youngest Thunderbolt, and Sudden Thunderbolt have been carried out.

It is clear that the gods were orchestrating this drama of development through the various heroes, including Blood Woman.

Eventually the father of Blood Woman notices her pregnant condition and demands to know who the father is. Although she steadfastly denies having known a man, it is to no avail, and her

father resolves to kill her, ordering the messenger Owls to take the maiden away to be sacrificed with White Dagger, the instrument of sacrifice. She, though, convinces the Owls to spare her life.

The color white in the dagger and saliva corresponds to the color for north and the sun's left side. The white-flower-thing refers to soul. This dagger is what offers soul to the gods as an instrument of ritual, offering the pure substance of blood. Yet the color white may also refer to remaining in a bloodless, bodiless, lifeless state, as opposed to embodying the life-giving qualities of red, such as blood, anger, and sex. It is the purity that opens the door to blood. Blood Woman's sacrifice was not a pure and sacred offering to the gods. Sexual transgressions were treated severely in K'iche' society. Her punishment was a murder, which was the demons' perversion of a genuine offering.

In place of Blood Woman's bloody heart, they return with a thick mass of resin, the blood of the croton tree, also called the dragon's blood tree. Both blood and sap have the same name in K'iche', *kik'*. Burning the resin incense, the death lords relish its smell and take no notice of the Owls leading Blood Woman to the surface of the earth. In this way, the lords of Xibalba were defeated because Blood Woman tricked them. The Owls lead her through a hole to the earth, and forever after, in exchange for performing this deed, they could fly on the earth.

The heart was the container for blood that was originally given by the gods. The demons, the dark side of the gods, were fed and nurtured on blood. The resin called *copal* or *pom* came from special trees, including the rubber tree. It gave off abundant smoke, and in this smoke could be seen ancestors and gods to whom the incense was offered. This particular resin was blood-red and seen as an equivalent to blood and the life force.

The Owls were creatures of the night and went between the underworld and the earth, bringing wisdom between humans and the divine. They were connected to both fertility and death (Miller and Taube 1993, 128). In Greek mythology owls are connected to the goddess Athena and to the moon. Athena brings in rational solar knowledge while the moon, with its lunar light, contributes intuitive knowledge. It is a reflection that rules the darkness (Chevalier and Gheerbrant 1996, 729).

Trickery is a repeating motif in the *Popol Vuh* and seems to be very important for success. One Hunahpú and Seven Hunahpú did not use tricks or seem to have the ability to think creatively, but only concretely. Blood Woman was curious and defied her father, thinking beyond what was apparent, through imagination. Of course, at this point in the myth, the protagonists were gods and had exceptional powers, if they took advantage of them. The Maya placed great value on humor and expressed it in many ways; having fun with tricks was one way.

Arriving at the home of Xmucané, the mother of the slain twins, Blood Woman declares herself to be her daughter-in-law, the wife of One Hunahpú. But Xmucané, convinced that her sons are dead, wants nothing to do with the pregnant maiden. Blood Woman tells her that her sons are still alive and says, "They have merely made a way for the light to show itself" (D. Tedlock 1985, 117).

The elder twins died to bring light to earth, to pave the way for the creation of a conscious human race, but they were unsuccessful heroes, leaving the task to their sons. Much like the three failed creations, the twins' task took a couple of tries to get it right and make a way for the light. Light was a metaphor for the birth of the sun and the full moon, which were represented by the twins as planets. Of course, Xmucané would be cautious bringing Blood Woman into her fold since she appeared to be a single pregnant mother, which is a taboo in Maya society.

Skeptical as she is, the grandmother sends Blood Woman on a test to gather a netful of maize from the field of One Monkey (Batz) and One Artisan (Chouen). When Blood Woman sees that the field has only a single maize plant, she begins to despair, then calls for the help of the guardians of the food, and they come to her rescue, providing her with more maize than she can carry. Animals come to her aid and carry the net for her.

One Monkey and One Artisan were clearly not able to grow much corn, representing a low level of fertility. The absence of grain provided a vehicle for Blood Woman to be tested, just as the demons tested the twins. The twins failed, but she passed her test and was able to fill the net with maize. In Maya theology, the net was a significant symbol for the divine order of the universe. Its fixed pattern represented the regularity of the seasons in the fabric of time. Thus, Maya goddesses were often depicted weaving on a cosmic loom (Christenson 2003, 136n304).

Returning with a great load of maize, Blood Woman proves that she is the wife of One Hunahpú. Yet Xmucané does not trust Blood Woman, thinking the maize was stolen, and she goes to the maize field to see for herself. Finding the one ear of corn still in the field, she realizes her daughter-in-law is enchanted, like herself, and thus accepts her as her relative.

Calling on nature to help her shows that Blood Woman was connected to nature and the earth, a part of the psyche that brings good instincts and was precisely what Xmucané, One Hunahpú, and Seven Hunahpú lacked. Xmucané, Blood Woman's mother-in-law, was cold, mistrustful, and mean and did not have adequate food or a flourishing garden, which meant the state of the world was not in balance with nature, which is perhaps the reason why One Hunahpú's wife died. The grandmother acted in a stingy and suspicious way, while in contrast, her sons, dead in the underworld, were too trusting and naïve. She, however, was the great diviner and played her part in the drama well, much like the myth of Aphrodite in relation to Psyche. She said, "They have merely made a way for light to show itself" (D. Tedlock 1985, 117), referring to the fateful workings of the psyche and indicating that they were part of the process and the foundation for further development. Blood Woman was a more developed aspect of the mother archetype, being from the underworld and having a connection to the darker forces, yet motherless herself. The feminine in this culture was in need of further development. Yet the twins' father was dead, so in equal measure things were incomplete. Xmucané recognized the divinity in Blood Woman in her ability to provide maize through magic.

Blood Woman's ability to use her feelings and her more developed connection to her instincts and the natural world opens up a level of cooperation with others, that is, animals, that seems to indicate a future possibility of establishing a culture of agriculture as opposed to hunting and gathering. **Blood Woman gives birth to the hero twins Hunahpú and Xbalanqué in the mountains. Although they are the children of One Hunahpú, the twins are not well received by Xmucané, their grandmother, or by One Monkey and One Artisan, who are jealous of their younger half brothers. The grandmother insists that the boys be thrown out of the house because they are too loud, and they are put first on an anthill and then in brambles. Their uncles hope they will die, but instead they sleep well.**

The boys seemed to survive under these harsh circumstances because they had their mother's connection to nature, to the wild, chaotic aspect that helped them deal with the uncertain and unpredictable as well as her ability to play tricks. The first trick played on them was being placed in an anthill. Ants and insects in general carry the soul in Maya thought. This part of the myth represents the motif of the discarded newborn child and the danger and threat to the emergence of the new life, the threat to the hero, a parallel to the story of Moses being sent down the river in a winnowing basket.

While the older brothers dance and make fine music and art, Hunahpú and Xbalanqué roam the forest, shooting animals with their blowguns. The spoiled older brothers snatch away all their game and leave them with only scraps of bone and gristle to eat. "Since One Monkey and One Artisan were great knowers, in their hearts they already realized everything when their younger brothers came into being, but they didn't reveal their insight because of their jealousy. The anger in their own hearts came down on their own heads; no great harm was done" (D. Tedlock 1985, 120).

They were jealous and treacherous. While inheriting clear vision and talents, excelling in everything they did, nothing came of them because of their envy. Their abuses of others fell back on them. Envy is a dark and poisonous affect. It seems this lesson warned against such behavior, that all could be lost because of it. "The jealousy of siblings is virtually institutional in Maya society. In K'iche' it is significant that *ch'ak'imal* 'younger-brother' is the word for 'jealousy,' while *atz* 'older sibling' also means 'specter'" (Edmonson 1971, 93).

One day the twins return from hunting empty-handed, telling their brothers that the shot birds are caught high in a tree. One Monkey and One Artisan agree to climb the Yellow Tree, but as they go up, the trunk miraculously swells and grows to a great height. The panicked elder brothers call out for help to Xbalanqué and Hunahpú, who tell them: "Untie your loincloths, wrap them around your hips, with the long end hanging like a tail behind you, and then you'll be able to move better" (D. Tedlock 1985, 121). Upon doing this, One Monkey and One Artisan are turned into forest monkeys, tricked by their younger brothers Xbalanqué and Hunahpú. But rather than being forgotten, these two monkeys become the patrons of artists, dancers, and musicians.

The Yellow Tree was used in the famous *Palo Volador* ceremony that was performed for years after the conquest. In the ceremony dancers dressed as monkeys climbed a tall pole and on long ropes circled and spun down, a ritual reenactment of this part of the *Popol Vuh* myth. Yellow represented the right side and the south, the sun, ripe maize, and the yellow spots on the jaguar's fur.

Hunahpú and Xbalanqué tricked their mean half brothers or used their guile, which is using one's shadow aspects consciously. The book says, "They were envious, they did not show their wisdom . . . and became monkeys because they became arrogant" (D. Tedlock 1985, 126, 130). The half brothers regressed to become animals, which reflected their unconscious shadow sides. From earlier in the story, Framer and Shaper's second creation attempt was carving beings from wood. Since these beings were incapable of understanding or honoring Heart of Sky, they were destroyed and turned into monkeys.

Monkeys are playful tricksters, not serious, but very clever, and in many cultures bring with them gifts of good heath, success, creativity, and protection. Being connected to the instinct, they have access to creative potential and are a precursor to humans. In this myth, these monkeys were scribes, artisans, carvers, and musicians, yet they had gone astray, beyond the bounds of justice. The monkey twins One Batz and One Chouen only played, which reflected the matriarchal, horticultural stage of cultural development, while the hero twins Hunahpú and Xbalanqué hunted daily, bringing in food to eat. The hero twins exhibited a strong work ethic, indicative of the agricultural stage requiring masculine labor. To put the world in its right order before the creation of humans, the hero twins had to subdue the lazy slothfulness of their half brothers. Transforming them into monkeys corresponded to the very nature they exhibited. Making them aware of this nature seemed to allow their talents to unfold over time. The monkeys became the important scribes and artisans of the Maya culture. Their wisdom became manifest. All the sets of twins carried different parts of the whole that was trying to form and organize itself out of the original chaos and lack of differentiation. Jung quoted Meister Eckhart, who explained, "Suffering is the fastest horse that carries you to perfection" (1997, 366).

The myth is created as a replica of the movement of the stars and planets, mostly Venus, which the Maya followed carefully. Each new section of the myth corresponds to the movement of Venus:

> When Venus and Mars appear in the east together Mars remains long after Venus has descended into the underworld, just as One Monkey (Batz) and One Artisan (Chouen) remained on the face of the earth when One Hunahpú and Seven Hunahpú went to Xibalba. (D. Tedlock 1985, 287)

The cycle of twins' actions correspond to the movement of the stars, descending and rising until the final apotheosis. The hero twins wanted a good relationship with their grandmother, one that was not possible in the presence of the stepbrothers:

> Thus, the twins seek to replace the treachery and jealousy of the household with love and respect. In Quiché view, this is not merely the establishment of a more comfortable home environment, but an essential prerequisite for the proper expression of divine will. In contemporary Quiché thought,

ancestors and deity do not tolerate open anger, jealousy, or pride and punish such severely. Until these characteristics are eliminated from the house of their mother and grandmother, the twins would not be able to act in concert with Heart of Sky, identified in the text as the inspiration for the twins' subsequent actions in defeating death and restoring their father-ancestor to power. (Christenson 2003, 146n345)

Two sets of antagonistic twins is not a common theme in creation myths. More common is one brother opposing another, like Cain and Abel, Jacob and Esau, Osiris and Set. Yet in this myth there is a predominance of doubling. The artisan monkey twins, who are the older half brothers of the blowgun hunters, Hunahpú and Xbalanqué, represent preconscious nature, while the hunter twins represent the movement toward consciousness. This is an interesting twist in the myth. One would think that artisans contributed more to the development of culture than hunters, yet the myth infers that what was lacking was an integration of the darker, unconscious force of evil. The culture heroes, Hunahpú and Xbalanqué, were successful and superseded the older monkey scribes, who could not fully take their rightful place until they were literally shown what behaviors they were acting out. This story illustrates seeing the shadow in projected form. Even the scribes in this culture needed to develop into the capable, wise participants they came to be.

The change from boys to monkeys represented a culture that was superseded, the maternal giving way to the early patriarchal system. Blood Woman was a bridging key here. The scribe-artisans, being their father's boys, lacked her connection to the underworld. Human instinct was missing along with a conscious ability to make choices. Instead, they were driven by complexes, which are *feeling-toned* expressions of our animal instincts related to archetypal patterns of behavior that grip the individual in an irrational way, causing the loss of one's humanity by becoming unconscious. Activated complexes run against the new social order being established and, therefore, have to be contained. Bringing them to consciousness helps contain them. The ability to see both sides must have been important in the creation of a race of humanity that would have to decide on its own to honor the gods and not forsake them in their idle play or be taken over by a darker authority like the complexes that gripped them.

The interaction with their brothers turned out to be good practice for the hero twins in their later confrontation with true darkness in the form of the underworld demons. While the scribe-artisan twins acted out in shadow ways toward their younger half brothers, the latter remained calm, contained, and consciously deliberate due to their conscious relationship to nature. "They tolerated it, for they knew their own nature, and this was a light by which they could see" (Christenson 2003, 142). The scribe-artisan twins' scene was reminiscent of the preconscious stage of Seven Macaw. Both represented the *prima materia* that was being worked on in this myth. The culture hero twins were novel in that they worked at hunting. Work is the key here, and the culture hero twins are compared to the artisans, who did not work. Working at hunting influenced the shift away from the maternal to a greater focus on the masculine. The breath that passes through the blowguns pointed to a connection to spirit, or archaic *pneuma*, and to Huracán, who personally guided the preparation of the world for the creation of humans. One by one, shadow and complexes were focused on, offered up as lessons, and transformed. These included Seven Macaw's vanity and power drive and the artisan monkey twins' selfishness and laziness. The process to transform these negative attitudes followed the same path one takes in individuation, where unconscious instincts are acted out until one becomes aware of them, sometimes by force. Then the attitude can change to become more constructive. The shift from the monkey twins to the culture twins represented a huge change in the development of the culture.

The hero twins call their transformed half brothers back home to sing for the grandmother, warning her of their change and telling her she must not laugh. They will only call them back four times. As they arrive and begin to sing, Xmucané cannot hold back her laughter; the monkeys look too hilarious with their red faces, long tails, and bulging bellies. Four times she laughs and finally they run off to the forest for good. These boys did nothing but play, even though they had great talents.

Wise and capable though they were, they became what they did best, tricksters who create laughter. They remained important figures in the Maya culture nonetheless. Represented by the eleventh day of the ritual calendar, these scribes and artisans were at times monkeys and at other times related to the sun (Longhena 1999, 120). The monkey twins were divine and had great knowledge, yet they obscured it. As scribal archetypes, when they acted according to their fate, they continued to represent this important function, as seen in the many Maya representations of monkeys as scribes.

Wanting to please and feed their grandmother, the hero twins then begin to cultivate the maize field.

This is a metaphor for preparing their ground for transformation, which was a shift to the beginning of the agricultural stage that supplants the hunting-gathering or horticultural stage. The boys were taking the responsibility of ensuring there was enough food and, in so doing, honoring their grandmother. Additionally, there are procreative and sexual overtones in the act of tilling the soil and planting seeds. Maize cultivation, religious thought, and the transformation of all aspects of the culture went hand in hand:

> Discovery of the laws of maize germination is accompanied by these new perceptions of being and cosmos, and the indivisibility of these three elements is seen in the fact that Hunahpú personifies them all at one and the same time. Besides symbolizing the process of the maize kernel that, falling into the earth, dies only to convert itself into the germ of a plant, Hunahpú exemplifies the destiny of the human being who, like the maize grain that dies, goes to the underworld and returns gloriously, as the young god-hero returned. In this allegory is proclaimed the belief in the immortality of the soul. (Girard 1979, 195)

Yet, instead of clearing the field, magically the tools work on their own, while the boys play with their blowguns. During the day the boys go to work in the field and watch the ground work itself. They ask the Turtle Dove to watch for the arrival of the grandmother and to alert the boys. That night, animals, small and great, come

and cause the field to grow up again. The twins want to know who is doing this and decide to hide in the bushes late at night and watch. They see all the animals gathered together, ordering the trees and bushes to rise. Seeing the twins, the animals, a puma, jaguar, deer, rabbit, fox, coyote, and peccary, run past them, and while the twins try to grab hold of each one, they cannot. By now there is fire or anger in their hearts, because they don't catch one, although they break off the tails of the deer and rabbit. Finally, a rat runs by, and they grab him in their net, and in their anger they burn his tail over a fire. The rat says to them, "I will not die by your hand! Gardening is not your job, but there is something that is" (D. Tedlock 1985, 128). The rat would not tell them without being fed first. He then tells the twins about their father's ball equipment hidden in the eaves of their grandmother's house. At that, they feed the rat and tell him that from then on he can have all the trash swept out of homes. They are very excited, conferring all night, and set a plan to retrieve the ball equipment with the rat's help. They all return home at midday. They ask their grandmother to prepare a meal and then to retrieve water to quench their thirst. While she is absent, a mosquito punctures the side of their grandmother's water jar to make it leak, thus delaying her return, while the rat clawed through the rope securing the equipment. The boys take the equipment and hide it on the road to the ballcourt; then they go to the river in time to see their mother and grandmother sealing the hole in the water jug.

In this depiction, magic was used intentionally by the twins. Being divine, they had such power. They asked for the help of the Turtle Dove to sit as a guard for them. This bird has qualities of simplicity, beauty, and innocence, an emblem of good tidings and peace. It was the symbol for Aphrodite, Ishtar, and Venus. It is a lovebird, emblematic of fecundity, fertility, and sexuality. It was also the fertilizing wind of the Holy Spirit that impregnated the Virgin Mary (Ronnberg and Martin 2010, 244). It signifies in this myth the quiet observer of Huracán in a gentler, more feminine form than the falcon, which is the black form of the Holy Ghost (Jung 1997, 136): "Winged beings, which since time immemorial have meant psychical facts, what one calls thoughts or ideas or intuitions. Anything that has to do with the mind has an air quality" (481).

The world before creation was infused with magic just as the inner world of psyche and its manifestation in dreams reflects this similar state of irrationality and magical happenings. All elements in the drama were players in the fateful task of creation. There are nine significant animals in this section, representing gods and days, prominent in the mythology as both active predators and sacrificers or passive prey and victims (Cohodas 1989, 228). They represent the natural instinctual aspect of the psyche, and here it is through the instincts that the message comes from the bottom up rather than top down. This, of course, is the piece that needed to be included in the final creation attempt. Just as Blood Woman survived because of her good instincts and emerged from below to the face of the earth, the instincts and knowledge of the twins' task came from the lowliest of animals, the rat, and arose to their ears. While the spark for creation came from lightning of Huracán from above, it had to circulate into the lowest realms to unify the totality of the cosmos, the upper, lower, and middle realms. From Turtle Dove to rat, they bring forth the soft, gentle bird, representing the feminine, and perhaps the soul and love, and the rat that is elusive and hard to pin down but very smart. Perhaps the dove is that aspect of the soft feminine that is missing in the myth. The animals appear and disappear like magicians, slipping through crevices in reality and in the psyche. They are restless beneath the surface of things, prolific and able to survive anywhere. Rats are rejected and hated; they represent those animals that are considered filthy and diseased. Psychologically, they work in the shadows of people's lives, helping overcome obstacles in their unconscious. Here rats were the carrier of the knowledge of fate.

The boys were not animals like their twin half brothers but instead were connected in a conscious way to animal instinctual knowledge. This knowledge helped them *sniff* out danger and know the right way to act to survive. The boys got angry and had fire in their hearts, which shows they incorporated some of their mother's red blood in the form of anger, an emotion they needed to be able to deal with the underworld figures they would encounter. This instinctual response in the form of appropriate anger would protect them. They were not acting out of shadow, like their half brothers; or ignorance that is unconscious of the shadow, like their father and uncle; or just plain nasty and angry, like their grandmother; instead, they used their appropriate anger for their creative endeavor. They remained composed and thoughtful.

While this myth was particular to a specific cultural group, it clearly parallels the process of individuation seen in Jungian analysis. The work of analysis helps the individual become conscious of and integrate the affects so that decisions can be made rationally, and the individual is less impacted by unconscious forces. Here the twins acted both as analysts and analysands as they worked on the archetypal energies represented by the other characters in the myth and worked on those same energies within themselves. Each layer of this myth demonstrated the psyche's intention to become conscious through differentiation and separation, the sorting out of attitudes, affects, and behaviors that did not serve the healthy establishment and function of the culture. Through example, it offered a blueprint of the wrong and right values for the individuals in that culture and in their lives.

What was retrieved from the eaves of the house was the rubber ball, the image of the Self left there by their fathers, who seemed to intuit that they would not complete the task ahead of them; that responsibility would fall to their sons. Like their father and uncle, the hero twins played ball on the ballcourt, but before they did, they swept out the court of their fathers. To sweep out means to clean out all that was before. Sweeping was a way to keep out the demons of Xibalbá. This action represents the alchemical process of cleaning out what is not useful or impinges on clarity and consciousness. It is a process of examining the old ways, ideas, attitudes, and behaviors. These are the complexes and elements of shadow that no longer serve the individual or culture. Here the way of the fathers was no longer appropriate. In traditional Maya culture, sweeping and clearing out of old pottery would take place at the end of the year during the five unlucky days before the beginning of the New Year. This is an apt metaphor for the hero twins sweeping the ballcourt. Sweeping was very important in the Mesoamerican cultures. This motif appears again in the Aztec creation myth of the birth of Huitilopochitli, the god of war. His mother, Coatlique, was sweeping when she became pregnant with him. The old ways needed to be discarded before the new ways could be introduced. To succeed in containing the demons in the underworld, the twins relied on their own clarity, consciousness, and instinct, related to their own relationship to the creator god. For an individual in Jungian analysis, this would be called establishing an ego-Self axis. This means that an individual's ego has lined up with the stronger inner core of the personality, the part that reflects the archetype of wholeness and wisdom. By integrating the unconscious parts of the personality that have remained in the shadow or are manifested as complexes, the ego becomes more substantial and is able to stand strongly in relation to the forces of the unconscious in a balanced way, accepting what is positive and helpful and rejecting what is negative and destructive.

The grandmother was left with a leaking jug. This is a reflection on the capacity of the developmental stage of that time to contain the culture. The old ways were not holding. The vessel represents the containment of culture, the containment of the psyche, and it was leaking. The twins, with the help of the mosquito caused the leak. "Among the Tlingit, the mosquito's characteristic sucking of blood corresponded to the shaman's capacity to 'suck out' sickness or evil from his patients" (Ronnberg and Martin 2010, 232). Mosquitoes live in marshes or where water is stagnant, attacking and feeding off humans and animals in an aggressive way, causing disease. Once the channels of water are opened to flow freely, mosquitoes disappear. The mosquito in the story opened the way for water to flow freely. Yet the water of life was now beginning to flow out, and it needed proper containment. For the grandmother, who was a goddess of creation, it was time to try again. This time, she needed the masculine energy to complete the process.

The masculine differentiates from the feminine and brings in logos in the form of consciousness that separates from the unconscious, like a spark of light out of the darkness. Not surprisingly, the group convened at midday when the sun was at its zenith. Differentiation is the beginning of patriarchy. While the shift from the matriarchy to patriarchy is not easy, the two frequently reside together culturally and individually, one layered on top of the other, the new as a thin layer over the old. According to archetypal theory, consciousness is built up over many generations and many cultures. The bedrock sits at the beginning of time, with the layers of cultures and religions as foundations to thinking and development. The old gods do not die but become the neglected demons and fantasy material of psychic life, as well as symptoms and diseases (Jung 1983, 37).

These lords are again infuriated by the incessant pounding above their heads and send their messenger Owls to summon the twins to the underworld in seven days to play ball. The message is delivered to the grandmother while the boys are absent, and she is heartbroken by this news, remembering the loss of her sons. Suddenly a louse falls on her and volunteers to deliver the message to the boys. The louse eats it and goes on his way until he meets a toad that can help him go faster if he too is eaten, to which he agrees. As they plod along the road, they meet a snake, called White Life, that eats the toad, which, in turn, is eaten by a falcon that perches on the edge of the ballcourt and squawks at the boys. Annoyed, they shoot the falcon with a blowgun. The falcon says, "The work is contained in my belly. But heal my eye first and I will name it" (D. Tedlock 1985, 132).

The message was delivered first by an owl and then by a chain of animals, from insect, to amphibian, to reptile, to bird, which is another common theme in myths and fairy tales. The owl is the messenger of the underworld gods, related to night, messengers between humans and the divine. For the K'iche', owls were considered to be the harbingers of sickness and death. Yet they were also related to fertility, bringing rain and maize. "The powers of death are also the powers of transformation, and the owl is symbolically bound to the renewal of life that is mythically implicit in death" (Ronnberg and Martin 2010, 254). "It was the owls that brought the first incense to the gods" (Stone and Zender 2011, 92). They have large eyes like the falcon and are able to see rodents in the dim light of night. As symbols of acute awareness, they are considered wise and crafty, with early connections to the feminine fertility and regeneration. Both the regeneration and fierce, warlike death aspects are grounded in the culture-building qualities of the goddess Athena. As a bird that sees and hears at night, the owl is a familiar companion of witches. "Siberian and Inuit shamans regard them as helping spirits, a source of powerful aid and guidance" (Ronnberg and Martin 2010, 254).

The louse is the lowliest of insect. Von Franz (1972, 2) discussed the louse as representing autonomous thought. These are the thoughts that, if not attended to, can become obsessions. Lice suck a person's blood, metaphorically depleting psychic energy just as obsessive thoughts do. Feeding on something else, they are nongenerative in themselves and can represent our dependent, or indolent, attitudes. In archaic cultures, people combed the lice from each other's hair as a friendly social gesture and many times ate them, perhaps adding a little protein to their diet. No animal is entirely bad, and in this case, the louse is certainly helpful. Helpful lice occur in other tales, as a supernatural pregnancy can come through fleas and other insects. Christenson commented on this animal series:

> The louse represents decay and corruption, while the toad is associated with the watery underworld and the fertility of the earth's interior as a source of renewal. The serpent is a common symbol of regeneration . . . and the falcon is a common symbol of the reborn sun at dawn. Thus the sequence of animals may presage the death and corruption of the twins in the underworld, followed by their rebirth to a new life and apotheosis as the sun and moon. (2003, 156n367)

The Maya used a hallucinogenic substance from the toad in their shamanic rituals to conjure the ancestors. The toad lives in the water and on land and can be considered a repulsive creature. Toads were thought to confer warts on anyone touching them. There is a Maya glyph referring to a woman that shows a toad swallowing the sun. In Aztec belief, "The toad monster Tlaltecuhtli, who swallowed the sun every evening, was also called Our Mother" (Cohodas 1989, 222).

Snake and bird are the famous Mesoamerican opposites that are represented together in the plumed serpent Quetzalcoatl (from Aztec culture), also known as Kukulkan and Q'uqu'matz (in Maya cultures). They live on land and in air, respectively:

> So birds usually symbolize thoughts, inspirations, enthusiasms, anything that is light or uplifting. And the dark animals, like snakes, moles, mice, and the aquatic animals, symbolize the heavy dark things: they denote sexuality, and all sorts of earthly desires or instincts or emotions. (Jung 1997, 54)

White Snake points to a spiritualized snake, the creature of the dark recesses and underworld that in this case is white, not black, representing the Mercurial snake of transformation that leads to greater consciousness, greater awareness, and control over the demons. "The snake is a widespread symbol of lightning in Mesoamerica" (Taube 1989, 358). Hence it is a symbol of primordial life force and rebirth. Snakes are considered to be a conduit for water, channeling water from sky to earth, and connected to both while their mouths open to form caves. They are also connected to the number 4:

> Maya nobility conjure up the vision serpent. This great undulating serpent rises from burning bloody paper, and from its mouth emerges an ancestor or, occasionally, a deity. The serpent itself, then, is what one sees in the clouds of smoke rising from the burning sacrifice. . . . The snakes, then, are the vehicle for the movement of the sun, the bearer of ancestors, and carry references to bloodletting. (Miller and Taube 1993, 150–51)

Shooting the falcon's eye harkens back to killing Seven Macaw, the vainglorious bird that believed he was the all-powerful god. In that case, his eye was a black mirror representing only self-reflection. The falcon is a working bird and selfless messenger of Huracán, a messenger between cosmic realms. It is noteworthy to see how involved Huracán was in this fateful process. With its big eyes, it is a far-seer and a potent hunter. The eye was also the symbol of Horus in Egypt; in Germany/Scandinavia, Wotan/Odin sacrificed an eye. Jung expanded on the theme of losing an eye:

Horus sacrificed one eye for his father. When his father, the god Ra, perceived Set in the shape of a Black pig, he had a piercing pain in one eye and became instantly blind. The mere sight of the devil, of the Black substance of the earth, was enough to put out one eye of the god. Then Horus the son sacrificed one of his own eyes to Ra, so his sight was restored, but Horus then had only one eye. Like Wotan, who sacrificed one eye to Mimir, the speaking fountainhead of the underworld—the unconscious, in other words—in return for a draft of the wisdom-giving water; and thereafter he had connection with the wisdom of the earth. (1997, 295)

The hunters used gum off the surface of the ball to bring back the falcon's sight. This gum was the same resin used as incense and was believed to represent blood and the life force.

The louse, the lowliest of creatures carrying the message, was stuck in the toad's teeth, which represented the bridge between outer and inner, important for the beginning of digestion and assimilation of not only food but, metaphorically, the world, as well.

In the process of retrieving the message, the boys punished the frog for not vomiting up the louse, crushing his backside, leaving all frogs in their seated position. Then they allotted specific food for each creature to eat from that time on.

The boys established order in the natural world as they proceeded through their lives, demonstrating that they were gods and sons of the creator deities. There were four animals in this passage: an insect, an amphibian that lived in the water, an amphibian that lived on land, and a bird. The scene covered an interesting cross section of life present at that point in the creation.

The message was a summons from below inviting the boys to be in Xibalbá in seven days to play ball with the underworld lords. Before leaving, they each planted an unripe ear of corn in the center of their grandmother's attic.

As has been discussed earlier,

The number seven has ritual significance in Maya theology. In this case, it may refer to the seven levels of earth that were believed to exist above the underworld. . . . It may also refer to the seven sacred directions of the Maya universe—the four cardinal directions plus the sky, center, and the underworld. (Christenson 2003, 159)

Seven is the number connected with the underworld jaguar war god. In many other traditions, seven refers to the dynamic perfection of a complete cycle: seven days, seven planets, seven petals on the rose, eternal life, human perfection, and so on (Chevalier and Gheerbrant 1996, 859–66). It is a very important universal number.

With the form of the house representing the cosmic conception of the universe, the maize plant in the center represents the *axis mundi*.

They told her that when the corn dries up, it will be a sign of their death, and when it flourishes, it will be a sign they are alive.

The act of planting an ear of corn reflects a ritual of renewal performed by a shaman, called father-mother in Maya culture. It was planted in the attic because that was where corn is traditionally stored. Xmucané was the great diviner-creator, watching as her grandsons clean up the complexes and prepare the world for her to step in and create humans.

The twins left on their journey taking the same road as their fathers and uncle before them. In their descent to Xibalbá, Hunahpú and Xbalanqué successfully passed rivers of pus and blood and other deadly obstacles until they came to the crossroads. This time the roads were black, white, red, and blue-green. At this time there was no yellow road but, instead, a blue-green one.

This may show that nature had become a part of the quaternity as the missing fourth and foreshadowed greater success on this journey. Yellow represents the Maya death god, Cimi. The shift from yellow to blue-green is symbolically significant. Blue-green is the color of the great water at the beginning of creation, the color of the holy quetzal feathers. It also represents the valuable stone jade and refers to what is most precious. The water god is blue-green, providing the moisture that starts the renewal process. It also represents the color at the center of the four directions where the sacred maize tree emerges.

Here Hunahpú sent a mosquito ahead of them to bite each of

the underworld lords to obtain their names. It was not really a mosquito but a hair plucked from the front of Hunahpú's knee. The insect first attacked the enthroned wooden images but then found the actual lords. As they were bitten, they cried out each other's names. In this way, the twins learned the names of all the underworld lords. From then on, mosquitoes sucked the blood of people on the roads.

These twins were much more suspicious and wily than their fathers, using tricks and their animal instincts to outsmart their enemy. In Mesoamerica, naming something is knowing it. When a thing is named, it becomes conscious and, therefore, less threatening. The process of naming gives an individual a certain power over the named thing, just as naming feelings and complexes does. Each of these gods represents an archetypal pattern that can have control over someone in the form of a complex. If one can name it, a person has a chance of saving himself or herself from it. Unlike these underworld demons that need to be named, the all-knowing, omnipotent, and omnipresent creator gods are and remain unknowable. In Maya mythology, they appear in many different ways and forms, and one cannot pin them down. Hunahpú magically created the mosquito to help. It was another parasite, like the louse, the lowliest of all creatures. An alchemical maxim states that "like cures like," and in this mythological example, the culture heroes have to fight like with like, or darkness with darkness.

The mosquito lives around stagnant water and can kill others by passing on illness. The metaphor for stagnant water is an apt one for the cultural dilemma that led to the descent into the underworld in search of renewal. To reiterate, this dilemma is the shift from the hunter-gather stage to the agricultural stage of cultural development. Parallel to this shift is the movement from the matriarchal to the patriarchal stage of psychological development with an increase in conscious awareness of and the domestication of human affects and instincts. One could say culture establishes itself with the incorporation of the super-ego, as seen in this myth. The demons are the forces that represent complexes that prevent change and the ability to lead a healthy, creative life. They keep one stuck in stagnant water. It was the twins' job to establish the proper balance between the forces in the cosmos to prepare the soil for the fourth creation.

When Xbalanqué and Hunahpú arrived at the palace of the underworld lords, they ignored the wooden statues and correctly greeted all of the death gods by name. They passed another test. When offered to sit on the bench, they refused, knowing it was a hot slab. They passed the first of a series of underworld tests. The astonished lords of Xibalbá then sent them with cigars and torches to the House of Darkness. The twins cleverly placed a red macaw feather on the torch and a firefly on the cigar to make them seem as if they were burning. At dawn the unburned torch and cigar were as new, thereby foiling the lords who were surprised and wanted to know where they came from and who gave them birth, since they seemed unique. The twins did not tell them.

Keeping the flame and light alive is a metaphor for holding on to consciousness. Using a macaw feather to do so harkened back to the lesson learned by Seven Macaw, who was killed to bring misbehaving, arrogant behavior back under control and reestablish the proper world order. In this instance, the feather was used on the torch to help maintain light and hold the powers of darkness at bay. Beyond this story but pervasive in the culture is the notion that Seven Macaw descended in death, transformed, and was reborn anew as the Principal Bird Deity, a positive force also connected to Itzamná, the old creator god not seen in the *Popol Vuh* but in the *Popol Vuh* frieze. The macaw feather foreshadowed the outcome of the twins' journey, to subdue the remnants of evil to put the world in its proper order for the creation of humans. One could say the demons represented the old order, the old gods who were relegated to the underworld as the new epoch emerged and new gods were established. The old gods became demons that do not die but fall back into the shadows. Not telling the lords their names was the opposite of tricking the lords so the twins could know their names. The twins did not give themselves away, and when they were not known, they were not controlled.

The twins then played ball with the death gods, eventually allowing themselves to be beaten. The death gods insisted on using their ball, which contained White Dagger, the knife of sacrifice,

and when the boys saw that, they complained of foul play, that the gods just wanted to sacrifice them, and threatened to leave. Instead, their rubber ball was put in play. They all agreed on a prize to the winners: four bowls of flowers, one with red petals, one with white petals, one with yellow petals, and one with whole flowers. The boys played very well but finally gave themselves up in defeat to the cheers of the Xibalbans.

The boys were led into Blade House, the second trial, where blades cut and slice. The blades were told if they did not harm the twins, from then on they would be able to cut the flesh of animals. Hearing that, they lowered their points. While passing the night, the twins called out for cutting ants to help gather flowers for the four bowls, which they did from the Xibalbans' own flower tree, behind the backs of the two bird guards stationed there. In the morning the demons were furious and punished the two guards by splitting their mouths open, and to this day the whippoorwills have a gaping mouth. The ball was dropped into play again, but it ended in a tie, so they agreed to play again the next day.

Flowers are used as offerings to the gods, and a fragrant flower was a sign of love. "White-Flower-Thing" is the word for "soul." The water lily, a frequent motif in Maya iconography, is similar to the lotus in Hindu mythology. The twins were beginning their Herculean tasks and were supported by the psyche. They knew they would eventually have to be sacrificed, as that was the task in the underworld and what was required for rebirth. Red, white, and yellow are alchemical colors reflecting development, with wholeness as the goal. The whole flower, like the alchemical golden flower, refers to the Self. According to Maya iconography, ants were industrious helpers that represented libido and carried the soul. They served nature by fertilizing plants. There is no individuality in an ant. They represented collective, community participation, working together with an attitude of humility for the sake of the whole, much as the twins strove to bring culture to a new form, domesticating the wild, disorderly nature for the benefit of the collective.

That night they faced another series of tests, but by their cunning they passed safely through the House of Knives, the House of Cold, the House of Jaguars, and the House of Fire. Finally, they were sent to the House of Bats, a room filled with fierce, knife-nosed bats. The twins hid inside their hollow blowguns for protection, but Hunahpú impatiently peeked out to see if dawn was approaching, and at that moment the killer bat Camazotz snatched off his head. One Death and Seven Death took Hunahpú's head and placed it on the ballcourt, while all the death gods rejoiced. Their victory over the twins seemed all but certain. They survived four houses in Xibalbá and got caught in the fifth.

The fifth represents the whole quintessential human. It is interesting that it was an animal, a bat that lives and hunts in the dark, that took Hunahpú's head. Losing one's head is a metaphor for falling into a complex. Bats are symbols of decapitation sacrifice in Maya mythology. It was the head and thinking that lost its power. One is taken back to the beginning of creation that began with the word and thinking. It was the thinking and perhaps sensation functions that needed to loosen so that feeling and intuition could emerge. The gods of creation tried to create a race with a heart, and it was literally the heart that was offered as sacrifice to the gods. Their names meant "calabash" and referred to the day of death in the Maya calendar. Hunahpú made the mistake of being impatient, and that is when the demon would strike, when one emerges too soon from sitting patiently in the dark place, trying to speed life's natural course. This mistake was a necessary part of the process because it set fate on its course. Pushing decisions ahead for one's own sake moves one up into one's head and disconnects from the natural instinct and humility of the body. Splitting away from the head indicates that Hunahpú was not quite conscious enough; instead, he gave way for the complex to take over. At this time, it is apparent that he still had some work to do; he was not quite ready to bring on the dawn. The knives are instruments of differentiation, and that is precisely the process that the twins and the cosmos were undergoing. Both blowguns and knives were used as weapons, but the difference was that knives were used at a close distance with much more of a relationship to the victim. They also released a larger quantity of blood, or life substance, which was what the demons ate for sustenance and what was to be offered to the gods for renewal.

However, in the late predawn hours, Xbalanqué, in his shame, had an idea and summoned all the animals to help by bringing their various foods. After much food arrived, the coati (similar to a raccoon) arrived with a large squash, and Xbalanqué placed it on the severed neck of Hunahpú like a new head. Magically, the squash took the form of Hunahpú's features, and he could see and speak, conferring with the others in council about what to do next. "His brains came from the thinker, from the sky as it was the Heart of Sky, Huracán who came down" (D. Tedlock 1985, 145). The sky god, Huracán, himself intervened to help form the new calabash head that was only able to speak, and by this time, it was beginning to dawn. The opossum, called Grandfather, was told to blacken the sky with soot to prevent the dawn, which he did four times. The sky turned red, then blue, when it began its being.

Huracán represents the Self as it oversees the individuation process and the development of culture. At dawn, the twins appeared together at the underworld ballcourt as if nothing had happened, even though Hunahpú had lost his head, much like his father. But they were clever and had the Self overseeing the process of this necessary mortification, dying and coming back to life, mirroring the creations of the world itself. The opossum was the old god, who was the darkness just before the dawn. He was connected to Xpiyacoc, also called Hunahpú Opossum. Old Man Opossum was associated with the dawn at the beginning of the planting season. The opossum presided over the five days at the end of the year, the Uayeb or unlucky days, but in the *Popol Vuh* he did not oversee the end of the year but the new sun. The coati is associated with the feminine, the Grandmother deity. Coatis are associated with gourds (Christenson 2003, 173).

The death gods began the game by throwing out the real head of Hunahpú to serve as the new ball. Xbalanqué struck the head so hard that it bounced out of the court and into the oaks or into the tomatoes, depending on the translation. A rabbit, previously told to wait in the trees, immediately bounded away, confusing

the death gods who mistook it for the ball. It was still dark. While their attention was distracted, Xbalanqué retrieved Hunahpú's real head and placed it back on his body. When the death gods returned, the twins threw the squash into the court as the sky was trying to dawn and reddening along the horizon. "The squash was punted by Xbalanqué, the squash was wearing out; it fell on the court, bringing to light its light-colored seeds, as plain as day right in front of them" (D. Tedlock 1985, 147). Thus, the confused and astonished death gods were defeated in their underworld court of sacrifice.

With their defeat, light-colored seeds brought forth for the first time the possibility of renewal, bringing the seed of light to the unconscious. Seeds are related to the dawn. With this, however, comes great danger. Seeds are connected to bones. The seed as the newborn child is what the psyche always tries to kill because an increase in consciousness, or the new life, is always a defeat for the unconscious. It is a time to carefully protect the new possibility. The rabbit is a symbol of fertility connected to the moon in mythologies the world over, reflecting the recurring cycle of darkness and light, ebbing and waning. Rabbits are associated with endless regeneration, sexuality, the Great Mother, and the eternal. While valued as hunting game, they are the playmate of the Moon Goddess and serve the gods. They are also sometimes depicted as a scribe containing wisdom in Maya iconography. The home of the Moon Goddess and rabbit was the moon, conceived in the underworld, in a wet environment like a cave. For this reason, the rabbit has the water lily pattern on its ear. On the opposite pole, as the dark moon, rabbits are known to be tricksters prone to drunkenness and lewdness. Just as the corn seeds needed to be planted at just the right time and not before to ensure a bountiful crop, the transformations and movement toward the dawn were perfectly timed.

Although Xbalanqué and Hunahpú were victorious, they knew that the death gods would not rest until they were killed. They knew it was time for them to die. The lords of Xibalbá constructed a great fiery oven and invited the twins, along with them, to jump over it four times. However, the twins consulted two knowers-seers, named Descended and Ascended, and were told what travails would come next and how to survive them (Christenson 2003, 177). In their names, these seers personified the process the twins were undergoing that is similar in many ways to alchemy:

> The first descent comes within the story of the Creation and is therefore left out of the account by most alchemists. Accordingly, they begin their work with the ascent and complete it with the descent, whose purpose is to reunite the freed soul (the *aqua permanens*) with the dead (purified) body, thus bringing the *filius* to birth. (Jung 1976, 339n313)

Everything was planned for them to die and come back to life and what was to happen to their bones. Knowing that the death gods only wanted their deaths, the twins bravely jumped into the pit and died. The gods of Xibalbá then ground their charred bones and cast them into the river rather than scatter them in a canyon or hang them in the top of a tree. The bones did not drift away but instead settled to the bottom, and in five days the twins reappeared as catfish-men.

The twins first had to descend before they could ascend in renewal. After the fire pit was crossed over four times, as if in a game, they jumped into the fire voluntarily. Here for the first time they consciously sacrificed themselves. They knew that this sacrifice was necessary if they were to win the ultimate goal. They had gone from unconscious sacrifice to conscious sacrifice; in other words, they were now working in relationship with the psyche, no longer the victims of it. This experience of burning up is similar to the alchemical *calcinatio*. In the Aztec creation myth, the gods jumped into the fire to start the sun on its daily journey across the sky:

> It is a symbol, which expresses on the one side utter destruction, a complete upheaval and disintegration, and on the other side a marvelous display of color and light; and on the primitive level, also the apparition of the divine. (Jung 1997, 30)

The bones were ground up and thrown into the river. They moved from *mortificatio* to *solutio* and were completely washed and remade from the water of life in the river in five days. They then emerged as fish, which is a symbol of the Self and of Christ, according to Jung (1978) in his book *Aion*. They were charged with the powers and wisdom of the depth. Fish are aquatic creatures, eaten as food, and may be connected to the water gods and rain making. Catfish referred to fishing rituals that existed throughout America of throwing bones into the river to bring forth more fish. A pervasive fish motif is fish-nibbling-on-water-lily-flowers.

The twins reappeared after five days. The number 5 refers to the *quintessencia*, the fifth essence or integrative element leading to wholeness. It denotes the whole person with limbs outstretched and the heart center, similar to the *axis mundi* uniting the sky, earth, and underworld, the five colors and senses. For the Maya it was a symbol of perfection, with the fifth day belonging to the earth gods. The central fifth in the cross represents the awakening of consciousness, solar fire as well as the fire of the underworld, when the sun is in the sky and then descends below the horizon. For the Maya, five refers to the month of Uayeb, or the five ill-fated days at the end of the calendar round, just before the arrival of the New Year. Quetzalcoatl remained four days in the underworld and was reborn on the fifth day. For the Aztec there have been five creations of the world. While five refers to the whole person, the concept of grinding up the bones and throwing them away refers to a complete end to the person. This is a description of what is experienced before renewal, what happens before transformation:

> The integration or humanization of the self is initiated from the conscious side by our making ourselves aware of our selfish aims; we examine our motives and try to form as complete and objective a picture as possible of our own nature. It is an act of self-recollection, a gathering together of what is scattered, of all the things in us that have never been properly related, and a coming to terms with oneself with a view to achieving full consciousness. (Jung 1989a, 263)

The knowers-seers were shamans who made this journey and knew the way. Their council gave wisdom and courage to the twins. Here the twins underwent a final initiation where they were killed and re-born. The entire journey for them was a shamanic initiation:

> [One] has to remain down in the dark, in that very
> comprehensible fear, until [one] can stand it. Usually such
> states of panic or great emotion last, or repeat themselves, as
> long as one cannot stand them. When one can stand them,
> they are overcome; if one can tolerate such a condition and
> remain quiet, it vanishes. It is as if one had taken the energy
> out of the emotional form and transformed it into a sort of
> consciousness. (Jung 1997, 426)

The following day they returned to Xibalbá disguised in rags as poor vagabonds or orphans able to perform magic. They burned down a house and immediately re-created it.

They first appeared as fish, then transformed into vagabonds, changing from the image of the Self (fish) to the rejected, despised, *prima materia*, or children without parents. This representation was the opposite of their glory but instead was their shadow side, which had to be included for the sake of wholeness. This is how the *deus absconditus*, the hidden god, synonymous with Mercurius, the alchemical agent of change, often appears. It is the force that offered the summons to the descent:

> When the libido is withdrawn from external objects and sinks
> into the unconscious, the soul is born again in God. This
> state, as he rightly observes, is not a blissful one, because it is a
> negative act, a turning away from life and a descent to the *deus
> absconditus*, who possesses qualities very different from those of
> the god who shines by day. (Jung 1976, 253)

In myths, gods frequently appeared as beggars when they come to earth. Wotan appeared as a vagabond wearing a hat low over his eyes, and Zeus and Hermes appeared at Philemon and Baucis's hut as poor hungry beggars. Buddha left his privileged life to become an ascetic beggar. Jesus was born into humble circumstances.

Hearing of their wonderful dances, a dance in honor of the cre-ator god, the twins were told to sacrifice a dog and then bring it

back to life. This they did, following which they sacrificed a man
and also brought him back to life. Xbalanqué then decapitated
Hunahpú and tore out his heart, only to restore him once again.
The principal death gods, One Death and Seven Death, were
overjoyed and ecstatic at this miraculous dance and, in the throes
of their enthusiasm, they asked to be killed. The twins performed
heart sacrifice on One Death and then grabbed Seven Death, but
they did not revive them:

> As soon as they had killed the one lord without bringing him
> back to life, the other lord had been meek and tearful before
> the dancers. He didn't consent, he didn't accept it: "Take pity
> on me!" he said when he realized. All their vassals took the
> road to the great canyon, in one single mass they filled up the
> deep abyss. . . . They all bent low in surrender, they arrived
> meek and tearful. Such was the defeat of Xibalbá. The boys
> accomplished it only through wonders, only through self-
> transformation. (D. Tedlock 1985, 154–55)

The Xibalbans fled into the canyon to hide, crammed together.
Then the ants came as if herded there and the Xibalbans gave
themselves up. This defeat was accomplished by the boys only
through their self-transformation.

The demon's power was limited while the twins emerged reborn
without a past or parents. They were now truly heroes who had integrated their shadow sides and complexes. The story itself said the
twins accomplished their task, vanquishing the gods of the underworld through self-transformation, containing the shadow and complexes that previously had free rein. Only through their suffering and
newly developed relationship to the opposites could they find success. Death is defeated by one's complete acceptance of it as a natural
process. By doing so, one is transformed.

It was through trickery, cunning, and help from the psyche from
having integrated shadow that the twins completely vanquished the
evil kingdom of Xibalbá. Hunahpú had been sacrificed three times.
Their songs and dances referred to the ritual dances common in
their culture as a way of honoring their gods. The dog was a frequent

sacrificial victim. It was domesticated as a household and hunting animal, and it was also fattened to eat. "Maya mythology includes a being with dog-like features whose task was to guard the entrance to Xibalbá, the realm of the afterlife, much like Cerberus, the dog of Greek mythology" (Longhena 1999, 161). It was appropriate that ants showed up again to herd the demons with their out-of-control behavior into a collective corner, tamed and contained, setting the stage for the beginning of an established culture with limitations and acceptable modes of behavior. For the individual, it is imperative to establish a resilient ego that is able to withstand the force of the complexes desiring to take charge and push the ego into the background. This substantial ego complex acts as the gatekeeper to the unconscious:

> The identity of the model ego figures in youth and of what we normally call figures of the Self in mythology indicate that the impulse which mainly builds up the ego is that center which in later life we call the Self. In the first half of life it acts as a force which builds up the ego. (von Franz 1972, 108)

When the boys went to retrieve them in their newly humbled state, they revealed their names and the names of their fathers. They suffered because of them. The twins said, "We are here to clear the road of the torments and troubles of our fathers. And so we have suffered all the troubles you've caused us. And now we are putting an end to all of you" (D. Tedlock 1985, 155-57).

"To clear the road of the torments and troubles of our fathers" referred to resolving cultural collective complexes (Singer and Kimbles 2004). "This fulfills the prophecy of Blood Woman, in which she declared that the lords of Xibalbá would no longer be allowed to receive human hearts in sacrifice but rather would have to accept the red sap of the croton tree" (Christenson 2003, 187). Previously the death gods received the fresh blood from accidents and illnesses on earth; now they would only receive the dirty blood that dripped down from above. The Maya gods, on the other hand, received the fresh, clean sacrificial blood. It was only then that the twins revealed their names, when it was safe to do so and they were in control. The twins first killed the vainglorious Macaw, and now evil itself, which was represented by complexes and the split opposites, or the black and white viewpoint of unconsciousness. They brought in consciousness as the dawning light of the gods they are, the sun and moon. **The Xibalbans begged for mercy and told them where their father and uncle were buried. The twins then agreed to spare the people of Xibalbá but told them that they would never again be powerful, as stated clearly in the quote and poem that follows: "All of you listen, you Xibalbans: because of this, your day and your descendants will not be great. Moreover, the gifts you receive will no longer be great. . . . Such was the beginning of their disappearance and the denial of their worship":**

> Their ancient day was not a great one,
> These ancient people only wanted conflict,
> Their ancient names are not really divine,
> But fearful is the ancient evil of their faces.
>
> They are makers of enemies, users of owls,
> They are inciters to wrongs and violence,
> They are masters of hidden intentions as well,
> They are black and white,
> Masters of stupidity, masters of perplexity,
> As it is said, by putting on appearances they cause dismay.
> (D. Tedlock 1985, 158)

This is a good description of shadow that attacks from within as well as outwardly in the form of projection. It also reflects the face of the old, worn-out god that is passed over by a new god and a new stage in cultural development. The demons are described as having "left faces," meaning crazy or insane (Christenson 2003, 188n441). This is also related to violence or harm.

During this time, the grandmother was praying and calling out in front of the corn ears that were dying and coming back to life. She was beside herself with confusion and grief and joy as she named the corn "Middle of the House, Middle of the Harvest, Living Corn, and Earthen Floor" (D. Tedlock 1985, 185).
Xmucané was the goddess of fertility and the seasons, while her

weeping may be the rain that fertilized the ground and maize stocks (Christenson 2003, 188). The corn now took on the name Middle, showing that the twins found the middle way, carrying the opposites between the upper and lower worlds, between black and white. They represent the transcendent function in this myth. The middle realm was the earth, where a new humanity could be created to reside.

The twins then spoke to the remains of their uncle at the place of the ballcourt; then they put Seven Hunahpú back together again and asked him to name his body parts. He could do very little and only named his mouth, nothing else, so they had to leave him at the Place of the Ball Game Sacrifice. They reassured him that he would continue to be respected and worshipped: "You will be the first to have your day kept by those who will be born in the light, begotten in the light" (D. Tedlock 1985, 159). Thus, their deaths were avenged. Hunahpú and Xbalanqué then rose into the heavens:

> And then the two boys ascended this way, here into the middle of the light, and they ascended straight on into the sky, and the sun belongs to one and the moon to the other. When it became light within the sky, on the face of the earth, they were there in the sky. (159–60)

The four hundred boys killed by the giant Zipacna ascended to become the Pleiades.

Seven Hunahpú could not *name* all his body parts. He named only his mouth on his skull and nothing else. He was left there to be worshipped; the day that was dedicated to the worship of the ancestors is called Hunahpú. Not being able to name the parts of his body above or below the mouth indicated that he had no connection to his head or body. When one cannot name all the parts of oneself, one remains fragmented into many pieces and quite unconscious of the whole. Psychologically, this is the work of analysis, to be able to name and know as many parts of oneself as possible, to bring what one can from the unconscious into consciousness. The process involves bringing personal as well as collective material over the threshold into consciousness to expand one's ego and awareness, while containing the dark impulses that invariably have an influence while they remain hidden. Seven Hunahpú remained undeveloped and unconscious of his wholeness. Seven represents the jaguar god, the divinity of the lower realm with the symbol of night. He is an old god who belongs in the lower ground, representing the preconscious attitude. He was left in the sacred ground at the ballcourt while his nephews brought in the light of consciousness and rose into the sky as the sun (Hunahpú) and full moon (Xbalanqué). His brother One Hunahpú was not discussed here, but there are other myths dealing with his transformation. As the calabash head in the fork of the tree of life, it rose up to become the Primary Maize God, which was another aspect of the creator god. Hunahpú was worshipped on the calendar day of his name in memory of the ancestors.

THE CREATION OF HUMANITY

After the underworld demons that threaten the order of the world were vanquished, the myth continued to describe the beginning of the creation of humanity that took place after the sun, moon, and stars ascended into the sky but remained dim until the actual dawning. The creator gods reconvened again and pondered together in the darkness about their next creation attempt. Four animals discovered yellow and white maize: the fox and coyote, and the parrot and raven, in two holy mountains called Broken Place and Bitter Water. They used this as the important essence to create humans. Maize became the flesh of humanity, while water became the blood. She Who Has Borne Children and He Who Has Begotten Sons ground the maize nine times to form the first mother-fathers. These people of corn possessed great knowledge and understanding and correctly gave thanks to their creators. However, Heart of Sky and Heart of Earth were troubled because these corn men saw everything clearly, through earth and sky to the limits of the universe. The gods were not pleased with this, so they diminished their knowledge and blurred the vision of the first people so that they could see clearly only what is near.

The predawn time was still about the mythic heroes in combat with demons and the negative energies that prevent the balanced creation of humanity. With the creation of the first humans and the coming of the dawn, the myth moved into human or historical time. Two sets of parallel animals found the maize in two mountains, again illustrating doubling:

> The fox and coyote are cunning nocturnal animals that the K'iche' associate with discovering and digging up hidden or secret things. The bright blue/green parakeet may be connected with the blue sky of the day as well as the living maize. The black raven, in contrast, represents the darkness of night and the interior of the earth where the maize seed is planted, germinates, and first begins to grow. (Christenson 2003, 193)

The maize was found by two sets of animals, one set from the earth and one from the sky. The combination of the raven and coyote is a common couple seen in the creation stories of many Native American mythologies. Coyote and fox are tricksters: "Coyote is both creator and destroyer, a shapeshifting character whose seemingly random actions and pranks have unforeseen consequences" (Ronnberg and Martin 2010, 276). Fox is also a wily trickster and thief:

> Called "son of the earth" by the Incas, the fox's ability to hear through the earth about far-off events made him a diviner-curer, just as the fox-guide's subterranean knowledge led North American and Siberian shamans through paths not ordinarily open or visible to humans. (278)

The raven and parrot represent the dark and colorful sacred spirit. The raven is helpful and destructive, wise and wily. They are thieves like their animal counterparts:

> Consider the progenitor and shaman Raven, who brings humans into being by coaxing them out of their (clam) shell, steals daylight for them through trickery or by opposing the falcon of night, brings them fire and water, teaches them how to sow seed

and to hunt—and then plays with his creatures and occasionally eats them. (248)

The parrot is the colorful bird that is similar in many ways to the raven. It talks, imitates, and plays tricks. The four animals that entered the two mountains were similar in their independence and trickery and in bridging the underworld with earth and sky. It was the use of trickery and magic, instinct and intelligence that allowed the hero twins to succeed in vanquishing the vainglorious Macaw, their arrogant and envious half brothers, and the underworld demons. These four animals had these qualities too. They entered into Broken Place and Bitter Water, the place of shadow, where the yellow and white corn was found. Broken Place and Bitter Water may refer to the brackish water of the sea before creation that laid stagnant and out of which the first mountains emerged (Christenson 2003, 193). Maize is found in the place that is not perfect but full of the darker emotions, perhaps reflecting experience in the combination of gods and demons:

> Yellow is associated with the south, misfortune, death, and the dry season. . . . White is associated with the north, new life, and the rainy season. This passage . . . may refer to the inauguration of the agricultural cycle of harvest and new growth. (193)

Yet yellowness also refers to abundance, richness, health, and fatness (195).

Psychologically, it is the birth of the new life that emerges into the cycle of birth, death, and rebirth, replicating the process the hero twins experienced in their journey. Humans will contain the opposites yellow and white, feminine and masculine, life and death, nature and spirit. The darker elements have been introduced by the gods and become part of the very nature of humans. The broken place is a cleft between two pieces or a place that has experienced some sort of trauma. To break in two is to differentiate out of the original wholeness. "Bitter" refers to affects, such as the feelings of sadness, anger, shame, and envy. These are important human responses that make up the *prima materia* of the analytical work. They are the affects that will destroy a culture. They are present and, therefore, need to be carried consciously for a healthy whole to emerge, both individually and collectively. Here in this creation, they are added to the mix at the moment of creation; bitter water is mixed with maize. The water became blood while maize became flesh. The maize was ground nine times by Xmucané, She Who Has Borne Children, and it is the first time she acts without her consort, Xpiyacoc, thus, emphasizing the feminine ability to give life. Nine carries great ritual significance for the Maya, being the number of months or moons for gestation.

There are nine levels to the underworld. It is considered to be a magic number in medicine and witchcraft (Longhena 1999, 76). The first four men were brought into existence by means of the word, just as the earth was revealed through the lightning-like emergence of the word in the beginning of the myth.

The creator gods made humans with all their wisdom and vision. They knew everything and could see everything. This disturbed the gods because they were concerned that humans would not reproduce or work and honor them. Through their council, the gods agreed that the mirror of humans' clear vision would be clouded with breath so their vision and knowledge would be limited to what is directly in front of their faces. The gods take back the clear vision, leaving humans to struggle to regain clarity.

The *Popol Vuh* itself was thought to be an instrument of clarity, and the K'iche' believed they carried within their blood the potential for this divine sight. If consulted, the *Book of Council* would offer the individual and culture the knowledge of the cosmos and the gods. Similar themes of reducing clarity are present in Gnosticism and in the Kabbalah. In Christianity the expulsion from the Garden of Eden removed humanity's clear connection to God, and the confusion created by changing language at the tower of Babel prevented the people of the Old Testament from achieving equality with God. In psychological terms, regaining clarity means becoming conscious of one's shadow and complexes through the individuation process. The ego is strengthened through the collision with the outer world and its challenges and responses. Further, one establishes an ego-Self axis, which leads to maintaining a constant relationship to the Self, in other words, to a spiritual life that requires the correct attitude of honor and respect toward the ineffable, unknowable source of creation, destruction, and wisdom. Yet experience of absolute clarity returns fleetingly when, as synchronicity, the archetypal energies break through into reality, demonstrating the unification of psyche and matter. In mythological terms it is a reconnection to what was lost during the creation. It seems amazing that the same instinct and desire for knowledge, unfolding in this creation myth in a pattern described by Jung as the individuation process, appears in this remote culture, away from the influence of the rest of the world, where similar creation myths were also expressed. It is a clear example of the reality and autonomy of the psyche.

The creators then supplied the first men with four beautiful wives to be their companions. In the dark, each group set out in a different direction while fasting and seeking the dawn. Along the way they found their gods. At the appearance of the morning star they offered incense, and the sun appeared. At this moment the gods were turned to stone along with the images of the powerful animals such as the puma, jaguar, and rattlesnake. Ever since the first dawn, this is how these images have been seen.

Even though the first men were male, they were referred to as "our first mothers and fathers" (Christenson 2003, 196). The four wives are not made from the men but were made in their own right to be companions. Marriage was thought to be essential to the Maya. Only a married man was considered whole. Just as the creator gods, Xmucané and Xpiyacoc, acted in concert, the priests were called mother-father. This represents a significant stage in the individuation process when these opposites—mother and father or masculine and feminine—are held together in consciousness.

Three family lines scattered to the four corners of the earth to find their gods and then went east, where they awaited the dawn. (The fourth family line did not have children.) Venus, as the morning star, announced the dawn and the sun rose. The heat and light from the sun dried out the earth and turned the gods to stones. It would seem the gods were now fixed in the minds of the humans, able to be carried within. For it was said the gods now spoke to the humans in their dreams and to their hearts, while they were carried literally as precious stones. For the individual, this may indicate the birth of the observing ego that now listens to and can reflect on the messages from the unconscious. For the actual gods, they became imagos or archetypes. This is the goal of alchemy and analytical psychology, that the Self or god-image be carried consciously within as the living stone, the *lapis philosophorum*, of alchemy. Von Franz added to this conception: "The Philosopher's stone was also thought of as being a divine child born out of the art of alchemy, using the simile of death and resurrection" (1972, 229).

"Five hundred and forty-two days later, the Maize Gods completed the structure of this, the Fourth Creation, by setting up the four sides and corners of the cosmos and erecting the center tree. The Maya called this tree *Wakah-Kan*, or 'Raised-up-Sky'" (Schele and Mathews 1998, 37). This tree has been called the *axis mundi* or tree of life in other mythologies.

With the birth of the Maize Gods, agriculture took center stage and culture moved into a solar, patriarchal phase, although the matriarchal influence remained just under the surface; masculine and feminine remained conjoined in its wholeness. Human life could be sustained in a predictable way through agriculture, and culture could develop. Yet it was through sacrifice and blood offerings, important for ongoing life and consciousness, that the relationship between humans and the gods was maintained. "The ancient Maya offered their blood. . . . They returned a portion of their life force to the powers of the cosmos" (Christenson 2003, 202).

This is the end of the story but not the end of the cycle, as that will go on long after when this world comes to an end and another is thought, or perhaps this time, felt, into existence as the burden of time passes from one god to the next.

CONCLUDING THOUGHTS

The *Popol Vuh* creation myth appears to be an extraverted expression of the same introverted process seen in alchemy and the individuation process as a "constant rhythm of successive creation and destruction" (von Franz 1972, 221). The goal of the inner process is to build up the immortal part of the personality and, for the culture, to build up its relationship with god. For the individual, this is the Self; for the creation myth, it is the tree of life, or the *anima mundi*. For the culture, it is a further step in consciousness and cultural development. The movement is circular and cycles through the four elements, earth, air, fire, and water, corresponding to the four colors, black, white, yellow, red with the further addition of blue-green. These were important elements in the *Popol Vuh* myth. The pattern of the flow in individuation as well as in alchemy is the reverse of what is seen in creation myths, however. In creation myths, culture is being built up, moving from above down, while for individual development the movement is from below up. To clarify this thought: a person's life energy circles from unconsciousness to consciousness, from below to above, and then circles back down into the body. In creation myths the energy moves from the all-knowing oneness, union of opposites to fall into opposites and then into unconsciousness, the body, and finally back to consciousness. The goal for both, however, is the same, the *coniunctio* or union of opposites with the development of what is called by the alchemists the philosopher's stone, glorified, or diamond body. This is the relationship to one's inner Self or the divine nature. It is the creation of the immortal body, resurrected from the mortal body and is "no longer submitted to the decay of this world" (von Franz 1972, 230).

In the *Popol Vuh*, out of the first thought or spark of imagination came aborted attempts at creation, leading finally to human life and shared, mutual experience. Much of the drama in the myth expresses taming the archaic and unconscious elements expressed first by the clay and wood figures, the vainglorious Macaw, then the monkey twins, and finally the gods in the underworld. The myth resolves itself with the development from father to son, to the successful hero who embodies spirit and instinct and the final resurrection into the sun, moon, and tree of life—the vegetative symbol of life—the *anima mundi*, the world soul. Although one cannot say that this is an example of an individuation process, as it is not personal but collective, it is nevertheless a template on a macrocosmic level of what is experienced in each individual's microcosmic journey. The twins in the myth and as metaphor in the individuation process must come to consciousness for the creation to be sustained. The purpose of life is to pay respect and make offerings to the gods, in other words, to not forget them. These gods are the archetypes that affect our daily lives. Creation myths are a reminder to all of us of what must be done to maintain the healthy balance between ourselves and the many levels of the cosmos.

CHAPTER 7
COMPARATIVE THEMES

To examine a thin slice of what has come to all through the mythical voice, four themes from the amplified section of the *Popol Vuh* were compared to similar themes in other myths from around the world. It was not necessary to go into great detail describing the other myths because there is so much already written on this subject (Austin 1993; Campbell 1973, 1982a, 1988a, 1988b, 1988c, 1989a, 1989b, 1991a, 1991b; Eliade 1991a, 1991b; Fernández-Armesto 2004; Frazer 1963; Hollis 1995; Jung 1967, 1977a, 1977b, 1984, 1997; Leeming and Leeming 1994; Neumann 1970; van der Leeuw 1963; von Franz 1972). The intention was to point out cross-cultural similarities with the *Popol Vuh*. The comparison demonstrated hermeneutically the similarity in emanations from the psyche of humans without regard for the disparate cultures and geographical locations from which they arose. This lends strength to an argument in favor of the reality of the collective unconscious. It also places the *Popol Vuh* in its correct position as a significant creation myth in the archive of world mythology.

Of the many themes possible, I limit this discussion to the twin motif, sacrifice, immaculate conception, and combat. There were many other significant motifs, but they were not selected because they were more prominent in the earlier or later parts of the myth, for example, in the themes of creation from thought or word, failed creations, and loss of clear vision. The theme of the hero's journey was touched on in an earlier chapter, and it is certainly also pertinent to the *Popol Vuh*.

THE THEME OF TWINS
This was, of course, a main theme in the *Popol Vuh*. The idea of twinning emerged very early with the initial differentiation of the gods into opposites. As the one splits into two, different aspects of the whole begin to be seen. Von Franz stated, "This duality of psychological contents is a general archetypal theme" (1972, 77). The twoness is

a differentiation out of the original chaos so dialogue can take place along with a beginning consciousness of the aspects of the archetype. This is relevant for the culture as well as for the individual. In this myth, these aspects tend to be more complementary than conflicted: in other words, they are different aspects but not opposed, as is often the case with other twin motifs from other cultures. In this myth, the original parents, being archetypes of wholeness, split into twos yet represent four aspects each. These were Heart of Sky and Heart of Earth. They, in turn, gave creation to a perhaps earlier, elderly husband and wife, Xpiyacoc and Xmucané, the first generation of creator gods also called the Grandfather and Grandmother, the divine matchmaker and midwife, or He Who Has Begotten Sons and She Who Has Borne Children, Blue-Green Plate and Blue-Green Bowl. They were diviners and gave birth, although it is not explicit how, to the first set of hero twins, One Hunahpú and Seven Hunahpú. One Hunahpú married, and that couple gave birth to One Chouen and One Batz, the monkey twins. Later One Hunahpú's head impregnated Blood Woman, who gave birth to the second set of hero twins, Hunahpú and Xbalanqué.

The elder set of hero twins were father and uncle, while the second set were brothers, although Xbalanqué contained elements of the feminine, the "X" in his name, and became the moon that was considered feminine. These twins were not antagonistic but were complements of each other. Just as it is important for individuals to become aware of their darker shadow elements, there are light aspects to shadow also that need to become conscious. These twins worked together and looked after each other, seemingly as one archetype. Evil was projected out onto other figures that they fought. The first set of twins failed, but the second set of twins succeeded in their task. One could say the second set was a more differentiated form of the first set. Or all sets of twins may have been emanations of the creator gods in their various forms. There are other antagonistic twins in Maya mythology, the paddler twins, for example.

A set of gods from central Mexico, Quetzalcoatl and Tezcatlipoca, represented the light and dark sides of the primary archetype. In their journey through the underworld as seen in the Codex Borgia, they were twins (Miller and Taube 1993, 175). They were antagonistic to each other, representing creation and destruction. Quetzalcoatl, as the plumed serpent and god of wind, was inspiration connected to water and also a culture hero in his human form. There are similar serpent deities elsewhere. A serpent deity in Maya is called Kukulkan; in Hopi, Palulukong; in Zuni, Kolowisi. Tezcatlipoca, on the other hand, was called smoking mirror and was a god of the earth, where Quetzalcoatl was god of wind. Tezcatlipoca was the embodiment of change through conflict, a proponent of human sacrifice, while Quetzalcoatl was not and instead was a culture hero.

"The motif of the hostile twin brothers belongs to the symbolism of the Great Mother. It appears when the male attains self-consciousness by dividing himself into two opposing elements, one destructive and the other creative" (Neumann 1970, 97). This same motif of the twins appears in the Bible's Genesis story of Cain and Abel, the two sons of Adam and Eve. Cain was a crop farmer while Abel was a shepherd. Cain killed Abel, so this clearly was an antagonistic twinship, although in this regard it is similar to the Hunahpú and Xbalanqué pair struggling against their monkey twin brothers. Both these myths seem to reflect a shift from matriarchal to patriarchal states in cultural development, from laziness to hard work reflected in the playfulness of the monkeys and easy workload of the shepherd. Both the hero twins and Cain cultivated the crops to bring in food. Jacob and Esau are another set of antagonistic biblical twins. Their antagonism had to do with stealing the birthright, and it could be said that Christ and Satan and Christ and Judas were brothers in opposition: one good, the other evil.

In Egypt, the creator gods Shu and Tefnut produced a second set of twins, Nut and Geb. Nut was the sky while Geb was the earth. They had two sets of twins, Osiris and Isis, and Set and Nephthys. Osiris and Set were hostile brothers. In a Seneca creation myth, one brother was a competent creator while the other was incompetent and resentful (Campbell 1988b, 208). In a Huron creation myth, sky woman is pregnant with twin boys, one evil and one good. The evil one refused to be born properly and broke through the side, killing his mother, then eventually killing his brother. In the end he made a place for the good dead in the west (Leeming and Leeming 1994, 130–31).

Von Franz (1972) included many other friendly twins, for example, the North American myth from the Ojibwe, part of the Algonquin tribes, that has twin gods on earth who do the creating with the high god behind them unseen. The earth gods are named Mennebosh and the Otter (66). There are friendly twin heroes in the Watunna creation cycle from the Upper Orinoco (Campbell 1989b, 332). In Babylonia, Gilgamesh had his shadow brother and friend Enkidu, and the Greek hero Heracles had a twin brother named Iphicles. Apollo and Artemis were brother and sister opposites. Prometheus and Epimetheus represented forethought and afterthought; Krishna and Arjuna were friends but more mentor-student. Other friendly twins were Castor and Pollux, Helen and Clytemnestra, Faust and Mephistopheles, Dante and Virgil, and the Navajo monster slayer twins, Monster Slayer and Child of the Water. "The principle of opposites which formerly divided the hostile brothers has now become the principle of brotherhood. . . . In every case the man-to-man relationship strengthens consciousness and invigorates the ego principle" (Neumann 1970, 181).

THE THEME OF SACRIFICE

Sacrifice includes what comes from oneself or from another. It is giving something up, making an offering or a ritual killing. It is either propitiatory or activating quid pro quo. Common practice in Maya culture was ritual self-sacrifice where women and men, mostly nobility, would draw ropes with magucy spines on them through perforations in their tongues, earlobes, upper arms, or penises to draw blood. Paper sheets would capture the blood, which would then be burned as blood offerings to the gods. Excruciatingly painful as these self-torture episodes must have been, it was not uncommon for the person to fall into an ecstatic state and be taken over by the Vision Serpent bringing in the words of the ancestors or gods. Both self-sacrifice and ritual sacrifice of another allowed the precious blood to be returned back to the realm of the gods to nourish and enliven them. Life was a reciprocal relationship between gods and humans.

Captives were also sacrificed for various rituals and offerings to the gods.

Psychologically, sacrifice is necessary for the development of maturity, and it keeps one in proper relationship to the gods, or the archetypal forces:

> The eternal return is part of the cycle of sacrifice (*sacre + facere*, to make sacred), bringing new life through death, plowing under that life might burst forth anew. . . . The killing necessary for life is thus rendered sacred because it is not random or gratuitous; it is part of a larger pattern. (Hollis 1995, 55)

In the *Popol Vuh* the gods themselves laid out the template through an example of what behavior they expected from humans, to be honored and respected through continual ritual sacrifice. The first three worlds and their creations were sacrificed because they were not considered adequate or capable of honoring the gods. The vainglorious Macaw and his two monster sons were destroyed or sacrificed. In the amplified chapter, the elder twins, One Hunahpú and Seven Hunahpú, were sacrificed for failing in the underworld, and later on in the story, so were the hero twins, Hunahpú and Xbalanqué. They died a number of times before reemerging and beginning the process of creation of the fourth world and humans. Hunahpú had his head sliced off by the bat, and the boys voluntarily jumped into the fire, died, and returned to use magic on the demons. For demonstration purposes, Hunahpú was sacrificed, yet again. The various sacrifices resulted in greater power and consciousness, strengthening of the ego, and the ultimate vanquishing of the demons, or complexes.

In the Aztec creation myth, as discussed earlier, the gods pondered together how to establish the sun and moon in the sky and who would be the new gods to light the sky. Two gods volunteered for the task. They had to jump into a large sacrificial pyre to immolate themselves and be transformed into the sun and moon. One god, Tecuciztecatl, was dressed in all the finest clothes, carrying a costly bundle, while the other, Nanahuatzin, was simple and ordinary, old and syphilitic, and his bundle was made of reeds and maguey spines with his own blood. The wealthy god was asked by the gods to jump first, to become the sun. He ran toward the pyre but wavered and backed off. Four times he tried without success. Then the gods asked the Nanahuatzin to jump, and he ran straightaway into the pyre, becoming the sun in the sky. Seeing him jump, the Tecuciztecatl jumped as well and died, becoming the moon. The gods were pleased except they worried that the moon was as bright as the sun, which should not be, so one of the gods threw a rabbit into the face of the moon to dim it. Then when the sun and moon wavered in the sky, not moving because the new sun, Tonatiuh, demanded the blood of the other gods, Quetzalcoatl insisted that all the rest of the gods be sacrificed to get the sun to move across the horizon. He cut the heart out of each of the gods with a sacrificial blade and placed them in sacred bundles for humans to worship. In this way the fifth sun, Nahui Ollin, the sun of motion, was created (Taube 1993, 43–44).

In another Aztec myth depicting the birth of the war god, Huitzilopochtli, his evil sister, Coyolxauhqui, was sacrificed by him at his birth along with most of his stepbrothers. This is commonly seen as the myth of how the sun fights with the night and wins, killing the moon and her four hundred brothers, the stars.

Beyond the Americas, Odin or Wotan sacrificed his eye for wisdom in the Norse myth. From Greece, Dionysus, son of Zeus and Semele, was torn to pieces at the jealous instigation of Hera. All these pieces of his body were then eaten by the Titans except for his heart, which was recovered. From that experience, he was put back together and reborn, taking the name Zagreus, which means "dismembered." Attis, a Phrygian vegetation god, was a sacrifice of the Middle Eastern goddess Cybele. Similarly, Adonis was also a Syrian vegetation god, representing the life-death-rebirth cycle and was sacrificed for Aphrodite. Tammuz was a Babylonian god who was put to death a number of times, returning to life until he finally remained in the underworld. Osiris was another vegetation god who was killed by his evil brother Set. He was initially tricked into climbing into a coffin made for him by Set, who sent it off down the Nile into the sea, where it landed in Syria at Byblos. A beautiful-smelling erica tree grew around the coffin. Attracted to its scent, the king had it felled and made into a pillar for his palace. Hearing of this pillar, Isis, Osiris's sister-wife, searching everywhere for her husband-brother, begged the king to release the coffin, which he did. When she returned with it to Egypt, Set, still angry, proceeded to cut him to pieces, scattering them across the land. Isis painstakingly searched for all of them, finding everything except his penis. He then became the god of the underworld (Campbell 1982a, 21–22). Horus, the son of Osiris and Isis, avenged his father's death by wounding Set and in the process sacrificed his eye, which, when offered to his father's mummy, restored him to eternal life (29). Jesus was the Christian version of the sacrificed vegetation god.

The Sumerian god Marduk descended into the underworld to sacrifice Tiamat, throwing one-half of her body to the sky to make the heavens and one-half below to create the firmament (Leeming and Leeming 1994, 25). In the Ceram creation myth from the Molucca Islands in Indonesia, a man named Ameta magically created a little girl, Hainuwele, from the blood dripping from his cut finger. Later in the myth when the girl was grown, she participated at the center of the ritual dance activities during nine nights, and each night she gave the group valuable objects. The nine participating families became envious of her wealth, and on the ninth night, the group decided to dig a hole and push her in. Missing her, Ameta found her dead and buried at the center of the dance grounds, locating her by sticking palm leaves into the ground. This way he found her hair and blood. He dug her up, cut her body into many pieces, and buried all but the arms in the ground. Suddenly, all the food staples of the Ceram people grew. Ameta gave her arms to the goddess Satene, who returned to the dance grounds and, holding up the arms, demanded each of the nine families try to walk through the gate made by her arms. Those who succeeded became people, and those who did not became animals (43–44). It is clear from this myth that nothing valuable becomes ours without equal or symbolic expenditure.

THE THEME OF COMBAT

Combat is an interesting archetypal theme, which is prominent in this myth as well as in many others throughout the world. It overlaps with the theme of sacrifice but is also quite distinct. Combat engages the concept of duality manifested in the opposites fighting against each other. Themes of good versus evil or gods versus demons are common. The twin heroes in the *Popol Vuh* who fought were warriors fighting against the powers of evil to eradicate the undesirable attitudes, such as vanity, arrogance, envy, and laziness. These mistaken attitudes threatened to destroy the culture that the twins, as representatives of the gods, were trying to establish. In an individual, these same attitudes prevent maturity or consciousness.

There were incidences of combat repeated in two separate sections in the myth. This repetition makes the structure of the myth obvious. Throughout, the culture heroes were superior to their enemy in terms of cleverness, magic, and vision. The first combat section pertains to vanquishing the Macaw and his two conceited sons. The second section pertains to the older twins, One Hunahpú and Seven Hunahpú, and their sons, the culture heroes, Hunahpú and Xbalanqué. In the battle of opposites, all who were defeated were outside the order of the culture they were striving to establish. The resolution of the combat was to vanquish the undesirable attitudes and bring consciousness into the world through the metaphor of the heroes ascending to become sun and moon. In the second combat section in the *Popol Vuh*, the ball game was the field of battle.

The archetypal theme of combat, so critical to the Maya creation myth, can also be seen in many myths from other cultures. In Mesoamerican culture, we see combat sequences in some of the key Aztec myths. The Aztec warrior god was Tezcatlipoca, who was the god of the smoking mirror and opponent of Quetzalcoatl, the savior god. In the creation of the worlds, the two battled with each other as earth and wind or matter and spirit. Tezcatlipoca, however, contained more of the earth. In the first sun, Quetzalcoatl struck Tezcatlipoca, turning him into a jaguar. In response, he struck Quetzalcoatl, the ruler of the sun and wind, and ended his rule. Tezcatlipoca was a creator as well as a destroyer, sowing discord and conflict, yet through conflict, he effected change. He lost a foot battling with the earth monster (Miller and Taube 1993, 164). Related to the Big Dipper constellation, Tezcatlipoca is important for hunters and gathers.

In a similar mythic battle motif from Greece, Ochiai (1986) described the battle between Apollo and the mythic python, son of the primordial mother and exponent of chaos, dwelling in a cave or underground location. The monster could take different forms, such as dragon, crocodile, lizard, sea monster, boar, lion, and a death spirit propagating death, illness, plagues, and famine. He was greedy and vicious with untamed instincts, conspiring against the creation of the world and an ordered culture. The enemy was finally destroyed after being outsmarted, deceived, or bewitched. Then the monster was imprisoned in the underworld while the hero, Apollo, was celebrated as a culture hero and worshipped as a sun god (86–100).

In the Babylonian creation myth, Marduk battled against the female monster Tiamat. The Greek hero Perseus fought and destroyed the Gorgon, Medusa, while Thor, the Norse god of thunder, fought the giant Hrungnir to reclaim a hostage, Orwandil. Theseus fought and killed the Minotaur as revenge for the slaughter of youths who were demanded for sacrifice. The Minotaur was a demonic perversion living deep in a labyrinth, much like the winding path into the underworld. Combat between the hero and a gigantic monster is seen in the myths of Indra and Herakles. Quetzalcoatl and Tezcatlipoca, working together in a moment of unity, killed the earth monster, Tlaltecuhtli. Osiris, as the night sun and pharaoh in the underworld, fought with the Apophis snake for survival to ensure that the sun would dawn in the morning. In Christian lore, Saint George slew the dragon. The Vedic god Shiva was the principal god of destruction. While Vishnu was the preserver and restorer, through one of his incarnations as Rama Chandra, he took the form of a warrior who defeated the most powerful demon in the universe (Coomaraswamy and Nivedita 1967, 93–94; Daniélou 1991, 171). He also incarnated into Krishna, the hero of the *Bhagavad Gita* in the epic story the *Mahabharata*. On the battlefield with Arjuna he opened him to a godly vision and explained why he must fight the enemy, proceeding to fight a terrible battle, a universal battle (Campbell 1973, 231–34; Coomaraswamy and Nivedita 1967, 202–7). The Iranian god Verethragna was a warrior god, aggressive and victorious against the forces of evil. In a Navajo creation myth, twin warriors fought their way to Father Sun, being tested along the way at each of the four directions (Campbell 1973, 131–32). The Sumerian myth of Gilgamesh was one of a warrior hero who had to battle along his journey to attain the watercress plant of immortality.

In the Wapangwa creation myth, after the creation of the birds, animals, and the first humans, the animals were hungry and wanted to eat the Tree of Life, but the humans defended it. This set off a huge battle between them where they bit pieces off each other, and those bits flew up to become the sun, moon, and stars (Leeming and Leeming 1994, 285).

THE THEME OF IMMACULATE CONCEPTION

The idea of conception without sex, without the active participation of the man, is a common theme. Psychologically, it seems to point to a disconnection between the feminine, specifically with the body representing nature, and the masculine representing spirit or logos. The opposites remain too far apart and are unable to connect into a pair. This was apparent in the *Popol Vuh* at the time of Blood Woman's immaculate conception. She was impregnated by saliva that was spat into her hand from the head of One Hunahpú in the calabash tree. He was disconnected from his body and was only a head; therefore, the impregnation was through logos, through imagination, and not yet an embodied act. Spirit gave birth to matter. This scene resembled the original creation of the word that emerged out of chaos that was spoken between Heart of Sky and Sovereign and Quetzal Serpent of the waters. At that time the earth did not yet exist; there was no middle ground. The insemination of Blood Woman was an act of creative, spiritual union between opposites with the possibility of bringing in a new third force, the embodied culture heroes, who would have the qualities of the gods and demons. It was they who would pave the way for humans, who then also possessed both godly and demonic qualities. "Human beings acted as the 'centering' agents of cultural and religious life. . . . The human body was considered the nexus and unifying structure of the universe" (Carrasco 1990, 21).

An Aztec or Mexica example of immaculate conception is found in the myth of the birth of Huitzilopochtli, the supreme god of war and an aspect of Tezcatlipoca. His mother, Coatlicue or Snake Skirt, who was the goddess of fertility, life and death, and rebirth had already given birth to four hundred sons who were led by her warlike daughter named Coyolxauhqui. Coatlicue was impregnated by a ball of down feathers while she was sweeping at Coatepec, Snake Mountain. Her children were furious with her and decided to kill her. As Coatlicue was about to be killed, her newborn son, Huitzilopochtli, emerged fully armed from her belly and killed his sister and his other four hundred siblings, who after death became the moon and stars (Miller and Taube 1993, 64). He dismembered her and threw her down the mountain. This was ritually repeated when sacrificial victims were thrown down the steps of the temples.

An immaculate conception also occurs in a Kwakwaka'wakw myth from British Columbia:

> The future mother of its hero was weaving, facing the rear of her house when the Sun's rays, shining through the cracks in the walls, struck her back and she became pregnant. She gave birth to Mink, whose name, this time, was Born-to-be-the-Sun, since it was known how his mother had conceived him. (Campbell 1988b, 202)

In a Navajo creation myth, Changing Woman had been born miraculously where for four days a dark cloud had been seen resting. She had been born of Darkness, and Dawn was her father. Then when she grew up and was still a virgin, she gave birth to twin boys (Campbell 1998b, 244). From Greek mythology, Danaë was impregnated by Zeus in the form of golden rain and gave birth to Perseus. Gaia had her son Kronos castrate Uranus for punishing his children, the Hekatoncheires, because of their unsightly appearance. From the wound, blood dropped onto Gaia and she became pregnant with the Giants and Erinnyes. Similarly, in Nordic mythology, Ymir, the primogenitor of the giants, produced two children, also giants, from the sweat of his armpit.

In India, Vishnu gave half a pot of nectar to the king's wife, who then gave birth to Rama, an incarnation of himself. Vishnu then gave a quarter of the nectar to the king's second wife, who gave birth to Rama's brother. He gave the remaining nectar to his brother's wife, who also had twins, Lakshmana and Batru-ghna. Each of the children had a part of Vishnu's essence (Roberts, Roberts, and Katz 1997, 338).

In Christian theology, the Virgin Mary was immaculately inseminated by the Holy Ghost and gave birth to Jesus. This is a significant example of matter giving birth to spirit without outside help from a physical father, as if the mother conceived a birth on her own. In Egypt, when Isis was not able to recover Osiris's phallus, she fashioned one out of gold to conceive Horus, who was the pharaoh in life just as Osiris was the pharaoh in death.

CHAPTER 8

CONCLUSION

The importance of creation myths is not to be underestimated, and
this one is barely known on the American continent where it originated. The creation of the cosmos can be looked at as the origin of
consciousness in the world. Similarly, when creation myth motifs
arise in the dreams of individuals, it is very difficult material pointing
to a huge change required of that person. There will inevitably be a
movement toward greater consciousness (von Franz 1972, 8). Many
times these dreams contain motifs of initiation, expressing the sacred
encounter between humans and the gods.

Out of the original state of stillness emerged the word, a spark of
intuition, a spark of lightning, that Heart of Sky took to Sovereign
Quetzal Serpent, and they talked. Through their dialogue they set in
motion the sowing and dawning. The stillness represents the preconscious state before the creative impulse sets off the positive and negative charges in the psyche that release life energy or libido. One becomes two, and there can now be a dialogue or conflict, as opposites
come into play with differences, opinions, and concurrence. Motion
and rhythm begin the sway, back and forth, as the cosmic dance that
swells and cycles, contracting and retracting. It projects outward,
then withdraws into depression; it stands above its creation watching, observing, almost dissociated from its creation but demanding
attention and honor. How does it learn to relate? How do humans
learn from the creator, and, with their free choice, how do they respond in return? When does it all cease and need to be started anew?
Is that when the gods themselves have projected everything they dis-
like onto the humans and now want a new creature? Did the gods
not like to see their animal natures in the faces of the quadrupeds
that roamed the newly revealed earth? Were the mud people a reflection of a soft, unformed part of the creators? What about the stiff
and inflexible wooden people that were violently destroyed by their
household objects and then cleansed away through a flood? Could

those have been other shadow aspects of the gods themselves? Angry, destructive, decisive the gods were, yet in council they all agreed on what they hoped for, but it was not yet available.

Who should take this task on, they wondered? Why not heroes, children of the gods, one step closer to the earthly realm? But they have to have choice, or it would not work. They are reflections of the gods but with a relationship to the earth, living on the earth, not in the sky. With choice they too fail, but from failure they learn—at least from generation to generation. They are messengers sent to eliminate shadow or to bring it to consciousness: vainglorious Macaw, his sons, the lazy and childish monkey twins, and finally the demons themselves. Are these all aspects of the creation, aspects of the gods projected into matter? When the gods have become conscious of their myriad undesirable aspects, the torch is passed to a new creation through the awakening dawn, bringing light to the face of the earth. Mother-fathers and their progeny are made from the very substance of the gods, maize—not from their instinctual nature alone, not from the mud of the earth or wood from the trees, but from them, from their blood, their life force. It is a strong bond that demands much both ways. It becomes humans' task to live in the world of duality and try to metabolize the huge shadow left by the gods from their messy experiments—gods that emerged out of stillness, not knowing what to expect. They were not and are not perfect.

How does one grow a god? That is the eternal question. It is the human task, as Jung pointed out in his book *Answer to Job* (1989a, 355–470). Humanity suffers and struggles with the unconscious projections of its gods, trying to understand what it believes it can see clearly and what it cannot. Humanity is left in a dilemma with its own infallibilities, those bits from the gods that have fallen into individuals along with gnosis, their wisdom, say the Gnostics. Humans struggle for clarity but seem to find only the breath on the mirror. Free choice with obscured vision is a dangerous combination. With the major forces swirling around humanity from good day to bad day, as predicted in the divinatory calendar, all will come to a halt, and then time and the gods will start again, perhaps in the outer world but definitely in each person's inner world, a new creation, new cultures, but always a creation myth encouraging the birth of new life and fresh vision.

The themes, symbols, and drama of the *Popol Vuh* creation myth are unique to the K'iche' Maya, yet they are similar to what emerged in the mythology of greater Mesoamerica and geographically far-distant cultures throughout the world. Distance in space and time is not a factor in the appearance of these same images in individuals' dreams. They arise from the same soil, out of the collective memory of humankind. The dream voice selects images and symbols that will best reflect the message needed to effect a change of attitude and behavior in the individual dreamer. The repository of knowledge archived from metaphor, from prior emanations of the psyche, is used by this dream voice to nudge people forward on their paths of individuation, the path to wholeness. Creation myths lay out the templates for humans' relationship to the gods and cosmos as well as their relationship to each other.

Cultures are formed as projections of the cosmic plan, just as cities, each one's home, and each one's heart represent a microcosm of that great macrocosm. Myths speak with the loud as well as the soft voice. As the gods were turned to stone when the sun's light touched the face of the earth, as their voices became internal, humans might remember their origin and connection to the living gods through their dreams and that soft inner voice of wisdom that whispers when they dare to listen. The Maya see their creation myth as the avenue back to their gods solidified in their *Book of Council*. Understanding it opens the door to the clarity of vision lost at the creation of humans. From another culture, another time, one can strive for that same clarity by understanding the ancient voices of wisdom from our ancestors and those of other cultures. The one voice speaks to all through metaphor from the archive of humanity's memories. The crucial question remains: Will we listen to that inner voice, that wise council; will we see the reality of the degradation of our current world, and putting our vanity and grandiosity aside, will humans and our world survive?

GLOSSARY

Archetypes are primordial patterns of human behavior and experience that are expressed as images, symbols, and ideas and reflect our biological instincts. These instincts are expressed as archetypes in recurring themes or motifs seen in mythology, fairy tales, folklore, and literature, as well as in human and cultural behavior. There are many archetypes, yet it is impossible to know fully what an archetype is. Only a portion of an archetype can be gleaned at any one time. They have been described as crystals with many facets. As one turns the crystal, another facet becomes prominent, representing another aspect of the archetype. All archetypes are connected to each other, like a large web of potential influence on human behavior (Jung 1977a). The word "archetype" derives from *arche*, "primal" or "first principle," and points to the creative source that cannot be represented or seen, and *typos*, "impression or imprint," which refers to a manifestation of the first principle. Jung said, "They are qualities not individually acquired but inherited . . . inborn forms of perception and apprehension, which are the *a priori* determinants of all psychic processes" (1981, 133):

> Since for years I have been observing and investigating the products of the unconscious in the widest sense of the word, namely dreams, fantasies, visions, and delusions of the insane, I have not been able to avoid recognizing certain regularities, that is, types. There are types of *situations* and types of *figures* that repeat themselves frequently and have a corresponding meaning. I therefore employ the term "motif" to designate these repetitions. Thus there are not only typical dreams but also typical motifs in dreams. . . . [These] can be arranged under a series of archetypes, the chief of them being . . . the *shadow*, the *wise old man*, the *child* (including the child hero), the mother

("Primordial Mother" and "Earth Mother") as a supraordinate
personality ("daemonic" because supraordinate), and her
counterpart the *maiden*, and lastly the *anima* in man and the
animus in woman. (Jung 1977a, 183)

Jung made reference to other archetypes when he said:

Some of the well-known motifs are the figures of the Hero, the
Redeemer, the Dragon (always connected with the Hero, who
had to overcome him), the Whale or the Monster who swallows
the Hero. Another variation of the motif of the Hero and the
Dragon is the *Katabasis*, the Descent into the Cave, the *Nekyia*.
(1989b, 38)

The purpose of archetypes, according to Jung (1977a), is to guide
the development of individual lives and reactions. Like instincts,
they help with survival. The archetypal images emerge in dreams to
help correct faulty or outdated attitudes and to enlarge the personality. When an archetype is activated, it releases the most overwhelm-
ing emotions, opening the individual up to the numinous, or what
is experienced as a religious experience. This becomes the bridge
between humans and the sacred and takes them into mythic time:

Frazier, in *The Golden Bough*, thought to explain the observed
resemblances as "the effect of similar causes acting alike on the
similar constitution of the human mind in different countries
and under different skies.". . . Adolf Bastian employed the
term "elementary ideas" (*Elementargedanken*) with reference
to the products of this universally human ground, while in his
second term, "ethnic ideas" (*Volkergedanken*), he recognized
the differences of their appearances among the greatly differing
cultures. (Campbell 1988a, 57)

As an anthropologist, D. Brown, in his book *Human Universals*, extensively studied this same idea but from a more materialistic point
of view. While most anthropologists study differences, he embarked
on studying the similarities that emerged in cultures across the globe.
His conclusions can be broken down into five statements:

The first is that universals not only exist but are important to any broad conception of the task of anthropology. . . . Second, universals form a heterogeneous set. A great many, for example, seem to be inherent in human nature. Some are cultural conventions that have come to have universal distribution. . . . Third, the study of universals has been effectively tabooed, as an unintended consequence of assumptions that have predominated in anthropology (and other social sciences) throughout much of this century. . . . Fourth, human biology is a key to understanding many human universals. . . . Fifth, evolutionary psychology is a key to understanding many of the universals that are of greatest interest to anthropology. The feature of human biology most of interest to anthropology is the human mind. (Brown 1991, 5–6)

Brown discussed the current hypotheses used to explain culture and perception that included Chomsky's (1988) views on anthropological linguistics and his theory called *universal grammar*, and the evolutionary anthropologist Fox (1989), who also espoused universals but at the process level. "Both Chomsky and Fox assume or find that these deeper and more significant universals, which on the 'surface' do not necessarily or even typically manifest themselves in substantive universals, are rooted in human neurobiology" (1991, 43). Brown continues: "D'Aquili and Laughlin argue that these cortical functions not only give us the capacity to mythologize but that by virtue of what they call the 'cognitive imperative' humans are *driven* to organize unexplained external stimuli into some coherent cognitive matrix" (99). Evolutionary theory attempts to pull these threads together. Assuming that society and culture are the result of human action and humans themselves are the result of human evolution, the assumption is that cultural structures stem from biology and the function of the brain. An early example of this is the evolutionary jump from *Homo erectus* to *Homo sapiens neanderthalensis* circa 40,000 BCE or even earlier that resulted in the first glimmers of symbolic thought. Evolution was clearly at work. The key is that humans are myth-making creatures that construe, structure the world, stand in relationship to it, and suffer when they lose a meaningful relationship to it.

But what is strikingly missing in these anthropological and linguistic views is the qualities that make humans unique animals: their desire, imagination, soul, and capacity to approach and express these mysteries symbolically. Jung (1981) recognized the importance of these elements in humans' lives as well as the innate need to maintain an understanding of and relationship to the cosmos. Though these are the intangibles on the outer ridges of life, far from empirical scientific evidence, Jung documented their very existence through the use of phenomenology, comparing the emanations of the human mind that emerge from dreams, visions, psychoses, mythology, and comparative religions:

All the most powerful ideas in history go back to archetypes. This is particularly true of religious ideas, but the central concepts of science, philosophy, and ethics are no exception to this rule. In their present form they are variants of archetypal ideas created by consciously applying and adapting these ideas to reality. For it is the function of consciousness not only to recognize and assimilate the external world through the gateway of the senses, but to translate into visible reality the world within us. (1981, 342)

Seeing patterns and universals, Jung formulated a theory of the psyche into a psychology of human behavior that helped explain the reasons for the existence of these emergent images, how and why they are formed into myths, and why they are important. The fundamental energy that motivated the formation of these patterns, or archetypal images, lies at the core of what makes one human.

Codices are ancient manuscripts of text in book form. Those from Mesoamerica were made from long strips of bark paper or deerskin covered with a thin coating of lime plaster to give the pages a smooth surface. The pages were then folded like an accordion into a book. The author painted and wrote hieroglyphics on the pages (Christenson 2003, 32–33). The four remaining Maya codices are the Paris, Dresden, Madrid, and Grolier artifacts. These four depict deities, calendars of divination, astronomy, and rituals. The *Popol Vuh* is a copy of an original and is a creation narrative. Other codices from Mesoamerica are the Mixtec texts, the codices Borgia, Nuttall, Bodley, and Vindobonensis. The Florentine Codex is Aztec. All were written down postcolonially from precolonial recollections.

Collective unconscious is the part of the unconscious that refers to the collective, impersonal, and universal experience of the human species that is inherited in the form of archetypes (Jung 1977a, 42–53; 1977c, 279). These preexistent forms become apparent in the mythological images and motifs that can emerge in differing cultures independent of historical tradition or migration. It is a term coined by Jung to differentiate what humans share collectively from what is personal to each individual, which is called the "personal unconscious."

The unconscious for Jung (1976) was not philosophical or metaphysical but purely psychological. His understanding of its presence developed through phenomenological observation of himself, in working with patients' dream and visionary material, from motifs in the fantasies of psychotics, and from comparative religions and mythologies. Many of these images from individuals harkened back to early mythological images and themes, those of which the individual was not aware. This curiosity led him to postulate that there was a reservoir within the mind/brain of humans that, in its neurological way, catalogued new cultural experiences and changes to the archetypal expressions, making them available to consciousness. This reservoir was beyond the material held in the personal unconscious, which contains all repressed personal elements:

> In addition to the personal unconscious contents, there are other contents which do not originate in personal acquisitions but in the inherited possibility of psychic functioning in general, i.e., in the inherited structure of the brain. These are the mythological associations, the motifs and images that can spring up anew anytime anywhere, independently of historical tradition or migration. I call these contents the collective unconscious. (Jung 1976, 485)

For Jung (1989a), myths serve the function of revealing the collective unconscious. Because it is inherently unconscious and, therefore, not knowable directly, myth is a vehicle for its expression. Yet one needs to learn the language offered up through myth, which is in the form of metaphor. To best do this, it is helpful to read myths from many cultures to compare the structure, the development of the action, the themes, and the symbols. Myth acts as an intermediary or messenger between the unconscious and conscious realms and is primarily significant when the meaning goes beyond the literal to the symbolic. It is up to the reader to move from the literal to the symbolic to understand the deeper meaning offered up by the unconscious. In this way the potency of the archetypes is revealed to the individual and the culture. As delineated earlier, most scientists stop their investigation at the literal level of meaning. They rarely move into the psychological layer of meaning revealed through the symbols. This is where humans are able to connect to the external world, beyond themselves as individuals, to give meaning to life. It allows one to step from the temporal world into the sacred world, to connect the gods within to the gods without (Jung 1989a).

What is meant by the concept of god? Since this concept is included in myths, it is important to define what it means and to differentiate how it is used for a particular culture even though its broad definition can be seen as universal and archetypal. This book relies on Joseph Campbell's definition from the *Mythologies of the Great Hunt* volume of his multivolume *Historical Atlas of World Mythology*:

> Unsentimentally defined, a god is an envisioned name and
> form metaphorical of a transpersonal state of consciousness,
> conceived as functioning in relation to human values locally
> recognized, whether actively (creating, supporting, negating),
> or at rest in contemplation. Since every god is thus in name
> and form culturally specific, none may properly claim exclusive
> identity with whatever may be beyond name and form as the
> transcendent ground of all being and beings, i.e., as that which in
> the Orient is referred to as beyond and without forms, hence the
> "void" (śūnya), or a *brahman*—for which we have in our Western

tongues, unfortunately, no word but "God," which has led, not only to a general idolatry of our own historically conditioned god as "God Eternal," but also to an equally improper notion of the gods of other mythologies as in this same way idolized: which they are not. Even the Bushmen recognize the temporally relevant (metaphorical) nature of their divinities. (1989b, xvi)

It can also be said from a Jungian perspective that the God image arises out of the archetype of the Self, which represents totality, wholeness, and wisdom. An experience of the Self is numinous, which reframes ego reality in a substantive way. It has this capacity to reframe one's reality because it affects one deeply and causes a change of perspective.

Complexes contain a set of archetypal motifs or images at their core, with a web of related behavior patterns around that core. They are described as "feeling-toned." When a complex is activated, one feels it deeply. Depending on one's early experiences, certain complexes take on heightened affectivity. These will be the ones a person is affected by and will benefit from working on to bring into consciousness and under control. It is through these complexes as they emerge in the body and emotions that the archetypes touch ground in material reality, manifesting these common human patterns. The complexes that appear in dreams give personalized shape to the archetypal images so that these can be assimilated into the ego and consciousness. Complexes affect cultures and groups as well as individuals.

Consciousness denotes a relationship between psychic contents and the ego. Jung stated that "consciousness is the function or activity that maintains the relation of psychic contents to the ego" (1974, 421–22). From a Jungian point of view, it is the goal of analysis to bring the content of the unconscious into consciousness so that the ego may remain aware of it, as opposed to remaining as shadow in the unconscious. This includes personal as well as collective content.

From a neuroscience point of view, consciousness is related to the executive function of the mind, having an awareness of *self* in relation to the world, but how it is defined is quite broad and actually overlaps with stages of sleep. It seems that consciousness is a state of the waking mind-brain, heightened neuronal awareness, yet while part of the brain may be awake, another part may be asleep. What seems consistent is that consciousness is an objective state of awareness of oneself, yet there are varying layers of consciousness, from acutely aware to a subtle background awareness that may only become apparent later.

Creation myths are the mytho-religious stories that explain the creation and destruction of worlds including earth, humanity, plants, animals, and the universe. Deities and primordial energies are delineated. These myths are used to further the initiation of youngsters into the community of elders of a society. They lay down the framework for the cultural and individual belief in the relationship between humans and deities and whether that is a supportive or antagonistic relationship (von Franz 1972, 5–19). There are different themes that dominate creation myths, which are discussed later. Some show a helpful relationship between the gods and their creations, while others demonstrate greater distance, fear, or lack of trust. Creation myths lay the template for ritual activity of the culture and influence all aspects of cultural development and viewpoint. The elements and motifs vary because myth relates to the total social reality expressed in different ways due to the differing historical and cultural conditions.

Daykeepers are the shamanic priests who are "active practitioners of the indigenous religion who are initiated calendar diviners, dream interpreters, and curers" (B. Tedlock 1982, 42). They understand the sacred texts and calendars and read them for information about the nature of the days and future events. Each day represents a different archetypal energy, and it is the daykeepers' job to pay attention to the movement of the energies through the days.

Gnosis is a gnostic term referring to the fullness and perfect knowledge of the totality of the divine. It constitutes moral and intellectual perfection generally embodied in God. In a nutshell, it refers to wisdom.

Individuation denotes the process of becoming an individual distinguishable from others and the general collective psychology. It is singling out of one's uniqueness, and becoming conscious of and differentiating one's individual parts, that is, the complexes and shadow. The primary goal of psychological development is to recognize the opposite energies that reside within oneself to establish a solid sense of self and ego. With this solid footing, one can find balance between opposite energies and live with a healthy relationship and interaction between the ego and the greater Self, which is the wisdom of the psyche or the unconscious. Individuation furthers consciousness and is supported and encouraged in Jungian analysis (Jung 1977c, 225). This process is inherent in humans as a driving force that leads to change from within in relation to oneself and to the world. Although the process draws one into self-discovery, Jung believed that after an extended period of withdrawal of one's libido or energy from the world, it is imperative to return to the world to repay this loss with one's newfound thoughtfulness and creativity to further collective consciousness.

Self with a capital "S" describes the central archetype of the psyche representing meaning and wholeness. It is the psyche's symbol-forming faculty, which brings archetypal images into the personal level of awareness, dressed as complexes, and appearing as images in myths, fairy tales, and dreams. Encompassing both consciousness and unconsciousness, the Self is the center of wholeness, the center of the psyche, as well as its circumference. The Self provides the archetypal foundation from which the ego and consciousness develop, and it guides the process of individuation while also being its goal. Myths contain cultural representations of the image of the Self, which is exemplified in experiencing god or the fourfold structure of the cosmovision, with the *axis mundi* as the fifth element in the center, bridging the celestial, earthly, and underworld realms.

Soul is a concept used in many cultures but with many different meanings. Jung described the soul as being the face individuals turn toward, to experience their inner world as opposed to the persona, which is the face turned to the outer world (1974, 466). In *The Red Book*, Jung described three aspects of soul: heavenly, human, and animal (2009, 577). From a Western, Judeo-Christian point of view, soul represents the incorporeal part or immortal essence of a person, the transcendent aspect of a person. It is the soul that gives the body life, the seat of human will, understanding, and personality. Kabbalah describes the three different parts of the soul: *neshama*, the "I" that inhabits the body with wisdom, the breath, and the godly part of the soul; *ruach*, spirit and wind, emotions; and *nefesh*, desire, the animal part of the soul. Together the three manifestations of the soul form the Self (Furlotti 2023, 65, 73). Animism holds the belief that all biological and nonbiological entities possess souls and that there exists a world soul called the *anima mundi*. In Buddhism, the individual has no permanent self; instead, the belief is of an ever-changing self, a no-self, and therefore, a no-soul, as well. The Maya referred to soul as "the-white-flower-thing" and believed there were four forms of soul: one being the animal soul; another, the soul-destiny given to the child through the day name that became part of his or her animistic being. Soul can take the form of insects, containing the soul of the dead. Each person possesses an innate soul, either hot or cold or active or quiet, and each is expressed as one of the colors of the four directions: white, black, red, and yellow, which is sometimes blue-green. Soul comes into existence as the life force flows from the gods into the human realm through the cosmic tree trunk at the center of the world, mixing and creating the soul substance referred to as the flower. This process has a decidedly alchemical flavor.

> First, two complementary elements exist separately, one above and one below; second, both of them are united in a tree trunk where they swirl around each other; third, from their friction, a new being is born; fourth, the being is freed and extends over the face of the earth. The liberated one is a flower, a flame. Is this not the image of the two sticks rubbed together to produce a spark and light the fire? The fire is a flower. (Austin 1993, 72)

According to Landa (1579), the Maya believed in the immortality of the soul, that there was a better life the soul traveled to after death. Those composed of the good energy or *ch'ulel* went to a pleasant place of the ceiba tree, while those who contained the cold, dark energy or life force were tormented in the underworld described by Sharer and Traxler (2006).

Symbols are archetypal representations that act as transformers of psychic energy, or libido. As the powerhouses of the psyche, they are representations of wholeness and the union of opposites, thus carrying the potent and current connection between humanity and the greater Self. As psychic transformers, symbols create a charge, a sense of numinosity, like having come into contact with something truly other. Symbols help restore health and wholeness, healing the blockages within the personality, and help reconcile the opposites within us and within cultures. They ultimately lead to a working relationship with the greater Self:

> Consciousness must confront the unconscious, and the balance between the opposites must be found. As this is not possible through logic, one is dependent on symbols, which make the irrational union of opposites possible. They are produced spontaneously by the unconscious and are amplified by the conscious mind. (*Jung 1989a, 468*)

When a symbol no longer carries its potency because of a change in the culture or religious beliefs, new living symbols emerge from the psyche to maintain the human-spirit connection and to reconcile the opposites on both individual and cultural levels.

The archetypes frequently present themselves in the form of symbols, which are the images that carry the numinous charge of the instinct, yet the form they take comes from the ideas acquired from the conscious mind:

> A symbol is an indefinite expression with many meanings, pointing to something not easily defined and therefore not

fully known. But the sign always has a fixed meaning, because it is a conventional abbreviation for, or a commonly accepted indication of, something known. The symbol therefore has a large number of analogous variants, and the more of these variants it has at its disposal, the more complete and clear-cut will be the image it projects on its object. (Jung 1967, 124)

Any given symbol is the best possible expression for a relatively unknown fact that is proposed to exist, and it cannot be expressed in any better way. The energy carried by the symbol from the archetype grips and demands recognition, giving each individual the feeling of being part of a greater process. This experience has been described in many ways, such as religious, spiritual, ecstatic, transcendental, and revelatory. Jacobi wrote in her book *Complex, Archetype, Symbol in the Psychology of C. G. Jung*:

When the archetype as such is touched by consciousness, it can manifest itself either on the "lower," biological plane and take form, for instance, as an expression of instinct or as an instinctual dynamism, or on the "higher," spiritual plane as an image or idea. In the latter case the raw material of imagery and meaning are added to it, and the symbol is born. (1971, 120)

Jacobi explained, "Jung calls the symbol a psychic transformer of energy and points out that it has an eminently 'healing' character, that it helps to restore wholeness as well as health (1971, 100) . . . by removing and transforming the blockages and obstructions of psychic energy" (103). "It is only possible to live the fullest life when we are in harmony with these symbols; wisdom is a return to them" (Jung 1981, 342).

Religion begins with living symbols, and when they lose their potency and meaning in a culture, they become mere signs, no longer carrying the potency of the archetype behind them. New symbols that carry the bridging meaning for the culture between the temporal and sacred worlds need to be created, evoked out of the unconscious, and surrounded by an ever-changing religion. A religion that has been reduced to signs is referred to as mythology. For a culture, when its religion has lost its symbolic numinosity, it has lost its ability to touch believers deeply. Mythology may refer to someone else's religion; one's current religion consists of dogma and theology. All the mythology that is studied now with curiosity was at one time a potent religion. Through its study one can gain a glimpse into the history of the manifestation of the collective unconscious.

APPENDIX 2
LITERATURE REVIEW

The literature review for this book is quite extensive because it covers a number of different areas of research.

1. In the area of Maya culture and mythology the review includes the original text, four translations of the *Popol Vuh* into English, other Maya original texts, and secondary literature in the fields of archaeology, ethnology, art history, mythology, and culture that sheds light on cultural context and the symbolic meaning of the imagery and themes in the text.

2. In the area of Jungian psychology and amplification it includes Jung's *Collected Works* and secondary material, which, when taken together, explain Jungian concepts and the Jungian psychological approach to and understanding of mythology and the process of amplification. Examples of Jungian amplification are included along with symbol books and dictionaries. Contained within these texts is an extensive resource for the amplification of images and symbols. Texts examining the field of psychoanalysis and different paradigms for looking at Jungian phenomena and culture are included.

3. In the area of general mythology this review includes texts written by non-Jungian scholars describing the meaning and purpose of mythology from different paradigms and cultures, as well as texts on comparative mythology and religions. These are also a resource for amplification.

4. In the area of bridging from one culture to another relevant literature includes texts that discuss the issues involved and those that demonstrate working across cultures.

MAYA RESOURCES

There does not seem to be sufficient understanding of the symbols in the *Popol Vuh* or the meaning of the myth itself. There are four full translations into English of the creation myth: Recinos ([1950] 1991); Edmonson (1971); D. Tedlock (1985); and Christenson (2003). All four, along with scans of the original Spanish document, are used for this research, but the focus is on the two most recent translations.

Recinos ([1950] 1991), an ethnologist, linguist, and archaeologist, was native to Guatemala. In 1950, he made a new translation of the *Popol Vuh* from the original French version, and in 1991, Goetz and Morley translated the Recinos 1950 Spanish manuscript into English. The 1991 Goetz and Morley translation of Recinos's 1950 work was one of the earliest English translations of the *Popol Vuh*. It is the most straightforward translation, with less emphasis on capturing the poetry of the original.

Recinos, a distinguished diplomat who was fluent in both K'iche' and Spanish, was also a linguist, anthropologist, and ethnologist. He discovered some important omissions and changes in the first Spanish version published by Brasseur de Bourbourg in 1861. He therefore decided to make a new translation directly from the K'iche' portion into Spanish, which was published in 1947. To help with his understanding of words, he used dictionaries that had been compiled during the Colonial period. It was then that Sylvanus G. Morley, a foremost authority on the Maya, and Delia Goetz, author and translator, both of whom worked with Adrián Recinos, became interested in translating the text from his Spanish version into English. They worked together to preserve the peculiarities of the K'iche' text in the English translation. For instance, "the original manuscript is not divided into parts or chapters but runs without interruption from the beginning until the end" (Recinos [1950] 1991, xiv). This may be a peculiarity of their language or reflect the unbroken cyclic nature of their worldview.

Edmonson (1971), who was a professor of anthropology and linguistics at Tulane University, produced the second English translation. He translated the *Popol Vuh* and published it in 1971 as *The*

Book of Counsel: The Popol Vuh of the Quiché Maya of Guatemala.
Edmondson stated that the original may have contained almanac
pages used for divination, similar to the four remaining codices that
are from the Postclassic period just prior to the Spanish conquest.
Edmonson's translation differs from the others in that it is a running
transliteration of the K'iche' text alongside the English translation. It
is helpful to see the K´iché text lined up next to the equivalent English. One gets a very good sense of the poetic structure of the text.

D. Tedlock (1985), a professor of anthropology and English, wrote
the third translation of the *Popol Vuh*, the first unabridged English
edition. The author conveyed the poetic nature of the original K'iche'
language. Tedlock, as of this writing, is professor of anthropology and
religion at Boston University and a long-standing scholar of Mesoamerican anthropology. His translation is poetic and easily accessible. As an anthropologist living in Guatemala, he looked for someone
who could shed light on some of the darker passages in the *Popol Vuh*.
He met a daykeeper (much like a shaman or priest) named Andrés
Xiloj Peruch, who worked with him on elucidating the text. Although
Peruch read only Spanish, not K'iche', he was easily able to grasp the
orthography of the *Popol Vuh* text. With his help and the colonial dictionaries, Tedlock translated the Spanish version into English, leaving his particular mark of understanding on his version: "From the
beginning of our work on the *Popol Vuh*, Andres Xiloj felt certain that
if one only knew how to read it perfectly, borrowing the knowledge of
the day lords, the moist breezes, and the distant lightning, it should
reveal everything under the sky and on the earth, all the way out to the
four corners" (1985, 20).

Freidel, Schele, and Parker pointed out that different scholars arrive at their translations and conclusions through personal judgment
as they evaluate the evidence surrounding the text, as exemplified by
the differences in the four English translations of the *Popol Vuh*: "All
text-based analyses are ultimately to be judged by the coherence they
lend to larger bodies of evidence" (1993, 444).

Christenson (2003) offered the most recent, the fourth English
translation of the *Popol Vuh*. Christenson, an assistant professor in
the Department of Humanities, Classics, and Comparative Literature

at Brigham Young University, wrote a clear version, presented in a syntax that is contemporary, while trying to maintain some, but not all, of the poetic voice of the original. Additionally, the author provided a detailed and helpful history and explanation of the text in his introduction. It is important to use all four translations to flush out the details of meaning seen through the eyes of four experts. Each author translated the text using the current understanding of the meaning of the words; therefore, Christenson had his predecessors' research to draw from and makes this clear in his text. He also gave more specific details about the K'iche' Maya and the symbolic meaning of their words, which is helpful for this book.

Christenson has worked as a translator and art historian of Maya material since 1976. Working as an ethnographer, he too lived among the Maya and learned the meaning of K'iche' words from them. Currently, K'iche' is an oral language only, but most of the early vocabulary is still understandable to the modern K'iche'. Working with Christenson, Vicente de León Abac of Momostenango, a daykeeper, said: "To read the thoughts of ancient ancestors is to make their spirits present in the room and give them a living voice. Such powers must be approached with great seriousness, and all care taken to be faithful to their original ideas in any transcription or translation" (Christenson 2003, 18).

Christenson studied K'iche' and Spanish for many years. He described the language in the *Popol Vuh* as "replete with esoteric language, plays on words, and phrases chosen for their sound and rhythm as much as for their meaning" (2003, 24). He, too, relied on dictionaries as well as theological treatises written by Spanish priests during the Colonial period in Guatemala. He also published a second volume, which is a literal poetic translation of the text that stands opposite the Latin version of the original. Unlike the Recinos, Edmondson, and D. Tedlock translations, Christenson did not break the book into parts, only chapters. Recinos started with a preamble and then continued with it in four parts. Edmonson's translation has four parts; D. Tedlock's has five parts. Christenson has a preamble and then no parts, only chapter headings. Christenson is the only one who used the current language convention referring to the group as

Maya, instead of Mayan, which is reserved for a description of the language itself. The Tedlock translation is the most pleasing to read because he tried to maintain the poetry of the original language while making it quite readable. In the following comparison of the translation of one passage, Tedlock added a further dimension of meaning referring to respect offered to the father. Tedlock wrote, "And so it remained that they were respectful of their father's heart, even though they left him at the Place of Ball Game Sacrifice" (1985, 159). Recinos translated this same passage: "And here is how they extolled the memory of their fathers, whom they had left there in the place of sacrifice at the ball-court" ([1950] 1991, 163). Christenson translated this same sentence as, "Thus the heart of their father was left behind at Crushing Ballcourt" (2003, 191). The same text from his second volume including a literal translation is as follows: "Left behind his heart their father. Merely he was left at Crushing Ballcourt" (151).

It is important to consider the meaning the K'iche' Maya themselves held regarding the images before comparing them to the more universal meaning of symbols and images. Two important Maya texts, *The Book of Chilam Balam of Chumayel* (Roys 1973) and *The Ancient Future of the Itza: The Book of Chilam Balam of Tizimin* (Edmonson 1982), focus on ritual and history and are useful in providing a comparison to the use of images and symbols in the *Popol Vuh* and in understanding the calendar systems. They are two of the only remaining books that survived destruction by the Catholic priests in the early years after the conquest of Mexico and Guatemala. They come from Yucatán rather than the lowlands of Guatemala and were written by the Itzá Maya rather than the K'iche' Maya, although both groups shared similar culture and beliefs. The books were written in the Maya language but used Latin script to express sounds not found in Spanish. The *Books of Chilam Balam* date from the seventeenth and eighteenth centuries and contain much of what was remembered of the original culture before the conquest, including rituals and traditions. They are full of historical and ethnological information, with little intrusive European material. These resources contributed to an understanding of the gods and ritual cycles that inform Maya religious thought and the creation myth in particular.

The infamous friar Landa (1579), who burned all the Maya codices, later proceeded to write his book as a way of exonerating himself from his abusive behavior in the New World. In so doing, he provided an account of life among the Maya of Yucatán shortly after the Spanish conquest. It offers a very detailed and clear glimpse into the daily life and rituals of the Maya. Expanding beyond the borders of the K'iche' Maya into greater Mesoamerica, original codices of Mixtec origin are a valuable resource for the meaning of images and symbols from across the central Mexico region: *Borgia* (Días and Rodgers 1993) included rituals and divinatory information; *Madrid* (Vail and Aveni 2009) included lunar and solar calendar almanacs and astronomical tables; *Zouche-Nuttall* (Nuttall 1975) included political and religious history; *Dresden* (Villacorta and Villacorta 1930) included astronomical tables, ritual schedules, and almanacs; *Vindobonensis Mexicanus 1* (Anders, Jansen, and García 1992) included a ritual and divinatory document with genealogy; and *Fejérváry-Mayer* (Keane and Loubat 2013) dealt with the sacred Aztec calendar. There are a number of Aztec codices that describe daily and economic life without the mention of ritual or religion. These, interesting though they are, were not helpful for this research. The codices *Telleriano-Remensis* (Keber 1995) dealt with the ritual and solar calendar, migrations, and historical events; its partial cognate, *Vaticano A* (Anders, Jansen, and García 1996) depicted Aztec religions, customs, and history; *Florentine* (Sahagún [1577] 1953) was a very impressive and comprehensive document on all aspects of Aztec life; and *Primeros Memoriales* (Sahagún and Sullivan 1997), was a postcolonial Nahuatl-language manuscript describing rituals, gods, heavens, underworld, rulership, and things relative to humans. The information contained in these on cosmology, ritual, deities, and mythology provided valuable comparisons to Maya imagery and symbolism.

Texts from secondary material are helpful in elaborating on the cultural and cosmic viewpoints and gleaning the meaning of specific symbols and mythological themes. Perhaps the most important recent writings are Hansen's (2005, 2012, 2017, 2018) contributions on his archaeological work in the Mirador-Calakmul Basin. His discoveries pushed the time frame for the height of Maya civilization back hundreds of years into the Middle Preclassic period (1000–350 BCE). He offered a convincing argument for the reasons behind the Maya collapse. Thompson's (1990) work is a fundamental, comprehensive overview of Maya history and religion from the Yucatán to the lowlands from the Classic period on, dealing with demographics, trade, and ritual. It is rich with description, yet some of his ideas have been challenged and discredited over the years because new information has emerged and new conclusions have been reached. Nevertheless, it is a foundational and important work. As an epigrapher, he accomplished important groundbreaking work on deciphering Maya hieroglyphic writing focusing on ideographic rather than linguistic principles. Yet later he was not willing to accept the more accurate development of syllabic and phonetic reading of symbols. Nevertheless, he dominated Maya studies for years and contributed significantly in many areas, including ceramic sequencing.

Anthropologists Sharer and Traxler (2006), Coe (1999), and Demarest (2004) contributed comprehensive studies of the origins and development of the Maya civilization in all stages of its history and aspects of its culture. For a general resource of the Maya culture, Coe, professor emeritus of anthropology, wrote a clear and definitive overview on the Maya, including history, culture, and environment. He followed the rise of the culture from its earliest times through the many periods of its history. All groups of Maya are mentioned, including their interactions with each other, their trade, and warfare. Life, thought, and culture are examined along with construction, art, ritual traditions, and social classes. As an anthropologist, he included the information and facts about all aspects of Maya life and culture. He did not interpret the information. Many researchers focused on particular aspects of the Maya culture. In this work, it was also helpful to have a wide overview of the Maya. Demarest, professor of anthropology at Vanderbilt University, presents a thorough overview of the Maya's presence from the Preclassic to Colonial periods, including their successful adaptation to living in the rain forest; the ruling system of K'uhul Ajaws, the shaman-priest leaders who focused on ritual, religion, war, and architecture; and the eventual breakdown of the theater-state political system resulting in the collapse of civilizations. Longhena (1999) and Taube (1992) described and explained the nature of the Maya gods and script. These are concise resources with illustrations helpful for a differentiation of the many gods and symbols. Along this same line, Miller, an art historian, and Taube, an anthropologist (Miller and Taube 1993), provided an illustrated dictionary of Mesoamerican religion that elaborated on many of the gods and symbols. It is a clear and concise resource for amplification.

Bassie-Sweet (2008) argued that geography is the template for the Maya worldview, linking the mythology to the land. Other authors linked mythology to the sky and the Milky Way. Bassie-Sweet explained the relationship between the elements in the *Popol Vuh* and geographical locations. It is an interesting concept, yet speculating that the myth was older, developing, and changing over time with each telling, and was a foundational belief among many groups in Mesoamerica, might indicate that it did not emerge merely from one landscape but perhaps from common elements in the general landscape. Speculating that the four rivers at the center of this area gave rise to the four roads in the myth is a quite limiting and concrete viewpoint that excludes all other possibilities, especially the symbolic. The concept of four roads is quite universal.

Miller and Brittenham (2013) recently published a spectacularly beautiful book on the Late Classic Maya murals at Bonampak. These are the most complete murals found in the Maya world. Painted around 800 CE, covering three rooms and filling twelve walls, the murals offer an unusual and rare view into Maya courtly life. The scenes, although never finished, are colorful and dynamic, depicting the royal court engaged in rituals, dancing, and the human sacrifice of captives while tribute is accepted. Elaborate costumes, musical instruments, and weapons were painted in great detail. The text is a description of the murals and what is known about the Maya at the time. Miller did not offer a story even though a number of the figures appear on several panels.

Dissertations written by prominent anthropologists are a rich resource for understanding the Maya symbolism. Carrasco (2005), an archaeologist/ethnologist, studied the iconography of the Mask Flange Iconographic Complex. It is a sculptural representation of Maya deities that acts as a map of the culture's creation mythology and a representation of their conception of a world order, which is based on the life cycle of maize. The author offered an understanding of the symbol system of the Maya as represented by this form and additionally gave insights into the interrelationship between art and ritual, with sculpture being the expression of the divine, and ritual the means of honoring it. This dissertation adds to the understanding of the symbols and ritual systems depicted in the *Popol Vuh* from a study within the culture itself. He also wrote a book (1990) on the religions of Mesoamerica that is very helpful in understanding the overall religious viewpoint of the Maya compared to that of the Aztecs.

Taube (1988), a well-respected Mesoamerican anthropologist and ethnohistorian, was a professor of anthropology at the time of this writing. His important study of the Maya New Year's Festival focuses on the dangerous liminal period of five days at the end of the year and beginning of the New Year, representing the period of death, decay, and renewal. As a festival, it reflects the larger mythological, cosmological belief systems concerning the destruction and creation of the world. Taube compared the current festival seen today among the Maya with the structure and form elucidated in the codices, both ancient and colonial, reflecting Classic Maya mythology and cosmology. He included descriptions of the major Maya gods. A later book (1992) focuses exclusively on the Maya gods of ancient Yucatán, and his book on Maya and Aztec myths (1993) provides a quick and clear comparison. Although the *Popol Vuh* is a text of the K'iche' Maya, there are many similarities in the cosmogony and cosmology of all Maya groups, as well as other non-Maya cultures throughout Mesoamerica—the Aztec, Mixtec, Toltec, and Olmec, for example. It is a rich and concise resource for the study of Postclassic Maya gods and includes a list of the codices used as reference in formulating this descriptive list.

Newsome's dissertation focuses on the dreams of a Classic Maya ruler nicknamed 18-Rabbit whose dreams reflected how the dreamer's "soul enters the realm of the dead to receive the world-creating powers of the Maya gods" (1991, v). The iconography on the sculptures is examined and studied, revealing the similarity between this and the creation mythology of the Maya people. It shows the importance of the king in maintaining and re-creating the circular order of the world. The hieroglyphics on each pillar support the hypothesis that each one is a symbol for the mythological Tree of Life, which the gods erected to support the sky at the moment of creation.

Robicsek and Hales (1981) and Schele and Miller (1986) presented studies of the art, including the vase paintings with depictions of rituals, mythic cycles, and daily life. Robicsek, a thoracic and cardiovascular surgeon as well as adjunct professor of anthropology, collected all known examples of this style of Maya vase paintings and established the hypothesis that they were the pictorial codices of the Maya books of the dead. Hales, an anthropologist, worked with Robicsek to study the style and sequence and presented his observations and commentary on the hieroglyphic text.

After the deciphering of Maya hieroglyphs made it possible to understand their writings, Schele and Miller (1986) were able to glean a deeper view into the world and minds of the Maya through their art. These include polychrome figurines, vases, portrait masks, costume ornaments, and ceremonial wares as well as their architecture and monumental art, such as steles. From these and their rituals, assumptions about the nature of their universe can be construed. This is a helpful visual companion to the translated *Popol Vuh* texts themselves. Schele, an epigrapher and iconographer, played an important role in the decipherment of Maya hieroglyphics. She also produced a book of the drawings of stelae and inscriptions that help the viewer see the images clearly.

Kerr (2000) continued this project with his later work. His book is a pictorial representation of the images on Maya vases showing the characters and scenes from mythology and is a helpful supplement to the text itself. The figures are identified with their unique symbolic characteristics and markings that are themselves symbolic. An example is the cover image of this book of a vase Kerr photographed and is in his pictorial collection. The author purchased the vase after it was photographed. Benson and Griffin (1988), Hanks and Rice (1989), and Stone and Zender (2011) offered elaboration on the written word, art, and iconography. As the history of the Maya is laid out in written and pictorial form on the steles and vases, these publications helped further amplify the images.

As an ethnologist from Mexico, León-Portilla (1988) presented an insight into the thinking of the Maya people, focusing on their interest in and obsession with time and its cycles. This, of course, affects their mythology, their religious thought, the organization of their culture, and their worldview. They devised two calendars and a very detailed study of the movement of the planets and stars, which in turn impacted their religious and ritual cycles. Milbrath (1999) and Aveni (2009) added to this study of astronomy that is fundamental to an understanding of the Maya creation myth. Milbrath, a curator of Latin American art and archaeology and an affiliated professor of anthropology, did her postdoctoral work with Aveni. He, as of this writing, is a professor and one of the foremost scholars of anthropology and astronomy, contributing extensively to the field of archaeoastronomy.

Boone (2007) explored the meaning of the cycle of time and the books of fate. Gossen (1986) compiled a very interesting series of articles in his edited volume on symbol and meaning in Mesoamerican ideas, part of a seminar looking at symbol and structural approaches to interpretation. He covered both the Maya areas and central Mexico.

An impressive book written by Freidel, an archaeologist; Schele, an art historian, epigrapher, and iconographer; and Parker, a professional writer (1993), is a study of Maya stories, both mythological and historical, revolving around archaeology, anthropology, and astronomy to present an argument for the continuation of the Maya's culture to the present day. Their research begins by addressing language issues, orthography in the K'iche'language and its translation into Spanish. Through the authors' personal experiences while living in Yucatán, observing current ritual practices and culture, along with solid knowledge of what is known of the Maya past, that is, culture and mythology, forged an interesting theory of Maya thought and cosmos. This conclusion focuses on the *axis mundi*, or the symbol of the world tree, an important part of the Maya mythology and cosmology. This book, as impressive as it is, has been thoroughly criticized for incorporating speculation and elaboration that is not substantiated by known facts. Schele and Freidel (1990) delineated the history of the Maya civilization from its beginnings to its collapse. It is a rich resource in filling out the details of Maya life and the struggles of the rulers to hold on to power. Included in it is a very helpful glossary of terms.

Gillette (1997), with a master of arts in divinity and a master of divinity in religion and psychology, looked at the Maya traditions from a depth psychological, archaeological, and comparative religious point of view. He interpreted symbolically and compared the images and themes to other mythic traditions from around the world. His work is closer to what this book contains than all other resources.* He used a depth psychological and religious perspective to amplify Maya mythology, including parts of the *Popol Vuh*. His focus was on offering up what he understood to be Maya resurrection teachings, which he showed were achieved through ritual, sacrifice, and altered states of consciousness. His purpose in writing the book was to take from the past a means of accessing a spiritual core to effect transformation and present it as an example for people today.

B. Tedlock (1992), a highly esteemed professor of anthropology, presented a compilation of articles based on the topic of the dream as a universal phenomenon seen from many different cross-cultural perspectives, including the Maya. The author, a Maya daykeeper herself, revealed a wide understanding of the current symbolism of that culture. The other contributors were anthropologists and psychologists who did extensive work in their culture of choice. In the book, scientists who worked in the field presented their facts and discussed their conclusions about the meaning of images from the unconscious and their relationship or lack of relationship to common human and cultural phenomena.

There are quite a number of authors who focused on Mesoamerica in general by looking at the commonalities. Austin (1993, 1996), a preeminent scholar of anthropology in Mexico, provided a theoreti-

*This book originated as a dissertation (Furlotti 2014).

cal study of Mesoamerican mythology. He used one common myth cycle, the opossum's theft of fire from the gods, to construct a pattern of similarity through the area and challenged the notion that myth is specific to culture. He further stated that ancient myths have the potential to be used to understand current myths. In other words, he approached the concept of myths archetypally. He was one of the most clear and thoughtful contributors to this area of study and looked at myths more inclusively while also focusing on the important considerations in the methodology of examining myths.

Girard (1979), an ethnologist, extensively studied Native American culture, principally with a number of the K'iche' and Ch'ortí spiritual elders. He presented a unique view of the esoteric vision presented in the *Popol Vuh*, laying out the cosmic philosophy by explaining Maya interpretation of the origin of the universe, the gods, and humans as they reflect the development of agriculture and culture. The underlying metaphor reflects the Maya perception of the ethical role of the individual and culture as a whole. This book touches on many of the subtleties that are common to metaphysical aspects of Jungian psychological thinking. It includes a very helpful glossary of Maya terms.

D. Tedlock (1993) took the reader on a journey with his wife, Barbara, and the Maya daykeeper with whom they both studied, weaving a playful and beautiful vision of the Maya world and imagination through personal stories and myth, from the past to the present. Bierhorst (1990), a writer specializing in American Indian literature and a translator of Nahuatl (Aztec), combined twenty creation myths from different groups in Mesoamerica into themes and compared them. In a later book (1998), he translated an important Aztec codex, the Chimalpopoca, which includes mythology and the role of human sacrifice. These provide cross-mythology comparisons.

JUNGIAN PSYCHOLOGY AND AMPLIFICATION

The primary text for this section is a number of volumes in C. G. Jung's (1976–97) *Collected Works*. From a culturally specific understanding of the symbols and images that appear in the myth, the next step is to move to a more universal understanding of symbol. Von Franz (1972) briefly described the myth from a psychological point of view and outlined and described creation myths from all over the world and from many different cultures. She then broke myths down into common motifs. Jung (1977a) and Stevens (2003) elaborated on the concept of the collective unconscious to allow for a comparison to the material in the myth itself. Jung (1977a, 1977b, 1977c, 1981) wrote extensively on myth in his *Collected Works*. These books explain the relationship between myth, the collective unconscious, and the process of amplification used to uncover the meaning of the symbols and images presented in the material.

To understand what constitutes an archetypal image, Campbell (1982a) and von Franz (1972) discussed the images, placing them in relation to the individual and the collective. Both compared manifestations of the same images across cultures as a way to glean a basic understanding of the underlying archetypal pattern. These patterns constitute the motifs that this book has flushed out of the *Popol Vuh* and compared to individual and cross-mythological material. There may be a difference between the archetypal manifestation on cultural and individual levels, and it is important to consider the difference. Campbell (1973) and Jung (1977a, 1977b, 1981) focused on the relationship between the archetypal motifs and culture, while Edinger (1972), Hollis (1995, 2000), Van Eenwyk (1997), and von Franz (1996, 1997) supported the idea of archetypes and mythic or imaginal thinking as a way to understand the process of individuation and translate symbolic material into Jungian psychological thinking. These authors also elaborated on the purpose of mythic motifs and how they further the development of the culture and help the individual become more conscious and productive.

Harding (1993) wrote a classic Jungian text demonstrating the process of individuation as seen through the model of *The Pilgrim's Progress*. She delineated this process of moving from shadow, strengthening the ego, and finally establishing a connection with the Self. It is pertinent to the process of the hero twins traversing through the underworld and emerging into light, as seen in the *Popol Vuh* and many similar creation myths. As another example of explaining a part of a creation myth in Jungian terms, Edinger (1999) focused on the Book of Revelation in the Bible and interpreted it psychologically as an explanation for events in the world today. The process of the destruction of the world as explained in this book mirrors the destruction and re-creation of worlds in the *Popol Vuh* myth. Psychologically it represents the coming of the Self into consciousness. Neumann (1970, 1991) wrote seminal books explicating Jungian psychology through myth and symbol. In his study of the Great Mother, he compared this archetype in different cultural references throughout history, while in his book on consciousness, he convincingly demonstrated how myths, especially the world creation and hero mythic cycle, represent the many stages in the process of development. Shalit (2002, 2011), Marlan (2005), and Henderson and Oakes (1990) took up similar themes comparing mythic, archetypal material to the Jungian psychological theory of development.

Ellenberger's (1970) immense and detailed survey, *The Discovery of the Unconscious*, traces the history of the unconscious from shamanism and loss of soul to the early works of Mesmer and hypnotism, to Charcot, Janet, and finally to the psychological systems of Freud, Jung, and Adler, with many other historical contributors in between. It shows the development of scientific methodology from its beginnings to 1970. The work is an example of this methodology in which the author states, "(1) Never take anything for granted. (2) Check everything. (3) Replace everything in its context. (4) Draw a sharp distinction between facts and interpretation of facts. Whenever possible, . . . use primary source material" (v). It is a very good example of historical scholarship.

At the present time, there seems to be a movement to study archetypes from a neuroscience perspective. Hogenson (2009), a Jungian analyst, discussed the relationship between mirror neurons and archetypes, both being what he called "elementary action patterns." From this perspective, human action occurs without unconscious factors, leading him to question the need for a theory of the unconscious at all. Merchant (2009) explored the contemporary views on archetypal theory in light of recent neuroscience findings. From his findings, he questioned the existence of autonomous archetypes separate from affective, emotional experiences.

There is much interest among Jungian researchers in the literature on the relationship between archetypes and their usefulness to cultural and intellectual history. Pietikainen argued that archetypal theory can move beyond the "unfruitful discourse on genetic inheritance" (1998, 325) to be understood through "culturally determined functionary forms organizing and structuring certain aspects of man's cultural activity" (325). In this way the concept contributes to hermeneutical and cultural studies. Lindenfeld (2009) further discussed the archetypes as plastic forms that help shape culture and have a unifying effect that counteracts the fragmenting influence of modern life. This supports the trend in evolutionary psychology. This trend in psychology supports the function of natural selection and adaptation due to environmental factors and the idea that humans have inherent behaviors and emotions consistent with the notion of archetypes but not described as such. Hogenson discussed the Baldwin effect, an evolutionary view that "learned adaptations affect the accumulation of genetic traits through natural selection" (2009, 101), in contrast to Jung's Lamarckian view. This view presupposes the existence of a dynamic unconscious.

Political anthropologists such as Johnson and Earle (2000) disputed this line of thinking and instead looked solely at the socio-political reasons for development. Many of the anthropologists cited previously also did not go as far as to discuss the images as archetypes or focus on the motifs of the myth. They remained within the Maya culture; did not compare images, symbols, and their meanings to those of other cultures; and actually frowned on making such comparisons. They explain that symbols are unique to a culture and contain meaning from that culture alone, and extending the meaning beyond the culture causes one to lose the exactitude of the meaning. This point is exactly where the anthropologists and mythologists part company. One is specific, and the other, general.

For general amplificatory material, Chevalier and Gheerbrant (1996) published a symbol dictionary that amplifies images and symbols from a wide cultural perspective. The Archive for Research on Archetypal Symbolism (ARAS, www.aras.org) is an online archive that is a resource for the amplification of symbols and images from many cultures and time periods. Finally, Shalit and Furlotti (2013) edited a book on dreams and amplification that explains many of the Jungian concepts and offers many examples of the process of amplification.

GENERAL MYTHOLOGY

Motifs from the *Popol Vuh* can also be compared to myths from other cultures. Such a comparison demonstrates a similarity of motifs from culture to culture. Campbell (1982a, 1988a, 1988b, 1988c, 1989a, 1989b, 1991a, 1991b), a mythologist, wrote extensively on comparative mythology from cultures all over the world in his *Historical Atlas of World Mythology*, in which he compared the mythological images and themes from many differing cultures. In his other books he focused on the specific myths and described the psychological process of development seen through the lens of the myth. His understanding and the vastness of his collection are impressive. He began at the beginning of time and ran through to his last contributions in the late 1980s, presenting creation mythology and a comparison of early Neolithic life and the early developments of civilizations and their early forms of religion. He included shamanism and the many symbolic themes that are pertinent on an archaic level. Pre-Columbian mythology falls into this category. He explained his theory of early imprinting resulting from a basic instinctual reaction in humans and animals as being the foundation for the creation of similar themes in different cultures. He took up the argument of conditioned versus innate behavior, and psychological versus ethnological approaches to myth. Many who have studied his work have considered the arguments he presented to be quite convincing.

Moving to a psychological understanding, Campbell (1973) took up the theme of the hero and went into great detail outlining the journey leading to greater consciousness. From the edition of the *Eranos Lectures* in which he served as editor, Campbell (1982b) presented a compilation of papers on the subject of religious mysteries showing the similarity and universal factors in religious thought. The papers cover a wide range of cultures and mystery traditions such as those of India and Greece in the Eleusinian and Orphic traditions, as well as Christian, Egyptian, Iranian, and Islamic mysteries. The concept of transformation is examined from various religious traditions, including Christianity, Zen Buddhism, Islam, and Indian philosophy. These papers elucidate the cross-cultural movement of transformation in humans.

Frazer (1963) wrote an early comparative survey of human ritual, religion, magic, and succession of rulers in Greece, the countries around the Mediterranean, and the Middle East with a focus on symbolism and similarities. Much has been written since then to clarify some of the assumptions presented in this book, but it remains a fundamental basic resource. Freund (2003) in his study of comparative mythology discussed the origins of the universe from the mythological, religious, and scientific points of view, and from this study he arrived at the notion of a universality of ideas and beliefs throughout humankind. Included in his study are references to Jung, Freud, and Campbell. He was a novelist, poet, playwright, anthropologist, and professor emeritus, and his book arose from his own phenomenological interest in the subject. He categorized creation myths and gave short comparisons from different cultures.

There are many books like the ones by Markman and Markman (1992), professors of literature; Sproul (1991), professor of religion; and Eliot (1990) that offer general comparisons of Mesoamerican mythology or comparative creation mythology that are not useful because they contain inaccurate information, lack detail and precision, or put forth speculation that is not grounded in any significant theory. Waters (1989), a writer with interests in Native America as well as Jungian psychology and an understanding of the collective unconscious, wrote on Mesoamerican spirituality and mythology, including its cosmos, its gods' ritual calendar, and its images and symbols. His book on the Hopi (1977) carries a similar thread, and, in fact, he made an interesting argument about the similarity of mythology between the Hopi and Maya and their common origin. However, Waters was not an anthropologist, art historian, or ethnologist, and his writings include a degree of intuition and extrapolation that may extend beyond the known facts. For this reason, his work must be compared carefully to other sources and placed within the larger context of research.

Von Franz (1972), Jungian analyst, discussed and compared many types of creation myths from different cultures. Each type of origin reflects on the development of the culture. The types include creation by accident or as an awakening, creation from above or below, two creators, first victim, creation from germs or eggs, twofold or fourfold division of the universe, abortive attempts at creation, chains, and creation renewed or reversed. A number of these motifs are present in the *Popol Vuh* creation myth. Her symbolic amplifications were particularly helpful in research for this book. As a Jungian, she explained the concepts of archetypes and the collective unconscious and their impact on conscious development. She moved fluidly between mythic themes and psychology.

Eliade was a professor of comparative religions who wrote extensively on many different cultures and religious systems, including mythology. In comparing religious systems, he studied the function of symbolism as well. In a book he edited (Eliade and Kitagawa 1959), the authors discussed the issues of phenomenology, subjectivity, the collective unconscious, and the relationship between universals and historic communities. Eliade (1991a) used the symbol of the cosmic tree to explicate his point of view on comparative symbolism, which is particularly helpful to the study of the *Popol Vuh*. He wrote a seminal book on shamanism (1974), going into great detail in its description and explanation of the various stages and the encounters it entails. When looking at the idea of history in relation to time, archetypes, and repetition, Eliade (1991b) looked at whether it is linear or cyclic, as in the myth of the eternal return or cyclic periodicity. He compared religious and mythic systems, showing how the treatment of history affects their development. He compared archaic with modern or historic humans, as well as Hegel's Universal Spirit with Marx's class struggle, seen as two ways of dealing with the fear of history and its repeated, inconsistent brutality. Eliade's (1991b) statement that the Universal Spirit offers shelter from the terror of history gives a reason for the belief in the archetypes and greater Self.

More specific to the focus of this book is how the cyclic myth of sequential destruction and regeneration of the world is consistent with the mythic system in the *Popol Vuh*, which is an archaic system that blends myth with historical personages. It relates directly to the hero twins in the *Popol Vuh* and their descent into the underworld. The study of symbolism is significant in studying comparative religions as well as mythologies. Eliade (1978) used these concepts regarding symbolism in studying the occult and compares the beliefs and symbols in many earlier and contemporary systems of belief. He stated that only by comparing similar religious phenomena would a researcher be able to uncover the general structure and specific meaning that is the appropriate methodology for such a study. In his later book (1991a), he analyzed numerous symbols from many different cultures, both East and West, and discussed the significance of the symbol itself as an essential part of meaning making. He focused on the symbols of the center: time and eternity, the god who binds and knots, and shells and water. Finally, Eliade (1991b) took up the concept of archetypes as seen through cultures and history. His work is particularly helpful in understanding comparative symbolism and making a bridge from one culture and religion or mythological system to another.

A renowned professor of history of religions and professor of Eliade's, Wach (1958) believed in the importance of studying religions as a way of increasing understanding between differing cultures. He clearly laid out his method of study of comparative religions and agreed with Dilthey ([1910] 2002) that human religious life is a reality accessible and worthy of study and understanding. He pointed out that there are universal themes in religious thought that reflect both cultures and individuals. As a phenomenologist, he thought that understanding experience was of utmost importance and was the way to psychological interpretation. He laid out his ideas on three forms of religious expression: thought, which includes symbols, myths, and dogmas; action, which includes devotion and service; and fellowship, including community and culture.

A professor of comparative religions, van der Leeuw (1963) looked at religion from a phenomenological perspective. His book, *Religion in Essence and Manifestation*, is a fundamental and important text on the subject. In this volume, the author examined the relationship between humans and God through the outward and inward expressions of relationship to the other, from ritual to introspection. He delineated the forms that religions have manifested over time, including struggle, asceticism, obedience, humility, and love. He then discussed the various types of religious leaders. His final chapter is on the study of phenomenology, which is particularly pertinent to the methodology used here.

Pagels (1996), a Gnostic scholar, took up the origins of the figure of Satan, historically and religiously, offering both the positive and negative aspects of this archetypal figure. The contrary or shadow side of this monotheistic dark god is Christ. Her resources are Gnostic and Christian. It presents a helpful understanding for comparative amplification of the origins of this dark figure that appears in different forms in all cultures, including the demons in the *Popol Vuh*.

Specialists focusing on specific cultures such as that of Egypt (Hornung 1992; Clark 1959; Schweizer 2010) were helpful in shedding light on Egyptian mythology to use as a comparison. Edinger (1994) looked at Greek mythology from the point of view of Jungian psychology. Pertaining to Indian mythology, Coomaraswamy and Nivedita (1967), Zimmer (1989), and Daniélou (1991) presented detailed and scholarly descriptions of the creation myths and gods that were useful for comparisons.

Radin (1991), an anthropologist very familiar with Jungian theory, explored the ritual life of the Winnebago Indians of North America, showing how their rituals are a recapitulation of the mythic origins of that group. It is an interesting comparison to the ritual sequence set forth in the Maya creation myth.

Swedenborg ([1758] 1995; [1763] 1995) was a scientist and philosopher interested in spirituality and lived from 1688 to 1772. He has been described as a Christian mystic. He outlined his philosophy of creation, the nature of god, the process and structure of creation, the world, and the spiritual and celestial realms. He presented a fully formed religion filtered through Christianity. Many of his concepts seem similar to Jung's, and it is known that Jung was familiar with his writings. More recently, Nuttman-Shwartz (2007) wrote of the clinical connection between inner psychological process and the outer social myths that lead to change within the individual. She focused on how shared myth and archetypal images relating to the culture at large facilitated individual change. Jaenke (2006) went one step further to describe the relationship between the revitalization of communal life and individual dreams. She specifically focused on ritual images in dreams that lead to a healthy restoration of balance within the group.

BRIDGING FROM ONE CULTURE TO ANOTHER

Jung (1976, 1977a, 1996), through his exploration of alchemy, typology, and kundalini yoga, and Edinger (1990a, 1990b, 1995), through his explication of alchemy and literature, translated these theoretical paradigms into Jungian psychology. In the process, they demonstrate how to bridge different areas of thinking, which is the task of this book.

Bricker (1981), an ethnologist, took up the issue of historiography in relation to the Maya mythology. This was a very helpful book regarding understanding the importance of the historical substrate to mythology as well as the importance of the mythological substrate to the formation of history. There is an interrelationship. She offered a critique of previous archaeological works and theses pointing out that most have explained the past solely in terms of the present, which she believed has created inaccuracies in both the history and mythology. She compared contemporary myths and symbolism to their ancient counterparts and formed an argument that one can trace a connection between the two. Her book offers a way of thinking about how to translate across cultures and time periods and was useful in supporting the methodology used here.

D. Brown (1991), an anthropologist, wrote about the idea of universals as a heterogeneous set in human nature. He studied similarities in themes across cultures and seemed not afraid to generalize about them, unlike most anthropologists. He believed biology and evolutionary psychology are keys to understanding them. This book provides an important comparison on the anthropological level to Jung's concept of the collective unconscious.

By way of bridging from one culture to another, Starcher (1999), in his doctoral dissertation, demonstrated a connection and similarity between the chakra system and psychology, selected to use the methodology that Jung used in his kundalini seminars as a way of transposing Eastern philosophy and the chakra system to Jungian psychology. This method was used in this study to transpose an amplification of the *Popol Vuh* into the framework of Jungian psychology. Perera (1981), a Jungian analyst, amplified a Sumerian myth from a psychological point of view as another example of how to create a bridge in methodology from myth to psychology.

REFERENCES

Anders, F., M. Jansen, and L. R. García, eds. 1992. *Origen e historia de los reyes Mixtecos: Libro explicativo del llamado códice Vindobonensis.* Mexico City: Fondo de Cultura Económica.

Anders, F., M. Jansen, and L. R. García, eds. 1996. *Religión, costumbres e historia de los antiguos Mexicanos: Libro explicativo del llamado códice Vaticano A.* Mexico City: Fondo de Cultura Económica.

Austin, A. L. 1993. *The Myth of the Opossum: Pathways of Mesoamerican Mythology.* Translated by B. de Montellano and T. de Montellano. Albuquerque: University of New Mexico Press.

Austin, A. L. 1996. *The Rabbit on the Face of the Moon: Mythology in the Mesoamerican Tradition.* Translated by B. de Montellano and T. de Montellano. Salt Lake City: University of Utah Press.

Aveni, A. 2009. *The End of Time: The Maya Mystery of 2012.* Boulder: University of Colorado Press.

Bassie-Sweet, K. 2008. *Maya Sacred Geography and the Creator Deities.* Norman: University of Oklahoma Press.

Bastian, A. 1895. *Ethnische elementargedanken in der lehre vom menschen.* Berlin: Weidmann.

Bawaya, M. 2007. "Saving the Mirador Basin." *American Archaeology* 11 (3): 18–25.

Benson, E. P., and G. G. Griffin, eds. 1988. *Maya Iconography.* Princeton, NJ: Princeton University Press.

Bierhorst, J. 1990. *The Mythology of Mexico and Central America.* New York: William Morrow.

Bierhorst, J. 1998. *History and Mythology of the Aztecs: The Codex Chimalpopoca.* Tucson: University of Arizona Press.

Boone, E. H. 2007. *Cycles of Time and Meaning in the Mexican Books of Fate.* Austin: University of Texas Press.

Bricker, V. R. 1981. *The Indian Christ, the Indian King: The Historical Substrate of Maya Myth and Ritual.* Austin: University of Texas Press.

Brown, D. E. 1991. *Human Universals.* New York: McGraw-Hill.

Campbell, J. 1973. *The Hero with a Thousand Faces.* Princeton, NJ: Princeton University Press.

Campbell, J., ed. 1982a. *The Mystic Vision: Papers from the Eranos Yearbooks.* Princeton, NJ: Princeton University Press.

Campbell, J. 1982b. *The Mythic Image.* Princeton, NJ: Princeton University Press.

Campbell, J. 1988a. *The Way of the Animal Powers*. Vol. 1 of *Historical Atlas of World Mythology*. Pt. 1, *Mythologies of the Primitive Hunters and Gatherers*. New York: Harper and Row.

Campbell, J. 1988b. *The Way of the Animal Powers*. Vol. 1 of *Historical Atlas of World Mythology*. Pt. 2, *Mythologies of the Great Hunt*. New York: Harper and Row.

Campbell, J. 1988c. *The Way of the Seeded Earth*. Vol. 2 of *Historical Atlas of World Mythology*. Pt. 1, *The Sacrifice*. New York: Harper and Row.

Campbell, J. 1989a. *The Way of the Seeded Earth*. Vol. 2 of *Historical Atlas of World Mythology*. Pt. 2, *Mythologies of the Primitive Planters: The Northern Americas*. New York: Harper and Row.

Campbell, J. 1989b. *The Way of the Seeded Earth*. Vol. 2 of *Historical Atlas of World Mythology*. Pt. 3, *Mythologies of the Primitive Planters: The Middle and Southern Americas*. New York: Harper and Row.

Campbell, J. 1991a. *Creative Mythology: The Masks of God*. New York: Penguin.

Campbell, J. 1991b. *Primitive Mythology: The Masks of God*. New York: Arkana, Penguin Books.

Carrasco, D. 1990. *Religions of Mesoamerica: Cosmovision and Ceremonial Centers*. Lone Grove, IL: Waveland Press.

Carrasco, D. 2005. "The Mask Flange Iconographic Complex: The Art, Ritual, and History of a Maya Sacred Image." PhD diss., University of Chicago. UMI Dissertation Services (UMI No. 3187838).

Chevalier, J., and A. Gheerbrant. 1996. *Dictionary of Symbols*. Translated by J. Buchanan-Brown. New York: Penguin Reference.

Chomsky, N. 1988. *Language and Problems of Knowledge: The Managua Lectures*. Cambridge, MA: MIT Press.

Christenson, A. J. 2003. *Popol Vuh: The Sacred Book of the Maya*. New York: O Books.

Christenson, A. J., ed. and trans. 2007. *Popol Vuh: Sacred Book of the Ancient Maya*. Provo, UT: Center for the Preservation of Ancient Religious Texts, Brigham Young University. CD-ROM.

Clark, R. T. R. 1959. *Myth and Symbol in Ancient Egypt*. London: Thames and Hudson.

Coe, M. D. 1999. *The Maya*. 6th ed. New York: Thames and Hudson.

Cohodas, M. 1989. "Transformations: Relationships between Image and Text in the Ceramic Paintings of the Metropolitan Master." In *Word and Image in Maya Culture: Explorations in Language, Writing, and Representation*, edited by W. Hanks and D. Rice, 222. Salt Lake City: University of Utah Press.

Coomaraswamy, A. K., and S. Nivedita. 1967. *Myths of the Hindus and Buddhists*. Mineola, NY: Dover Publications.

Daniélou, A. 1991. *The Myths and Gods of India*. Rochester, VT: Inner Traditions.

Demarest, A. 2004. *Ancient Maya: The Rise and Fall of a Rainforest Civilization*. Cambridge: Cambridge University Press.

Días, G., and A. Rodgers. 1993. *The Codex Borgia: A Full-Color Restoration of the Ancient Mexican Manuscript*. New York: Dover Publications.

Dilthey, W. (1910) 2002. *Wilhelm Dilthey: Selected Works*. Vol. 3, *The Formation of the Historical World in the Human Sciences*. Edited by R. A. Makkreel and F. Rodi. Reprint, Princeton, NJ: Princeton University Press.

Edinger, E. 1972. *Ego and Archetype*. New York: Penguin Books.

Edinger, E. 1990a. *Anatomy of the Psyche: Alchemical Symbolism in Psychotherapy*. Chicago: Open Court.

Edinger, E. 1990b. *Goethe's* Faust: *Notes for a Jungian Commentary*. Toronto, Ontario, Canada: Inner City Books.

Edinger, E. 1994. *The Eternal Drama: The Inner Meaning of Greek Mythology*. Boston: Shambhala.

Edinger, E. 1995. *Melville's* Moby-Dick: *An American Nekyia*. Toronto, Ontario, Canada: Inner City Books.

Edinger, E. 1999. *Archetype of the Apocalypse: Divine Vengeance, Terrorism, and the End of the World*. Chicago: Open Court.

Edmonson, M. S. 1971. *The Book of Counsel: The* Popol Vuh *of the Quiche Maya of Guatemala*. New Orleans: Middle American Research Institute, Tulane University.

Edmonson, M. S., ed. 1982. *The Ancient Future of the Itza: The Book of Chilam Balam of Tizimin*. Austin: University of Texas Press.

Eliade, M. 1957. *The Sacred and the Profane: The Nature of Religion*. Translated by Willard R. Trask. New York: Harvest, Brace and World.

Eliade, M. 1960. *Myths, Dreams and Mysteries: The Encounter between Contemporary Faiths and Archaic Realities*. Translated by P. Mairet. New York: Harper Torchbooks.

Eliade, M. 1974. *Shamanism: Archaic Techniques of Ecstasy*. Translated by W. Trask. Princeton, NJ: Princeton University Press.

Eliade, M. 1978. *Occultism, Witchcraft, and Cultural Fashions: Essays in Comparative Religion*. Chicago: University of Chicago Press.

Eliade, M. 1987. *The Sacred and the Profane*. Translated by W. R. Trask. New York: Harcourt.

Eliade, M. 1991a. *Images and Symbols: Studies in Religious Symbolism*. Translated by P. Mairet. Princeton, NJ: Princeton University Press.

Eliade, M. 1991b. *The Myth of the Eternal Return: Cosmos and History*. Translated by W. R. Trask. Princeton, NJ: Princeton University Press.

Eliade, M., and J. M. Kitagawa, eds. 1959. *The History of Religions: Essays in Methodology*. Chicago: University of Chicago Press.

Eliot, A. 1990. *The Universal Myths: Heroes, Gods, Tricksters, and Others*. New York: Truman Talley Books.

Ellenberger, H. F. 1970. *The Discovery of the Unconscious: The History and Evolution of Dynamic Psychiatry*. New York: Basic Books.

Fernández-Armesto, F. 2004. *World of Myth*. Vol. 2, *The Legendary Past*. London: British Museum Press.

Fox, J. R. 1989. *The Search for Society: Quest for a Biosocial Science and Morality*. New Brunswick, NJ: Rutgers University Press.

Frazer, J. G. 1963. *The Golden Bough*. New York: Macmillan.

Freidel, D. 2018. "Maya and the Idea of Empire." In *Pathways to Complexity*, edited by M. K. Brown and G. J. Bey III, 363–86. Gainesville: University Press of Florida.

Freidel, D., and L. Schele. 1988. "Symbol and Power: A History of the Lowland Maya Cosmogram." In *Maya Iconography*, edited by E. P. Benson and G. G. Griffin, 44–93. Princeton, NJ: Princeton University Press.

Freidel, D., L. Schele, and J. Parker. 1993. *Maya Cosmos: Three Thousand Years on the Shaman's Path*. New York: Quill, William Morrow.

Freund, P. 2003. *Myths of Creation*. London: Peter Owen.

Furlotti, N. S. 2014. "The *Popol Vuh*, Creation Myth of the Quiché Maya, Amplified from a Jungian Psychological Perspective." PhD diss., Saybrook University. UMI Dissertation Services (UMI No. 3628164).

Furlotti, N. S. 2023. *Eternal Echoes: Erich Neumann's Timeless Relevance to Consciousness, Creativity, and Evil*. Asheville, NC: Chiron Publications.

German, John, ed. 2013. Update. *Santa Fe Institute Newsletter*, November/December.

Gilgamesh. 2004. Translated by S. Mitchell. New York: Free Press.

Gillette, D. 1997. *The Shaman's Secret: The Lost Resurrection Teachings of the Ancient Maya*. New York: Bantam Books.

Girard, R. 1979. *Esotericism of the* Popol Vuh: *The Sacred History of the Quiché-Maya*. Pasadena, CA: Theosophical University Press.

Gossen, G. H., ed. 1986. *Symbol and Meaning beyond the Closed Community: Essays in Mesoamerican Ideas*. Albany: Institute for Mesoamerican Studies, State University of New York.

Grube, Nikolai. 2001. *Maya: Divine Kings of the Rainforest*. Cologne, Germany: Konemann.

Hanks, E., and D. S. Rice, eds. 1989. *Word and Image in Maya Culture: Explorations in Language, Writing, and Representation*. Salt Lake City: University of Utah Press.

Hansen, R. D. 2005. "Perspectives on Olmec-Maya Interaction in the Middle Formative Period." In *New Perspectives on Formative Mesoamerican Cultures*, edited by T. G. Powis, 50–71. Oxford, UK: Archaeopress.

Hansen, R. D. 2012. "Kingship in the Cradle of Maya Civilization: The Mirador Basin." In *Fanning the Sacred Flame: Mesoamerican Studies in Honor of H. B. Nicholson*, edited by M. A. Boxt and B. D. Dillon, 139–71. Boulder: University Press of Colorado.

Hansen, R. D. 2017. "The Feast before Famine and Fighting: The Origins and Consequences of Social Complexity in the Mirador Basin, Guatemala." In *Feast, Famine or Fighting? Multiple Pathways to Social Complexity*, edited by C. R. Chacon and R. G. Mendoza, 305–35. Gewerbestrasse, Switzerland: Springer.

Hansen, R. D., D. W. Forsyth, J. C. Woods, T. P. Schreiner, and G. L. Titmus. 2018. "Developmental Dynamics, Energetics, and Economic Interactions of the Early Maya." In *Pathways to Complexity*, edited by M. K. Brown and G. J. Bey III, 147–94. Gainesville: University Press of Florida.

Harding, M. E. 1993. *Journey into Self*. 2nd ed. Boston: Sigo Press.

Henderson, J., and M. Oakes. 1990. *The Wisdom of the Serpent: The Myths of Death, Rebirth, and Resurrection*. Princeton, NJ: Princeton University Press.

Henwood, K., and N. Pidgeon. 2007. "Grounded Theory in Psychological Research." In *Qualitative Research in Psychology: Expanding Perspectives in Methodology and Design*, edited by P. M. Camic, J. E. Rhodes, and L. Yardley, 131–55. Washington, DC: American Psychological Association.

Hill, Gareth, ed. 1978. *The Shaman from Elko: Papers in Honor of Joseph L. Henderson on His Seventy-Fifth Birthday*. Boston: Sigo Press.

Hogenson, G. B. 2009. "Archetypes as Action Patterns." *Journal of Analytical Psychology* 54 (3): 325–37. doi: 10.1111/j.1468–5922.2009.01783.x.

Hollis, J. 1995. *Tracking the Gods: The Place of Myth in Modern Life*. Toronto, Ontario, Canada: Inner City Books.

Hollis, J. 2000. *The Archetypal Imagination*. College Station: Texas A&M University Press.

Hornung, E. 1992. *Idea into Image: Essays on Ancient Egyptian Thought*. Translated by E. Bredeck. New York: Timken Publishers.

I Ching [Book of Changes]. 1970. 3rd ed. Translated by R. Wilhelm. Princeton, NJ: Princeton University Press.

Jacobi, J. (1957) 1971. *Complex, Archetype, Symbol in the Psychology of C. G. Jung*. Translated by R. Manheim. Reprint, Princeton, NJ: Princeton University Press.

Jaenke, K. 2006. "Dreaming the Ritual Onward." *ReVision* 29 (1): 3–10.

Johnson, A. W., and T. Earle. 2000. *The Evolution of Human Societies: From Foraging Group to Agrarian State.* 2nd ed. Stanford, CA: Stanford University Press.

Jung, C. G. 1950–79. *The Collected Works.* Vols. 1–20. Edited by Sir H. Reed, M. Fordham, G. Adler, and W. McGuire. Translated by R. F. C. Hull. Princeton, NJ: Princeton University Press.

Jung, C. G. 1967. *Symbols of Transformation.* 2nd ed. Translated by R. F. C. Hull. Princeton, NJ: Princeton University Press.

Jung, C. G. 1974. *Psychological Types.* Translated by R. F. C. Hull. Princeton, NJ: Princeton University Press.

Jung, C. G. 1976. *Mysterium Coniunctionis.* 2nd ed. Translated by R. F. C. Hull. Princeton, NJ: Princeton University Press.

Jung, C. G. 1977a. *The Archetypes and the Collective Unconscious.* 2nd ed. Translated by R. F. C. Hull. Princeton, NJ: Princeton University Press.

Jung, C. G. 1977b. *Psychology and Alchemy.* Translated by R. F. C. Hull. Princeton, NJ: Princeton University Press.

Jung, C. G. 1977c. *Two Essays on Analytical Psychology.* Translated by R. F. C. Hull. Princeton, NJ: Princeton University Press.

Jung, C. G. 1978. *Aion: Researches into the Phenomenology of the Self.* 2nd ed. Translated by R. F. C. Hull. Princeton, NJ: Princeton University Press.

Jung, C. G. 1981. *The Structure and Dynamics of the Psyche.* Translated by R. F. C. Hull. Princeton, NJ: Princeton University Press.

Jung, C. G. 1983. *Alchemical Studies.* Translated by R. F. C. Hull. Princeton, NJ: Princeton University Press.

Jung, C. G. 1984. *Dream Analysis: Notes of the Seminar Given in 1928–1930 by C. G. Jung.* Edited by W. McGuire. Princeton, NJ: Princeton University Press.

Jung, C. G. 1989a. *Psychology and Religion: West and East.* 2nd ed. Translated by R. F. C. Hull. Princeton, NJ: Princeton University Press.

Jung, C. G. 1989b. *The Symbolic Life: Miscellaneous Writings.* Translated by R. F. C. Hull. Princeton, NJ: Princeton University Press.

Jung, C. G. 1996. *The Psychology of Kundalini Yoga: Notes of the Seminar Given in 1932 by C. G. Jung.* Edited by S. Shamdasani. Princeton, NJ: Princeton University Press.

Jung, C. G. 1997. *Visions: Notes of the Seminar given in 1930–1934 by C. G. Jung.* Edited by Claire Douglas. Princeton, NJ: Princeton University Press.

Jung, C. G. 2009. *The Red Book.* New York: W. W. Norton.

Jung, C. G., and A. Jaffe, eds. 1965. *Memories, Dreams, Reflections.* New York: Random House.

Keane, A. H., and J. F. Loubat. 2013. *Codex Fejérváry-Mayer: An Old Mexican*

Picture Manuscript in the Liverpool Free Public Museums. Edited by E. Seler.
San Bernardino, CA: Ulan Press.

Keber, E. Q. 1995. *Codex Telleriano-Remensis: Ritual, Divination, and History in a Pictorial Aztec Manuscript.* Austin: University of Texas Press.

Kerr, J. 2000. *The Maya Vase Book: A Corpus of Rollout Photographs of Maya Vases.* New York: Kerr Associates.

Kolbert, E. 2014. "Think Again: Repeat When Necessary." *Onearth: A Survival Guide for the Planet*, Winter, 26–27.

Landa, D. D. 1579. *Yucatan before and after the Conquest.* Translated by W. Gates. Mexico City: San Fernando.

Leeming, D. A., and M. A. Leeming. 1994. *A Dictionary of Creation Myths.* Oxford: Oxford University Press.

León- Portillo, M. 1969. *Pre-Columbian Literature of Mexico.* Norman: University of Oklahoma Press.

León-Portilla, M. 1988. *Time and Reality in the Thought of the Maya.* Norman: University of Oklahoma Press.

León-Portilla, M., and E. Shorris. 2001. *In the Language of Kings: An Anthology of Mesoamerican Literature—Pre-Columbian to the Present.* New York: W. W. Norton.

Lévi-Strauss, C. 1983. *The View from Afar.* Translated by J. Neugroschel and P. Hoss. Chicago: University of Chicago Press.

Lindenfeld, D. 2009. Jungian Archetypes and the Discourse of History. *Rethinking History* 13 (2): 217–34. doi: 10.1080/13642509092833833.

Longhena, M. 1999. *Maya Script.* New York: Abbeville Press.

Markman, R. H., and P. T. Markman. 1992. *The Flayed God: The Mythology of Mesoamerica.* San Francisco: Harper.

Marlan, S. 2005. *The Black Sun: The Alchemy and Art of Darkness.* College Station: Texas A&M University Press.

Merchant, J. 2009. "Reappraisal of Classical Archetypal Theory and Its Implications for Theory and Practice." *Journal of Analytical Psychology* 54 (3): 339–58. doi: 10.1111/j.1468–5922.2009.01784.x.

Meyer, R. 2007. *Clio's Circle: Entering the Imaginal World of Historians.* New Orleans: Spring Journal Books.

Milbrath, S. 1999. *Star Gods of the Maya: Astronomy in Art, Folklore, and Calendars.* Austin: University of Texas Press.

Miller, M., and C. Brittenham. 2013. *The Spectacle of the Late Maya Court: Reflections on the Murals of Bonampak.* Austin: University of Texas Press.

Miller, M., and K. Taube. 1993. *The Gods and Symbols of Ancient Mexico and the Maya: An Illustrated Dictionary of Mesoamerican Religion.* London: Thames and Hudson.

Neumann, E. 1969. *Depth Psychology and a New Ethic*. New York: Harper Touchstone.

Neumann, E. 1970. *The Origins of History and Consciousness*. Translated by R. F. C. Hull. Princeton, NJ: Princeton University Press.

Neumann, E. 1991. *The Great Mother*. Princeton, NJ: Princeton University Press.

Newsome, E. A. 1991. "Trees of Paradise and Pillars of the World: Vision Quest and Creation in the Stelae Cycle of 18-Rabbit-God K, Copan, Honduras." PhD diss. UMI Dissertation Services (UMI No. 9128316).

Nuttall, Z., ed. 1975. *The Codex Nuttall: A Picture Manuscript from Ancient Mexico*. Mineola, NY: Dover Publications.

Nuttman-Shwartz, O. 2007. "Myths of Women and Their Reflection in a Therapy Group." *Clinical Social Work Journal* 35 (4): 237–45. Doi:10.1007/s10615-007-0109-1.

Ochiai, K. 1986. "On Whom the Gods Tried Their Swords: A Semiotic Approach to the Combat Myths of the *Popol Vuh*." In *Symbol and Meaning beyond the Closed Community: Essays in Mesoamerican Ideas*, edited by G. H. Gossen 83–100. Albany, NY: Institute for Mesoamerican Studies.

Pagels, E. 1996. *The Origin of Satan: How Christians Demonized Jews, Pagans, and Heretics*. New York: Vintage Books.

Perera, S. B. 1981. *Descent to the Goddess: A Way of Initiation for Women*. Toronto, Ontario, Canada: Inner City Books.

Pietikainen, P. 1998. "Archetypes as Symbolic Forms." *Journal of Analytical Psychology* 43 (3): 325–54.

Radin, P. 1972. *The Trickster: A Study in American Indian Mythology*. New York: Schocken Books.

Radin, P. 1991. *The Road of Life and Death: A Ritual Drama of the American Indians*. Princeton, NJ: Princeton University Press.

Recinos, A. (1950) 1991. *Popol Vuh: The Sacred Book of the Ancient Quiché Maya*. Translated by D. Goetz and S. G. Morley. Reprint, Norman: University of Oklahoma Press.

Riger, S. 1995. "Epistemological Debates, Feminist Voices: Science, Social Values and the Study of Women." In *The Culture and Psychology Reader*, edited by N. R. Goldberger and J. B. Veroff, 139–63. New York: New York University Press.

Roberts, T. R., M. J. Roberts, and B. P. Katz. 1997. *Mythology: Tales of Ancient Civilizations*. New York: Michael Friedman Publishing Group.

Robicsek, F., and D. M. Hales. 1981. *The Maya Book of the Dead: The Ceramic Codex, the Corpus of Codex Style Ceramics of the Last Classic Period*. Norman: University of Oklahoma Press.

Ronnberg, A., and K. Martin, eds. 2010. *The Book of Symbols: Reflections on Archetypal Images*. Cologne, Germany: Taschen.

Roys, R. L. 1973. *The Book of Chilam Balam of Chumayel*. Norman: University of Oklahoma Press.

Sahagún, B. (1577) 1953. "The Sun, Moon, and Stars, and the Binding of the Years." In *Florentine Codex: General History of the Things of New Spain*, Book VII, translated by A. Anderson and C. E. Dibble. Reprint, Santa Fe, NM: School of American Research and the University of Utah.

Sahagún, B. (1577) 1978. *The Origin of the Gods*. In *Florentine Codex: General History of the Things of New Spain*, Book III, translated by A. Anderson and C. E. Dibble. Reprint, Santa Fe, NM: School of American Research and the University of Utah.

Sahagún, B. D., and T. D. Sullivan. 1997. *Primeros memoriales: Paleography of Nahuatl Text and English Translation*. Norman: University of Oklahoma Press.

Schele, L., and D. Freidel. 1990. *A Forest of Kings: The Untold Story of the Ancient Maya*. New York: Harper Perennial.

Schele, L., and P. Mathews. 1998. *The Codes of Kings: The Language of Seven Sacred Maya Temples and Tombs*. New York: Simon and Schuster.

Schele, L., and M. E. Miller. 1986. *The Blood of Kings: Dynasty and Ritual in Maya Art*. New York: George Braziller.

Schweizer, A. S. 2010. *The Sungod's Journey through the Netherworld: Reading the Ancient Egyptian Amduat*. Ithaca, NY: Cornell University Press.

Segal, R., ed. 1998. *Jung on Mythology*. Princeton, NJ: Princeton University Press.

Shalit, E. 2002. *The Complex: Path of Transformation from Archetype to Ego*. Toronto, Ontario, Canada: Inner City Books.

Shalit, E. 2011. *The Cycle of Life: Themes and Tales of the Journey*. Carmel, CA: Fisher King Press.

Shalit, E. 2018. "Revisiting the Well at the Dawn of Life." In *The Human Soul (Lost) at the Dawn of a New Era*, edited by N. S. Furlotti, 179–97. Asheville, NC: Chiron Publications.

Shalit, E., and N. S. Furlotti, eds. 2013. *The Dream and Its Amplification*. Skiatook, OK: Fisher King Press.

Sharer, R. J., and L. P. Traxler. 2006. *The Ancient Maya*. 6th ed. Stanford, CA: Stanford University Press.

Singer, T., and S. L. Kimbles, eds. 2004. *The Cultural Complex: Contemporary Jungian Perspectives on Psyche and Society*. New York: Brunner-Routledge.

Slochower, H. 1970. *Mythopoesis: Mythic Patterns in the Literary Classics*. Detroit, MI: Wayne State University Press.

Sosa, J. 1986. "Maya Concepts of Astronomical Order." In *Symbol and Meaning beyond the Closed Community*, edited by G. H. Gossen, 185–96. Albany, NY: Institute for Mesoamerican Studies.

Sproul, B. C. 1991. *Primal Myths: Creation Myths around the World*. New York: HarperOne.

Starcher, C. D. 1999. "The Chakra System of Tantric Yoga: "Sat-cakra-nirupana" Text Interpreted within the Context of a Growth-Oriented Depth Psychology." PhD diss., Saybrook University. UMI Dissertation Services (UMI No. 3110201).

Stevens, A. 2003. *Archetype Revisited: An Updated Natural History of the Self*. Toronto, Ontario, Canada: Inner City Books.

Stone, A., and M. Zender. 2011. *Reading Maya Art: A Hieroglyphic Guide to Ancient Maya Painting and Sculpture*. London: Thames and Hudson.

Stuart, D. 2011. *The Order of Days: The Maya World and the Truth about 2012*. New York: Harmony Books.

Swedenborg, E. (1758) 1995. *Heaven and Its Wonders and Hell: From Things Heard and Seen*. Reprint, West Chester, PA: Swedenborg Society.

Swedenborg, E. (1763) 1995. *Angelic Wisdom concerning the Divine Love and the Divine Wisdom*. Reprint, West Chester, PA: Swedenborg Foundation.

Taube, K. A. 1988. "The Ancient Yucatec New Year Festival: The Liminal Period in Maya Ritual and Cosmology, Vols. 1–2." PhD diss., Yale University. UMI Dissertation Services (UMI No. 9009428).

Taube, K. A. 1989. "Ritual Humor in Classic Maya Religion." In *Word and Image in Maya Culture: Explorations in Language, Writing, and Representation*, edited by W. Hanks and D. Rice, 351–82. Salt Lake City: University of Utah Press.

Taube, K. A. 1992. *The Major Gods of Ancient Yucatan*. Washington, DC: Dumbarton Oaks.

Taube, K. A. 1993. *Aztec and Maya Myths*. Austin: University of Texas Press.

Tedlock, B. 1982. *Time and the Highland Maya*. Rev. ed. Albuquerque: University of New Mexico Press.

Tedlock, B., ed. 1992. *Dreaming: Anthropological and Psychological Interpretations*. Santa Fe, NM: School of American Research Press.

Tedlock, D. 1985. *Popol Vuh: The Definitive Edition of the Mayan Book of the Dawn of Life and the Glories of Gods and Kings*. New York: Touchstone Books.

Tedlock, D. 1993. *Breath on the Mirror: Mythic Voices and Visions of the Living Maya*. Albuquerque: University of New Mexico Press.

Tedlock, D. 2010. *2000 Years of Mayan Literature*. Oakland: University of California Press.

Thompson, J. E. S. 1990. *Maya History and Religion*. Norman: University of Oklahoma Press.

Vail, G., and A. Aveni, eds. 2009. *The Madrid Codex: New Approaches to Understanding an Ancient Maya Manuscript*. Boulder: University of Colorado Press.

Van Der Leeuw, G. 1963. *Religion in Essence and Manifestation*. New York: Harper and Row.

Van Eenwyk, J. R. 1997. *Archetypes and Strange Attractors: The Chaotic World of Symbols*. Toronto, Ontario, Canada: Inner City Books.

Villacorta, C. A., and J. A. Villacorta. 1930. *The Dresden Codex: Drawings of the Pages and Commentary in Spanish*. Walnut Creek, CA: Aegean Park Press.

Von Franz, M. L. 1972. *Creation Myths*. Dallas, TX: Spring Publications.

Von Franz, M. L. 1978. *Time: Rhythm and Repose*. London: Thames and Hudson.

Von Franz, M. L. 1996. *The Interpretation of Fairy Tales*. Boston: Shambhala.

Von Franz, M. L. 1997. *Archetypal Patterns in Fairytales*. Toronto, Ontario, Canada: Inner City Books.

Wach, J. 1958. *The Comparative Study of Religions*. Edited by J. Kitagawa. New York: Columbia University Press.

Waters, F. 1977. *The Book of the Hopi: The First Revelation of the Hopi's Historical and Religious Worldview of Life*. New York: Penguin Books.

Waters, F. 1989. *Mexico Mystique: The Coming Sixth World of Consciousness*. Chicago: Swallow Press.

Young, Neil. 1979. "Thrasher." On *Rust Never Sleeps*. Reprise Records.

Zimmer, H. 1989. *Philosophies of India*. Princeton, NJ: Princeton University Press.

INDEX

Note: Page numbers that appear in *italics* refer to illustrative matter. The names of paired-up entities—particularly gods and mythical twins—are listed both together and separately, since they are discussed as pairs as well as individually.

Adonis (Assyrian myth): as dying god in creation myth, 52, 58; sacrificed for Aphrodite, 172

Agnus Dei: sacrifice of, 118

agriculture: as level in Maya myth, 123; in Mesoamerican myth, 64–65; and myth of eternal return, 56, 58; origins of, 97; supplants hunter/gatherer and horticultural stages, 136, 164. *See also* corn; maize; Maize gods

Ahau: on Maya calendar, 66, 108. *See also* calendar(s)

Albedo (whiteness, in alchemy), 117

alchemy, 101; colors in Western, 117, 119–20, 148, 152; goal of, with psychology, 164; Jung on ascents/descents in, 152; philosopher's stone in, 164, 165; torture and, 121–22

Alvarado, Pedro de, 14

Ameta (in Ceram creation myth): sacrifices Hainuwele, 173

analysis, Jungian: amplified in *Popol Vuh*, 104–66; on destruction and creations, 161–62; ego/Self axis in, and myth, 140; goal of, with alchemy, 164; and myths in *Popul Vuh*, 4, 158–59. *See also* archetypes; collective unconscious; Jung, C. J.; individuation

analytical psychology, 8–10; and alchemy, 164; and archetypes/collective unconscious, 30–32; on mythical creation, 101; on number one, 105. *See also* archetypes; collective unconscious; Jung, C. J.

ancestors: contemporary Maya strictures, 133–34; Maya worship/reach out to, 126; memory of, 104, 159

Anima: in Blood Woman, 126; disregarded, 7–8; in *hieros gamos*, 59; in men, 59

animals: aquatic, 143; as aspects of gods, 65–66; cooperation with, 85, 127, 131; creation of, 78, *79*, 100; *Homo sapiens sapiens* as, 6; humans fight against (Wapangwa myth), 176; as images and symbols, 1–2, 35; Maya cosmos as, 70; mythical qualities of, 138, 142; in *Popol Vuh*, 21, 59, 78, *79*, 80–82, 85, 86, 87, 88, 89, 90, 91, 100; regression to state of, 132; represent instincts of psyche, 138; sacrificed, 13. *See also individual names*

anima mundi (Tree of Life): and Self/creation myth, 165

Anima Mundi (world soul), 27, 165, 192

animus: One Hunahpú as, 126–27; of wholeness, 168; in women, 184

animus mundi (soul of nature):
disregarded, 7–8
anthropology, 41–42, 184–85
ants, 89, 148, 156. *See also* animals;
mosquito, psychological meaning
of
Aphrodite (Greek goddess), 137; and
Psyche, 130. *See also* gods; Greek
mythology
Apollo (Greek god): defeats python
(evil), 175. *See also* Greek
mythology
Apollo and Artemis (twins), 170. *See
also* Greek mythology
archetypes: concept of, 30, 32, 36,
38, 113; demons as, 115–16; gods
as, 163, 171; grandmother remains
as, 113; images and symbols as,
30–31; of mother (Blood Woman *vs.*
Xmucané), 130; and myth, 36–38;
negative Great Mother, 114; scribal,
107, 136; two complementary, and
myth, 106, 168 (twins); universality
of, 32; and universality of myths,
32–33, 44. *See also* collective
unconscious; Jung, C. J.
Archons, 55
Arjuna (Indian god), 175
Arrow Owl (war councilor/demons'
messenger), 84, 116
Ascended (seer), 90
Athena (Greek goddess): associations
of, 128–29, 141. *See also* god(s);
Greek mythology
Attis (Phrygian god): sacrificed by
Cybele, 172; as vegetative god, 123
Auilix (god), 93–94
Austin, A., 25, 31, 36, 37, 42–43
axis mundi, 105, 153, 164; maize plant
represents, 145

Aztecs, 12; ball game of, 115; on
Chouen, 106; color symbolism
for, 119; creation myth of, 48–49,
51–52; sacrificial rituals of, 49, 63;
significance of five for, 153

Bachofen, J. J., 122
Balam Acab (Jaguar Night) (mother-
father), 79, 93, 95
Balam Quitze (Jaguar Forest) (mother-
father), 79, 93, 95
ballcourt (path to underworld), 83;
burial beneath and fertility, 123;
cleaning out, 139; Crushing, 84, 121;
gods play on, 111; Great Abyss of
Carchah, 110
ball game, x; as field of combat, 174;
as matriarchal/agrarian, 112; as
metaphor for individuation,
111; One Hunahpú and Seven
Hunahpú play, 82–83, 84
baptism: as second birth, 113. *See also*
religion
bat: as Maya myth symbol, 149; takes
off Hunanpú's head, 149. *See also*
animals
Bat House, 84, 121
Batz· meaning of, 107. *See also* One
Batz and One Chouen
Bhagavad Gita, 175
Bible: animals in, 100. *See also* Jesus
Christ; religion
birds, 79, 82, 86, 87; mythic
significance of, 142–43, 144. *See also*
animals; *individual names*
Bitter Water, 159, 161
black: significance for Maya, 117–18.
See also colors
Black Road, 84, 89, 117, 120, 145;
significance of, 117, 119–20

insect. *See* mosquito
introversion: in creation myths, 100;
 vs. extraversion, 100
intuition: Huracán and, 99
Iqui Balam (Wind Jaguar) (mother-
 father), *79*, 93, 95
Ishtar (Egyptian goddess), 137. *See also*
 god(s)
Isis (Egyptian goddess): conceives
 Horus from golden phallus, 178
itz: as *ch'ulel* for tree sap, saliva, etc.,
 125, 126
Itzmaná (Maya god), 147

Jacob and Esau, 59, 169
Jacobi, J., 30
jaguar, 1, 70, *79*, 87, 90, 108, 119, 136,
 174; becomes god's image, 94, 108,
 163. *See also* animals
jaguar god of the underworld, 105, 159.
 See also god(s)
Jaguar House, 84, 90, 121
jealousy, between siblings: hero twins
 combat, 133–34; institutional
 among Maya, 132–32. *See also* One
 Batz and One Chouen
Jesus Christ: as brother to Satan/Judas,
 169; fish as symbol of, 76, 153; as
 sacrificed god in creation myth,
 52, 58; as vegetative god, 123, 173;
 virgin birth of via Holy Ghost, 178
Johnson, A. W., 40–41
Jung, C. J., 1, 2, 3–4, 8–10, 33, 42;
 on alchemy, 152; on archetypal
 conceptions of God, 121; on
 archetypal motifs, 30–31, 44;
 on collective unconscious and
 myth, 38; on creation myth and
 individuation, 163; on dangers of
 inflation, 102–3; on evil, 55; and

final death/rebirth of hero twins,
 154; on fire as symbol, 152; on fish
 symbolizing Christ, 76; on inferior
 function, 100; on integration of
 self, 153; on loss of eye in myth,
 143–44; "psychoid" realm of, 61;
 on trickster's behavior, 107; on
 two as first number, 59–60. *See
 also* analysis, Jungian; analytical
 psychology; archetypes; collective
 unconscious
Jupiter (Roman god), 112

Kabbalah, 162
K'ich'e (present-day Santa Cruz), 21;
 genealogy of lineages, 95; meaning
 of, 77; parallelism in language of,
 106; root of people, 93. *See also*
 Maya
kik' (blood/sap): distracts death lords,
 128
kinh (sun-day-time), 66, 68, 69, 70,
 71–72. *See also* time
Kirk, G. S., 43–44
knives: significance in myth/
 psychology, 149–50
Kolowisi (Zuni serpent deity), 169
Krishna (Indian god), 175
Kronos (Greek god): castrates Uranus,
 177
K'uhul Ajaws (shaman-lords), 12; role
 of, 13
Kukulkan (Maya god) (Q'uqu'matz),
 95, 143, 169. as feathered serpent,
 21. *See also* Quetzalcoatl

Lakshmana and Batru-ghna (Indian
 goddesses): offspring of Vishnu via
 nectar, 178
languages: begin to differ, 93

squash. *See* calabash

stars: arrival/creation of, 94, 97

structuralism, 39–40; biogenetic, 44

Sudden Thunderbolt, 127

suffering: Jung on, 133

Sun, 14, 58, 108; in Aztec creation myth, 171–72; birth of, 94, 97; jaguar represents, 108; as symbol in ball game, 109–10. *See also* jaguar; lunar myth; Moon; solar myth

super-ego: and establishment of culture, 146. *See also* analysis, Jungian; ego

sweeping: as motif in Mesoamerican myth, 139–40

Sweeping Demon and Stabbing Demon, *83*, 113

symbolic logic: myth and, 39–40

symbol(s): blood as, 124–25; colors as in Western alchemy, 119–20; eye as, 143–44; fire as (Jung), 152; fish as Christ/Self, 76, 152; general, of number seven, 106; gods' sets of, 109; Maya and cross-cultural, 30–31; myth and, 35, 38, 42, 61; owls as, 116; present in ball game, 109–10; snake as, 112. *See also* archetypes

Tammuz: as dying (Sumerian) god in creation myth, 52, 172

Tao (in Chinese religion), 60

Tecuciztecatl (Aztec god): in creation myth, 48, 51–52, 171–72

Tedlock, B., 42

Tedlock, D., 74, 120, 123

Teraphim, Hebrew: as oracle head, 123

Tezcatlipoca: Aztec god of duality, 48; compared with Quetzalcoatl, 168–69; defeats Quetzalcoatl, 174;

fights along with Quetzalcoatl, 175. *See also* Quetzalcoatl

theology(ies): significance of net for Maya, 130; significance of number seven among, 106, 144–45. *See also* God; god(s); religion

therapy/analysis: differentiation as stage of, 123; suffering can lead to, 121–22. *See also* analysis, Jungian

Theseus: kills Minotaur, 175. *See also* Greek mythology

Thor (Norse god): fights Hrungnir to reclaim Orwandil, 175

Thoth (Egyptian god), 107

Tiamat (Assyrian god): as first victim, 49, 173, 175

Tibetan Book of the Dead, 10

time: cycles of (Jungian), 12, 13, 15 (Maya), 65, 67, 68, 69, 73 (Greeks), 161; historical *vs.* eternal in creation myths, 46, 65; historical *vs.* predawn, 160; idea of as primary, 64; lunar/solar system of (Maya), 64; psychic (nonlinear/dream), 102; sacred, in myth, 42; and space, 71; universal mythic, 61. *See also* calendar(s)

Titans (Greek gods): Jungian take on, 55, 116. *See also* Greek mythology

Tlaltecuhtli (Aztec earth lord): earth and sky created from body of, 48–49; as Mother, 142; Quetzalcoatl and Tezcatlipoca vanquish, 175

toad, 88, 141; mythic significance of, 142, 144. *See also* animals

Tohil (god), 21; demands human sacrifice, 93–94. *See also* Quetzalcoatl

Tonatiuh (Aztec sun god): in creation myth, 52, 172